IMAGES
of America

McMULLEN VALLEY

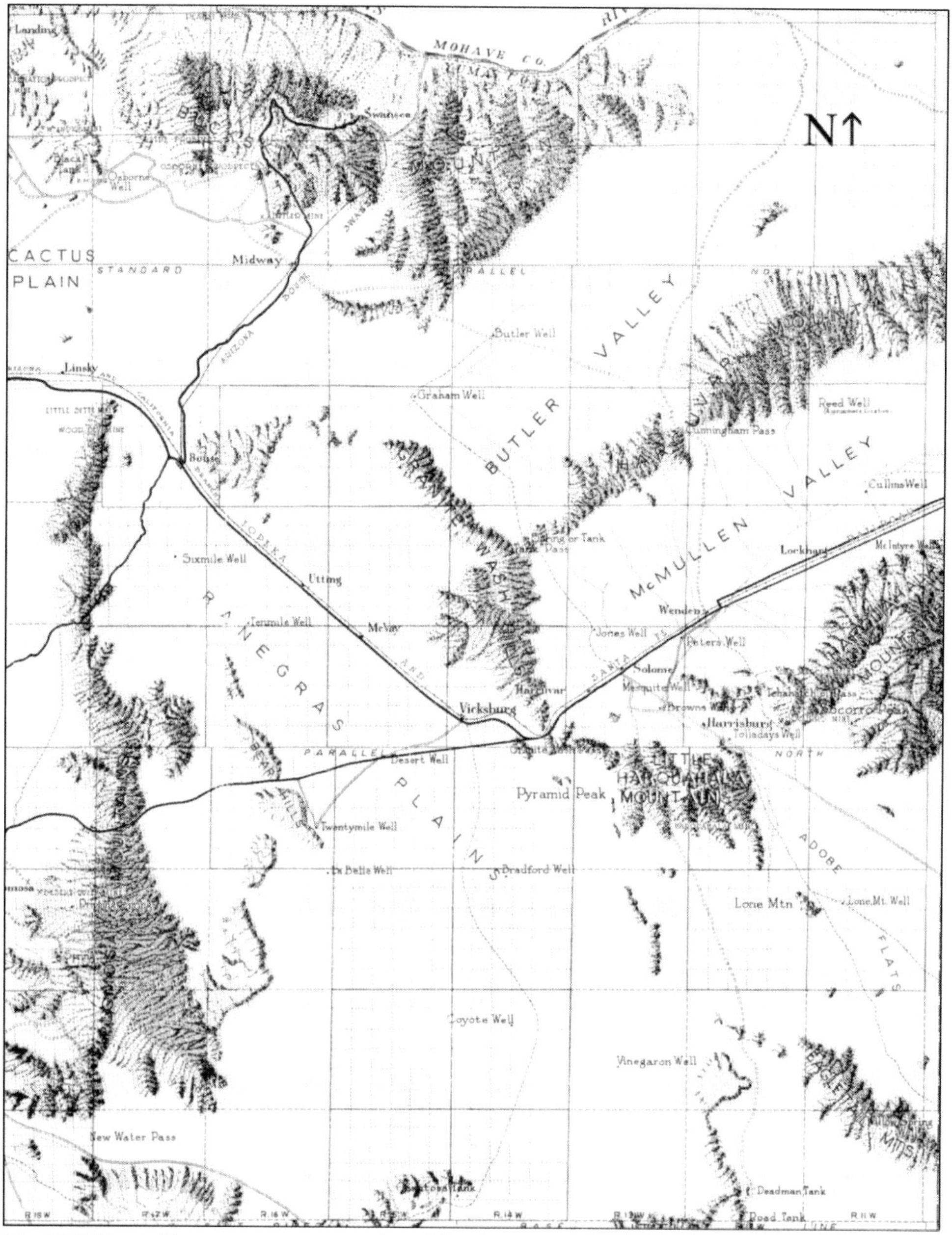

This 1920 Yuma County map was produced by the county highway department. The Santa Fe Railroad and the sand track that would become Route 60 run parallel along the southern rim of the McMullen Valley. The communities of Vicksburg and Bouse, technically located on the Ranegras Plain, have historically and culturally been considered part of McMullen Valley. (Great Arizona Outback Rumor and Innuendo Historical Society.)

ON THE COVER: Roy MacDonald, mining entrepreneur and promoter, picnics with his grandfather, John Rutherford (left), and his great uncle, J. R. Rutherford (right). MacDonald would bring promotional tours to a new level to entice investors to buy shares in his mines during 1930s. (Rohrig family.)

IMAGES
of America

McMULLEN VALLEY

E. W. Kutner, Sharon Rubin,
and the Great Arizona Outback
Rumor and Innuendo Historical Society

ARCADIA
PUBLISHING

ISBN 978-0-7385-5851-6

Published by Arcadia Publishing
Charleston SC, Chicago IL, Portsmouth NH, San Francisco CA

Printed in the United States of America

Library of Congress Catalog Card Number: 2008931753

For all general information contact Arcadia Publishing at:
Telephone 843-853-2070
Fax 843-853-0044
E-mail sales@arcadiapublishing.com
For customer service and orders:
Toll-Free 1-888-313-2665

Visit us on the Internet at www.arcadiapublishing.com

To the people of the Great Arizona Outback—past, present, and future.

CONTENTS

ACKNOWLEDGMENTS

The founders of the Great Arizona Outback Rumor and Innuendo Historical Society would like to thank its members and their families who have joined us on our mission to discover, restore, and preserve the history of the McMullen Valley. The writing and assembly of the photographs in this book would not have been possible without their guidance and encouragement.

We are grateful to the McMullen Valley Chamber of Commerce and Lee Vernon for sharing her research and that of the late Pauline Sanholdt. We greatly appreciate Linda Darland and Jeanne Youell for keeping us within the bounds of English grammar.

We wish to thank those who shared their history but also helped us connect with many others. Their enthusiasm to share recollections enriched the text and diversity of the images featured in the book: Dorie Appelhans, Frances and "Heavy" Baird, Hayden Brown, Kemper and Toni Brown, Pauline Dalton, Lowette Dihel, Clare and Jim Downing, Billie Farr, Cactus Kelli, Dorothy Matthews, Cheryl and "Mo" Montijo, Albert and Irene Nord, Lowell Rohrig, Bill Sheffler, and Doug and Louise Wolfe.

We wish to recognize the Arizona Historical Society (AHS) Museums in Tucson, Phoenix, and Yuma for helping us navigate and locate images in their extensive archives; Jim Turner, Chrystal Burke, David Tatum, Ashley Smith, Megan Reid, and Carol Brooks; Ryan Flahive at the Sharlot Hall Museum; and John Bennett at the Bouse Assay Office Museum. And of course, thanks to Jared Jackson at Arcadia Publishing, who sensed our little desert towns had a big story to tell.

Unless otherwise indicated, images have been drawn from the archives of the Great Arizona Outback Rumor and Innuendo Historical Society. All others are provided courtesy of the identified sources.

Disclaimer: Dates, names, locations, and other facts are deemed to be accurate but are not guaranteed. We welcome documented corrections and other input for future editions.

INTRODUCTION

The McMullen Valley, also known as the Great Arizona Outback, is roughly the necklace of communities in La Paz County strung along Route 60 that includes Salome, Wenden, Hope, and Vicksburg.

In the postwar years before the Interstate Highway System, Route 60 had been known as Route 66's southern sister. The highway epitomized the refrain "See the USA in your Chevrolet." Neon signage, roadside diversions, and full-service gas stations were all available on the major thoroughfare that ran between Phoenix and Los Angeles.

From the earliest mining days in the Great Arizona Outback, accessibility to liquid gold—water—played a vital role in the success of the valley. Long before modern-day hydrologists discovered the massive aquifer beneath our soils, early-day miners, farmers, and ranchers had hand-dug wells, often finding water within 25 feet of the surface. Water, abundant and easily available, was critical in our past and will determine our future.

With the dawning of the 21st century, the McMullen Valley entered its third century of European settlement. The pristine natural beauty of the northwest corner of the Sonoran Desert first observed by the early gold prospectors retains its exquisite, distinctive character. The clean air, clear skies, and bountiful water remain intact.

Overshadowed by Arizona's other tourist attractions, such as the Grand Canyon or Monument Valley, the Great Arizona Outback may not appear to be as spectacular, but should you stop to look around, you may realize that you have found an amazing place that retains the best of small-town America.

Many of the current residents are the descendants of independent, rugged, individual men and women who first came to the valley and surmounted a never-ending cascade of challenges. Their spirits were renewed nightly by the specter of the unobstructed view of the Milky Way.

The fact that the Great Arizona Outback is much like it has always been is a likely attraction for many of the visitors and retirees, fondly referred to as snowbirds, who flock here each winter. They come to explore the foothills of the Harquahala, Harcuvar, and Granite Wash Mountain wilderness areas. They discover abandoned mine shafts surrounded by the most extensive desert flora and fauna in the world.

They come to marvel at our mountain vistas. They hike in our desert, drive off-road vehicles, and ride horses. Many set up comfortable trailers and often luxurious "rock-star-like" motor homes in RV parks, while others camp at state and county parks. All of them patronize our local businesses to help make the local economy viable.

Wherever tourists travel these days, they eventually come face to face with the local residents' expression of civic pride. Terms like "World's Greatest City," "America's Favorite Town," or "The West's Best Community" abound. These slogans characterize the local citizens' personal perspective on their place in the universe. Monuments are engraved, signs embossed, and T-shirts printed that proclaim what is the most subjective truth about where they live, work, play, and eventually die.

So what conclusions are to be drawn about a place whose residents buy, sell, and wear T-shirts that proudly exclaim, "Salome—Conveniently Located in the Middle of Nowhere?"

Quite obviously, the middle of nowhere is not as remote as it once was. The outer suburbs of Arizona's capital have sprawled closer and closer, making them a 60-minute drive. To the southeast, downtown Phoenix remains approximately 100 miles from Salome. In all other directions, the communities of Quartzsite, Wickenburg, and the La Paz County seat of Parker can be reached in about 45 minutes or less, when obeying the posted speed limits.

Forty-five minutes is sufficient time for McMullen Valley residents to prepare for their arrival at the first traffic signal, fast-food drive-in, and supermarket or hospital emergency room. Perhaps the entire "nowhere issue" is best exemplified by the advice of the 911 operator who receives an emergency call about a rattlesnake bite: "Get in the car and drive as fast as possible. At best, you have about an hour."

From the very beginning of settlement, our desert has attracted optimists, visionaries, and dreamers. Foremost among them was Dick Wick Hall. Hall came to start the town of Salome and ended up writing the *Salome Sun* newspaper. In 1921, his work was discovered and published in the *Saturday Evening Post*, the magazine with the largest circulation in the country. His rhyming prose about the Salome Frog, "Salome—Where She Danced," and dozens of other witty and satiric tales caught the imagination of the nation.

For decades, Hall was compared to Will Rogers, the cowboy comedian, who developed a fondness for polo after becoming a Hollywood star. But Dick Wick Hall was from beginning to end a down-to-earth sort who could dream big dreams and pump gas at his service station at the same time. In his spare moments, he invented humorous road signage and turned his friends in Salome into characters of mythic proportions. Part Homer the Greek poet, part Homer Simpson, Dick Wick Hall paved the way for those who would follow.

Almost concurrently with Hall's thrusting Salome to fame and notoriety, just down the road in Wenden, the nation's top scientists chose to locate the world's premier solar observatory on the peak of Harquahala Mountain, overlooking the McMullen Valley. Administered by the Smithsonian Institute, as it was then known, the now-abandoned observatory remains a destination for adventurous hikers and off-road enthusiasts.

A decade later, entrepreneurial businessman Russell Sheffler, known as "Bus," came through Salome and believed he had found the locale for his visionary idea. When Sheffler made his first investment in Salome, he was simply seeking to empty his warehouse of "vending machines" that were not producing any income.

With his brother and partner Bill, Bus had supplied the gambling ships off the coast of California. When the ships were shut down, the Shefflers went looking for new markets. Sheffler's vision was to make gambling legal in Arizona and to build a modern destination resort in the desert on his property in Salome.

The Shefflers enlisted a respected Phoenix attorney named William Sullivan to coordinate their voter initiative to legalize gambling in Arizona. They brought in a Los Angeles architect to design and build a modern motel with a swimming pool. They put up blinking neon signage that could be seen for miles across the desert—all this years before Bugsy Siegel had ever seen the railroad town in Nevada called Las Vegas.

Like much of the West, the communities of the McMullen Valley contributed to the war effort. Camp Bouse, located in the adjacent Butler Valley, brought thousands of troops to the area. Known as "Patton's Boys," the soldiers enjoyed their hours of liberty at the civilian bars and restaurants across the valley.

As the nation and the Great Arizona Outback prospered in the postwar era, the subsequent baby boom, felt in the schools, brought forth a deceptively "grandmotherly" dynamo to take on the county.

E. V. Haydis was a dealer of high explosives who had been driving truckloads of volatile materials to miners across the valley since her youth. Elected to the county school board, she led the fight to bring a high school to the McMullen Valley. She took on and beat the recalcitrant officials of

Yuma County and went on to stump the panel on the 1950s quiz show *What's My Line?* In the Great Arizona Outback, she is remembered as the tough-minded optimist who brought a high school to Salome.

Over the next 20 years, the identity of the McMullen Valley as a vestige of "the old Wild West" seemed to be in ascendancy. Easier transport to urban markets enabled farming and ranching to expand. Large commercial cotton fields covered the McMullen Valley by the 1960s. Water and accessible natural gas and electricity attracted investors from Phoenix, and farm service businesses came in to expand employment opportunities.

Ever-increasing numbers of road travelers required services. Our desert towns provided gas, food, and lodging. Our point of distinction was the character of the strange and bizarre roadside attractions we had to offer: aviaries, cactus gardens, Native American curios, Gila monsters, and everything under the sun for sale, including woodpecker holes.

However, in the 1970s, things begin to fall apart. Utility and fuel prices rose, and commodity prices fell. Road business ebbed with the nation's first fuel crisis and the completion of the interstate. The outlook for the future was grim.

After 75 years of battling with Yuma County over roads, schools, and other services, the McMullen Valley and the adjacent population centers along the Colorado River were spun off from Yuma County with uncharacteristic speed.

Soon after La Paz County came into existence, a buyer appeared in the McMullen Valley and made the farmers and ranchers "an offer they couldn't refuse." Ben Matthews, a La Paz County supervisor and McMullen Valley farmer, said at the time, "I did what you would have done if somebody offered you twice what your house was worth."

The buyer was not some cable news magnate or Saudi prince but the McMullen Valley's ever-expanding, contiguous neighbor in Maricopa County, the City of Phoenix.

The over 14,000 acres of land purchased by the City of Phoenix for the McMullen Valley water was an insurance policy—a water assurance policy.

Fortunately, the McMullen Valley would be represented in the state legislature by a self-described "water buffalo" named Herb Guenther. Water buffaloes are very slow, very deliberate, and very conscientious, if not a little bull-headed.

In 2008, Herb Guenther serves as director of the Arizona Department of Water Resources. Recalling the David and Goliath battle to protect the McMullen Valley and its water of a quarter of a century ago, Guenther says, "Instead of the City of Phoenix stealing McMullen Valley's future, the law we passed, the Arizona Water Transportation Act made it so we could coexist. The City of Phoenix purchase would be honored but they were going to have to function as a good neighbor."

The Great Arizona Outback Rumor and Innuendo Historical Society looks forward to documenting what is certain to be the next exciting chapter in the history of the McMullen Valley.

The residents of the McMullen Valley remain sanguine. In the following pages, readers will see that they are a resilient and resourceful people. As if echoing what Dick Wick Hall might have written in regard to managing water in an arid state, Director Guenther seems to sum things up for now when he says, "I can lead you to water, but I can't let you drink."

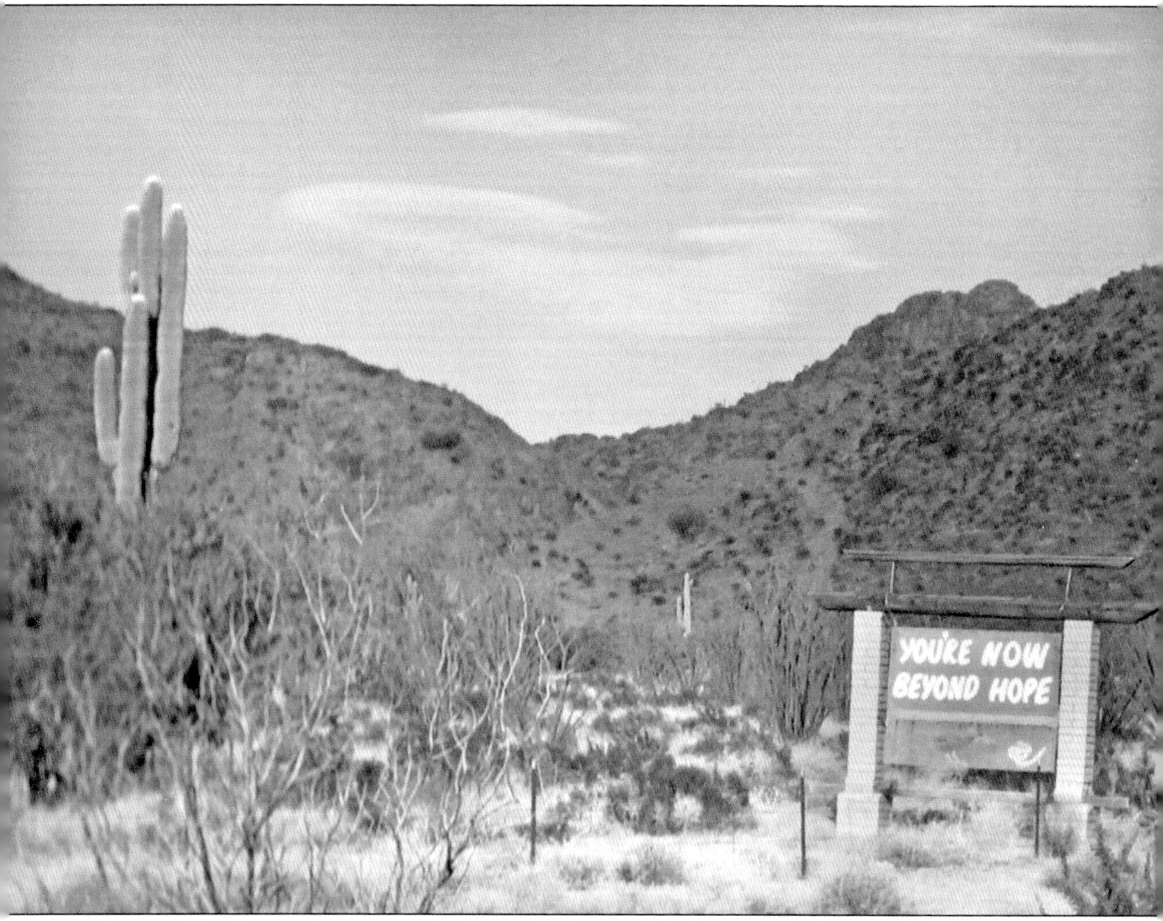

Located in Hope, Arizona, at the base of Granite Wash Pass (also known as Mountain Pass), this road sign is seen on Routes 60 and 72 from the west. As the sign paraphrases the immortal Dante, it harkens back to the spirit of Dick Wick Hall, Salome's founder and road signage pioneer. The sign exemplifies the humor and eclectic boosterism that have always been present in the McMullen Valley. (Sharon Rubin.)

One

The Magnetic Pull of Gold

Other than ancient petroglyphs at the western entrance of the McMullen Valley and in Granite Wash Pass and tales of an 1849 Native American massacre, there is little known about the area prior to 1857.

That year, James Birch received the U.S. Mail contract enabling him to finance the first regular stagecoach service between San Antonio and San Diego. Birch's stage route ran right through the valley.

In the 1860s, James McMullen drove the stagecoach between Congress and Ehrenburg. McMullen dug a well to serve both his teams of horses and his venturesome passengers. McMullen's well provided passengers with refreshing, cool, sweet water. Legend has it that water made his reputation, and water was the reason the valley took his name.

In the late 1870s, word of gold mining success across central western Arizona spread, propelling the vanguard of mining prospectors to flow into the foothills surrounding the valley. Within a decade, the mining camps of Harrisburg and Harqua Hala grew up. They brought knowledgeable fortune seekers, important territorial-era personalities including former governor Fredrick Tritle, George Ellsworth, and Carmelita Campbell. Men like John Agard and John Brayton Martin followed, starting out as prospectors but later trading their picks and shovels for legislative votes upon election to the legislature.

By century's end, while Fredrick Jackson Turner was declaring the frontier closed, the untamed McMullen Valley was just opening for settlement. Small prospectors, pioneers, and settlers began arriving. Every new arrival brought the expectation they would find what they were looking for, whether it was wealth, adventure, solitude, health, or simply peace and quiet.

Homesteaders, farmers, and ranchers began to stake out their futures in this surprisingly verdant desert valley. Before long, rumors of the railroad coming through the district spread. As the 20th century began, dreams were of boundless opportunities, and powerful steam locomotives could almost be seen on the horizon.

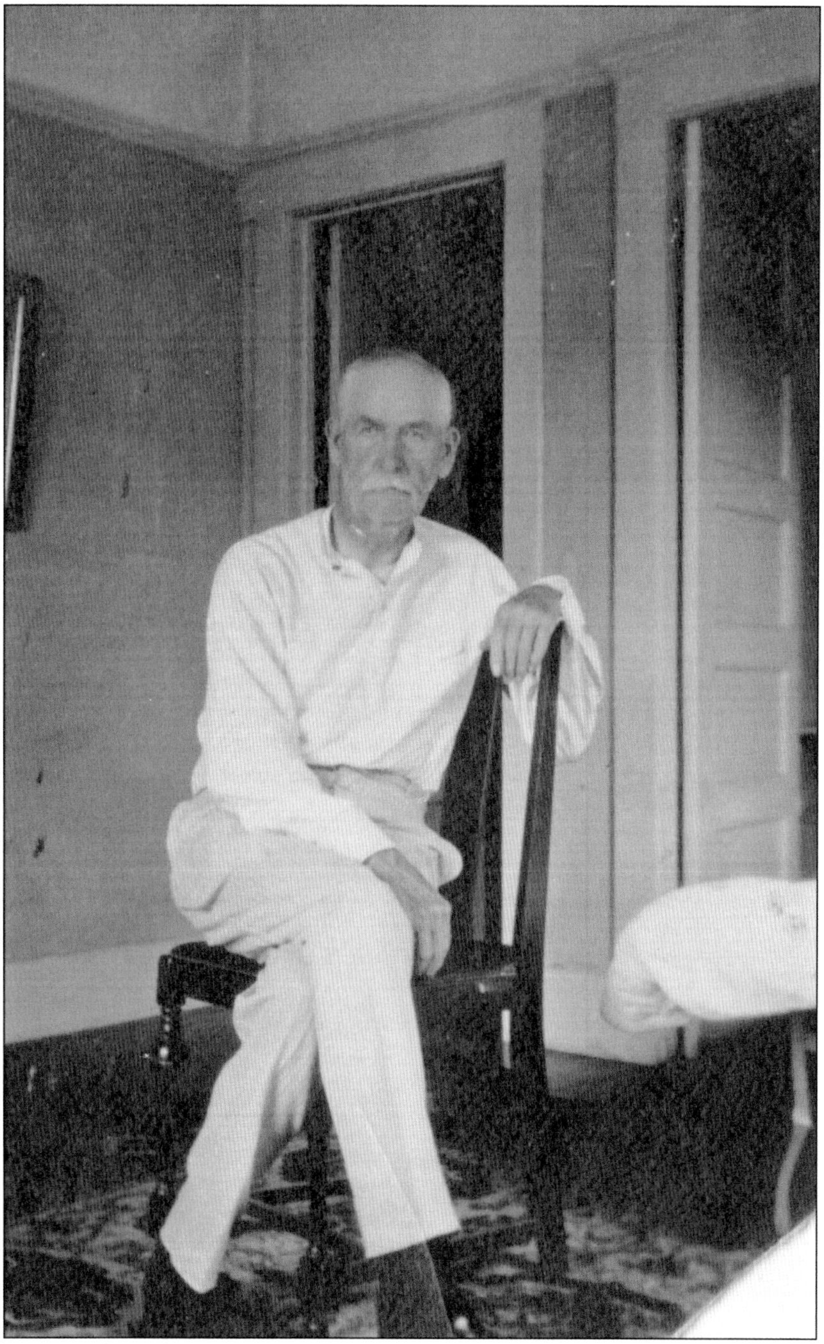

Few 19th-century legends placed themselves at the center of the action better than Wyatt Earp. Hanging up his badge and six-shooter in Tombstone in the 1880s, Earp headed for the gold mining camp at Harqua Hala. It was the place to be. Not ready to kick off his boots and put his feet up, Earp opened a saloon, running girls and offering working miners quality diversions. In his spare moments, he worked his own claims. As he was the first recorded retiree to settle in the McMullen Valley, Wyatt's active lifestyle established a pattern for successive generations of retired persons. Earp is pictured above in the 1920s. (AHS Tucson.)

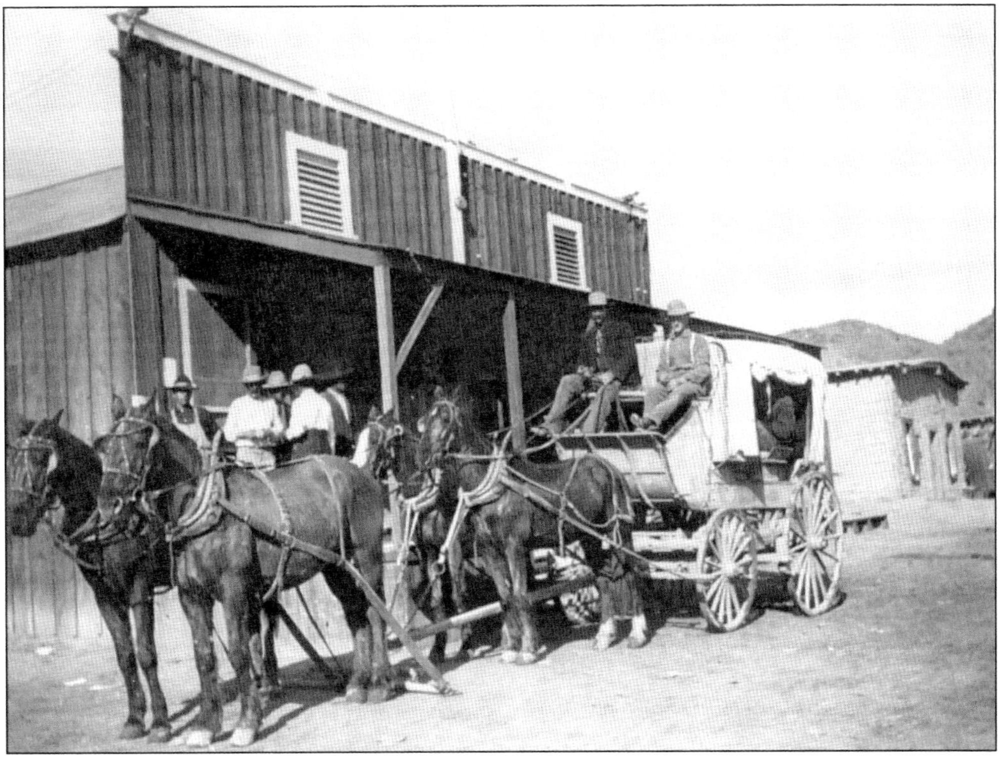

In the last decades of the 19th century, discoveries of gold, silver, and copper in the Arizona Territory exerted a magnetic pull. Adventurous souls came from every direction, employing all manner of transport. In the 1860s, James McMullen drove the stagecoach through the McMullen Valley. By McMullen's time, Alexander Butterfield had taken over the stagecoach line that eventually would become known as Wells Fargo. Until the end of the 1800s, passengers traveling east from California to ride the stage from Ehrenburg crossed the Colorado River on ferry barges like the one pictured below. (Both AHS Yuma.)

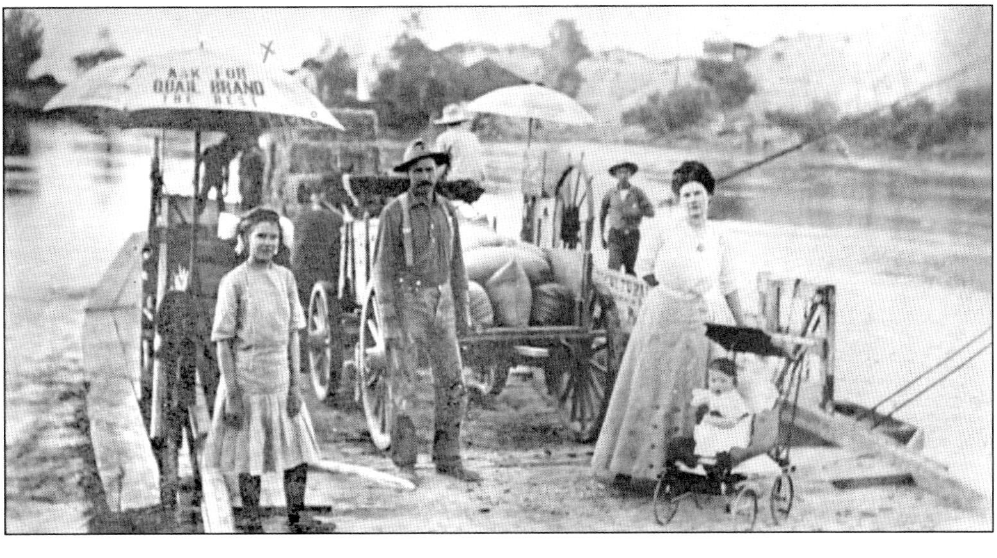

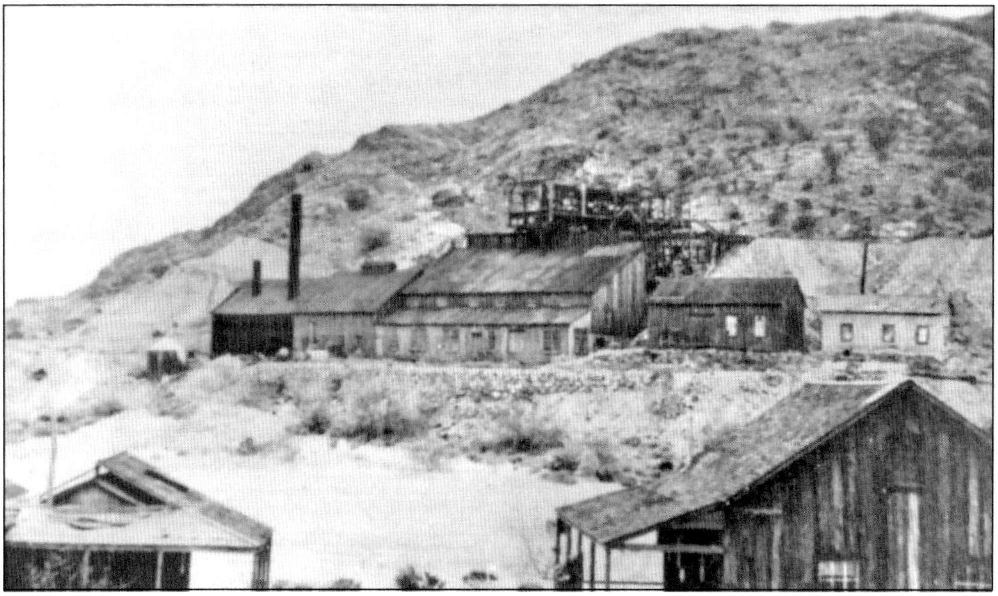

In 1865, the first copper deposits were discovered in the Harcuvar foothills. Cunningham Pass is named after the first successful prospector, Charles Cunningham. Across the valley, gold ledges would be found near the first mining camp at Harrisburg in the 1870s. Six miles south, discoveries at the Golden Eagle and Bonanza mines brought cries of "Eureka!" Pictured is one of the extensive facilities built there, called the Harqua Hala.

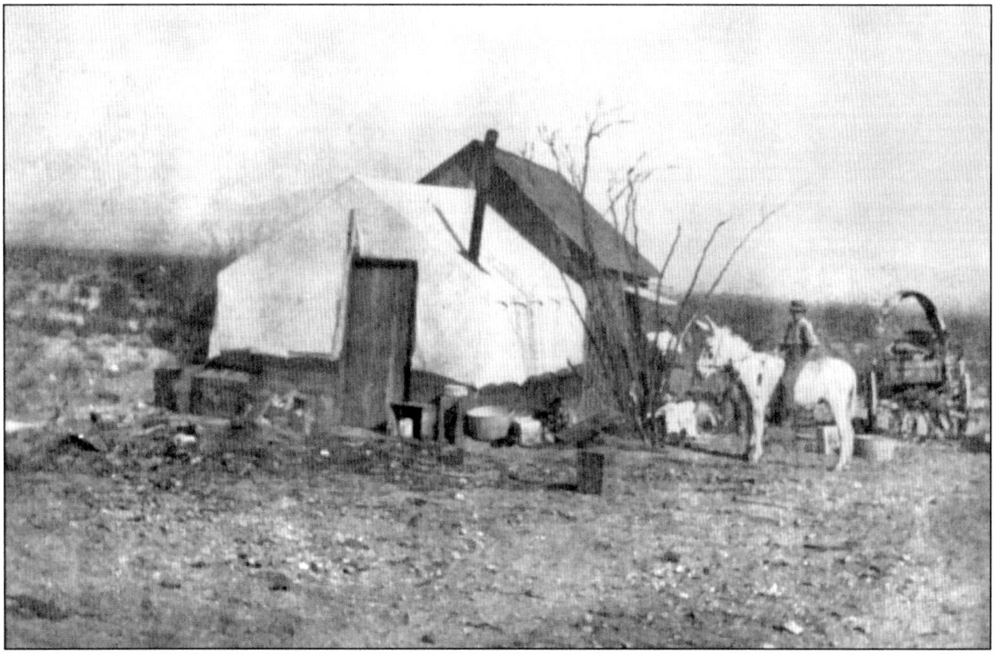

Not all miners were suited for camp life. Some chose to live in isolation, close to their claims. The approach to residential architecture was always practical and often innovative. Seasonal temperature extremes made tented/stick-built combinations (pictured above) one answer. Residential portability would become a regular feature of the landscape in the years ahead, as trailers, fifth wheels, and RVs rolled into the McMullen Valley for the winter.

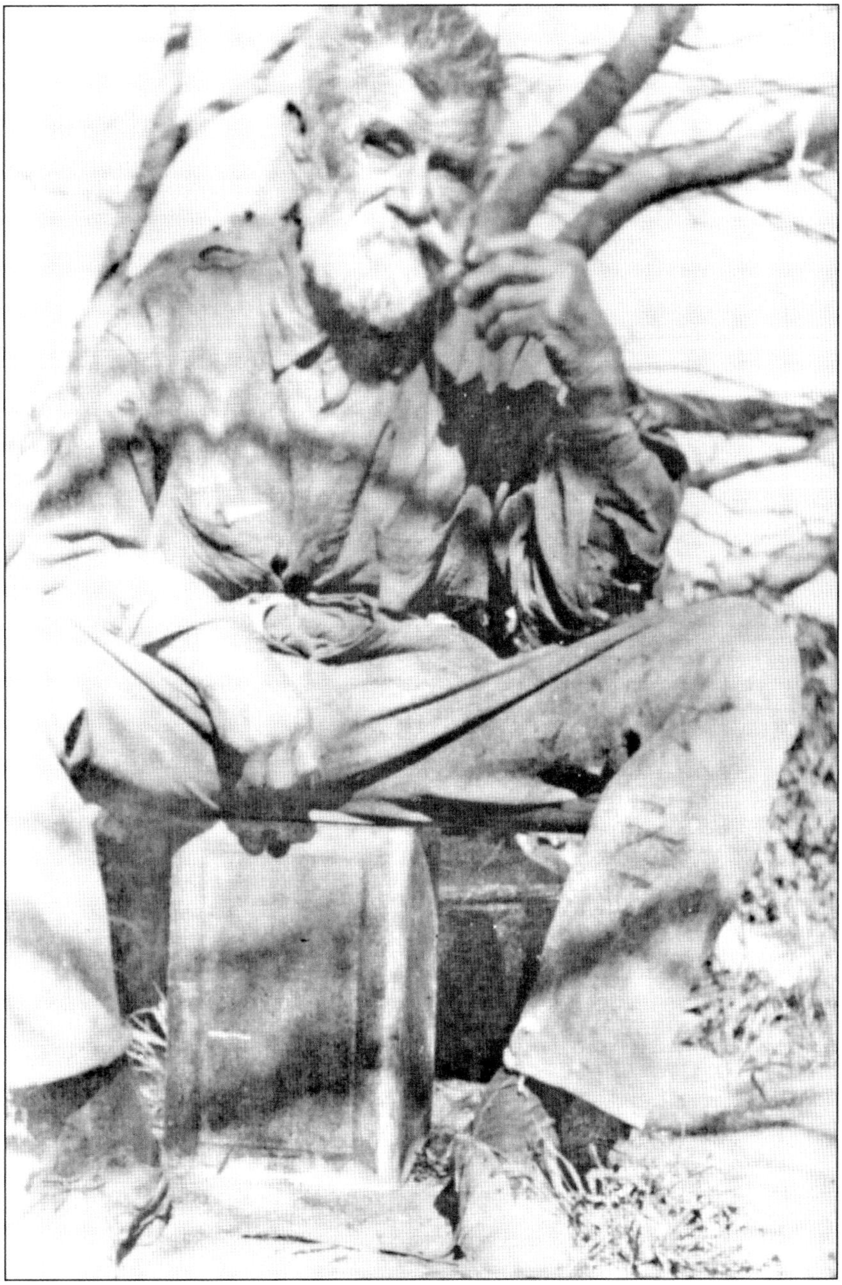

William Beard (also known as Bill Bear) was a legendary miner and one of the founders of the mining camp at Harrisburg. In 1886, with former Arizona territorial governor F. A. Tritle and H. E. Harris, he established the Harris Gold and Silver Mill and Mining Company. Bill Bear also served as Harrisburg's first postmaster. The substantially richer gold deposits at the Harqua Hala mines attracted investment capital from large mining companies. Still, without Harrisburg's abundant water supply, extracting Harqua Hala's rich yield of $6 million might have proved impossible. Few found fortune at Harrisburg, and many miners moved on. Bill Bear remained with his wife, Mary, cobbling out a life from the gold flakes found in the foothills they loved. Bill Bear remained a symbol of the golden days long after Harrisburg was abandoned.

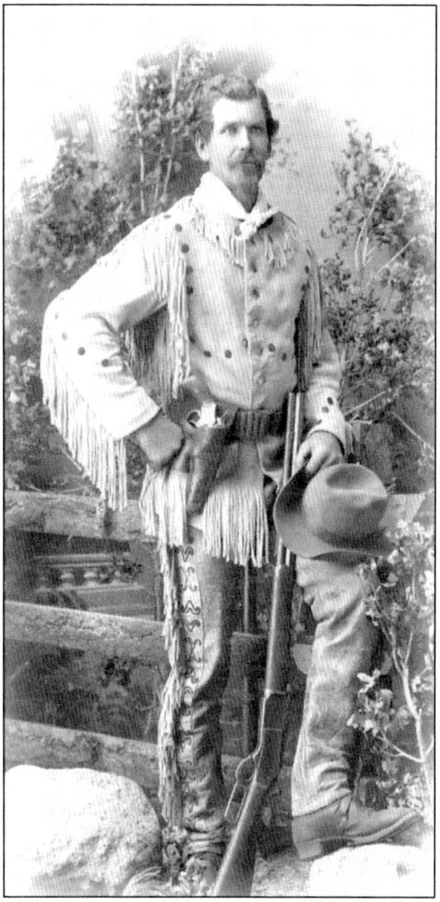

In his youth, John Reid, seeking adventure, affected the look of a man of the Wild West. Eventually he settled down, establishing a farm that yielded quality cattle feed for his herds and excellent potatoes. Reid introduced innovative irrigation techniques to his fields. With his wife, Mary, John is remembered as gracious and welcoming to successive waves of new settlers. (Sharlot Hall Museum.)

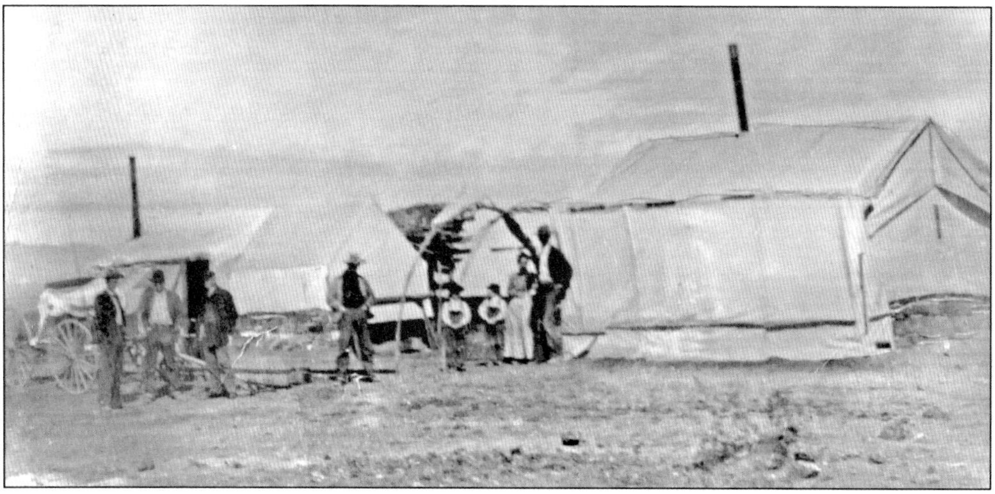

The Martin Camp at the San Marcos Mine was 6 miles from Harrisburg. The camp consisted of three large tents, each featuring a stone fireplace. One tent served as a kitchen and dining room; the other two were used for sleeping quarters. John Martin and his family slept in one tent, his work crew and close relatives in the other. The men worked the mine. Pictured are the Martin Camp and extended family.

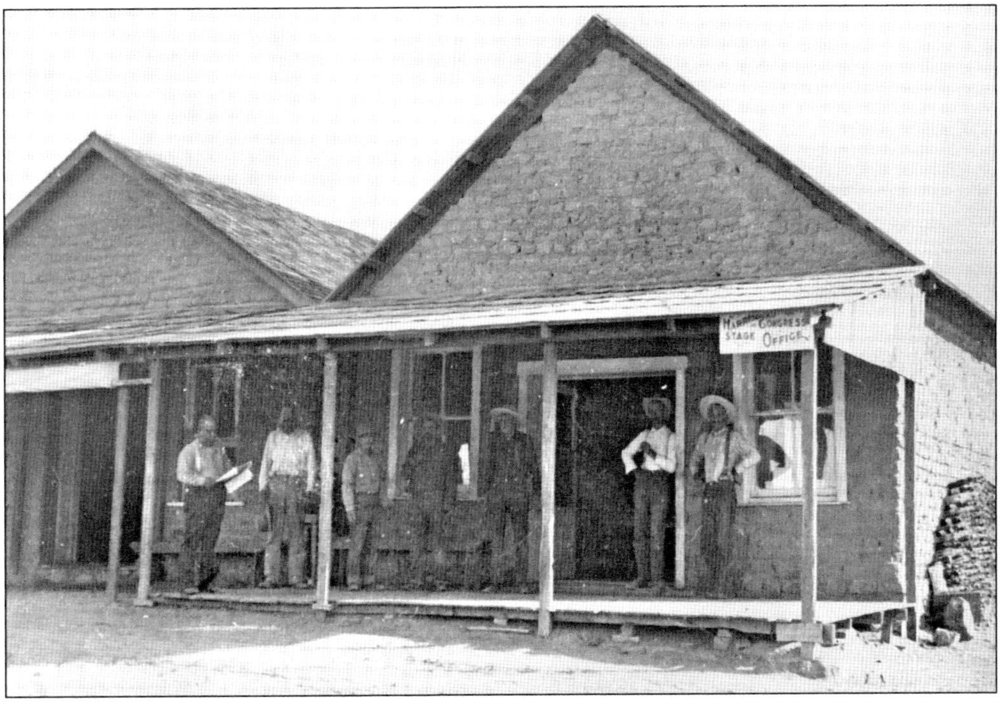

Built in the 1890s, the Harrisburg shopping center's twin look-alike buildings supplied life's necessities, enabling it to survive after the mine's decline. One building housed the general store, post office, and stage depot. The second structure was home to the saloon.

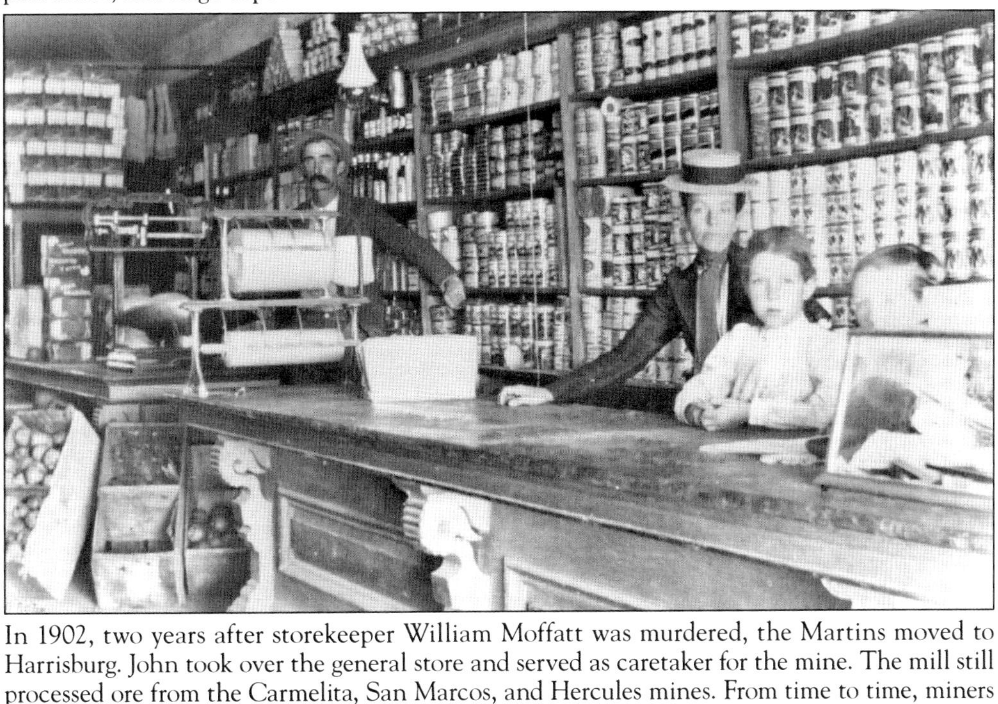

In 1902, two years after storekeeper William Moffatt was murdered, the Martins moved to Harrisburg. John took over the general store and served as caretaker for the mine. The mill still processed ore from the Carmelita, San Marcos, and Hercules mines. From time to time, miners appeared, took a lease, worked the mine, gave up, and moved on. Pictured from left to right are John, Sadie, Gladys, and Marcella Martin.

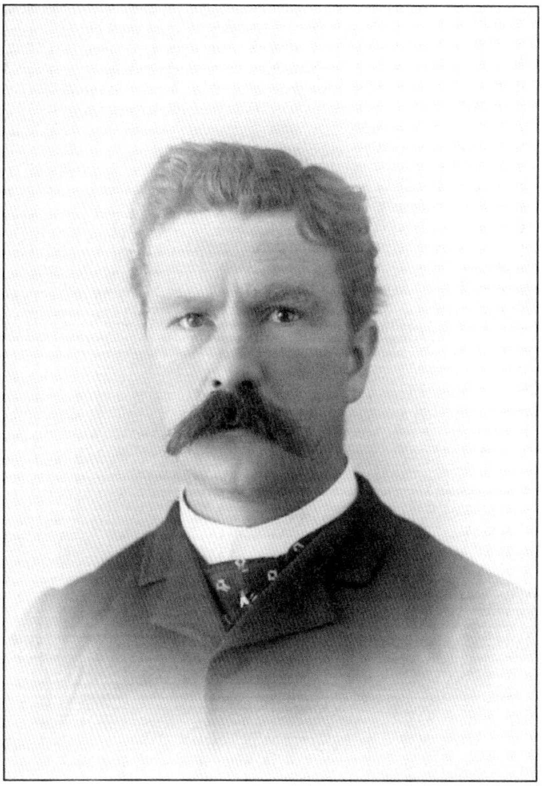

John Agard was an early prospector. He worked at all the major mines as well as pursuing his own claims. Briefly serving in the territorial legislature, Agard returned to live out his long life in Cunningham Pass, observing the transformation of the McMullen Valley into settled communities adjacent to a railroad and a paved highway.

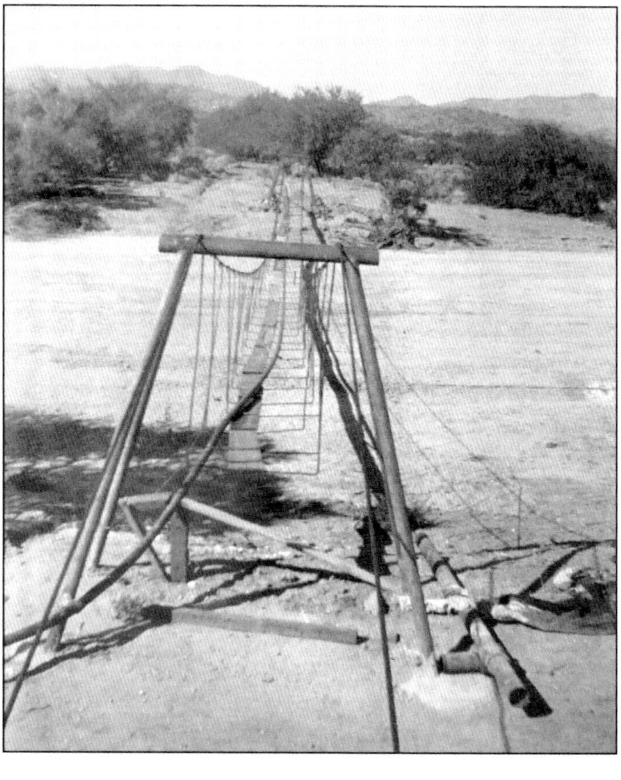

The unlimited water supply at Harrisburg enabled the gold at Harqua Hala to be mined successfully. Sophisticated engineering was required to pipe the water six miles through the foothills. Spanning the Centennial Wash (often dry but sometimes irrepressible with thundering waves of water) presented the biggest challenge. This combination aqueduct/suspension bridge proved to be a durable and long-lasting answer.

Carmelita Campbell was unique in the mining world. A Latina from Chile, she helped to transform her husband, John C. Campbell, into a successful territorial politician. After he left her for another woman, Carmelita settled on the Centennial Wash on her own to pursue her fortune. She was a dynamo, feared and respected by the men she employed at the Carmelita Mine and 50 other mining claims she developed. (Sharlot Hall Museum.)

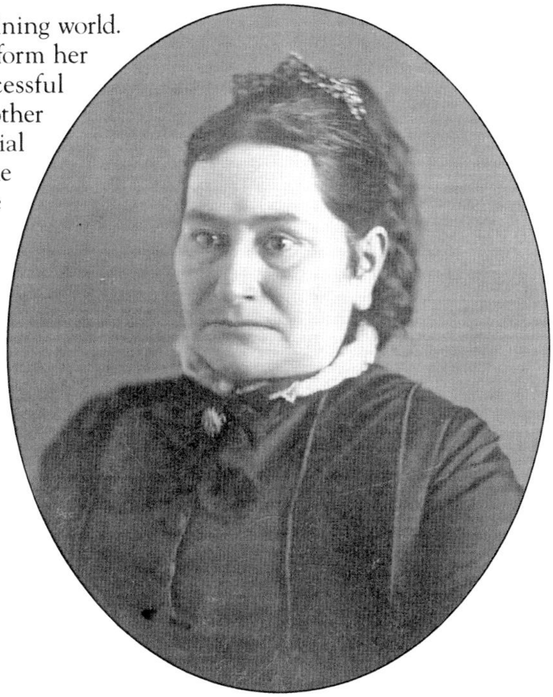

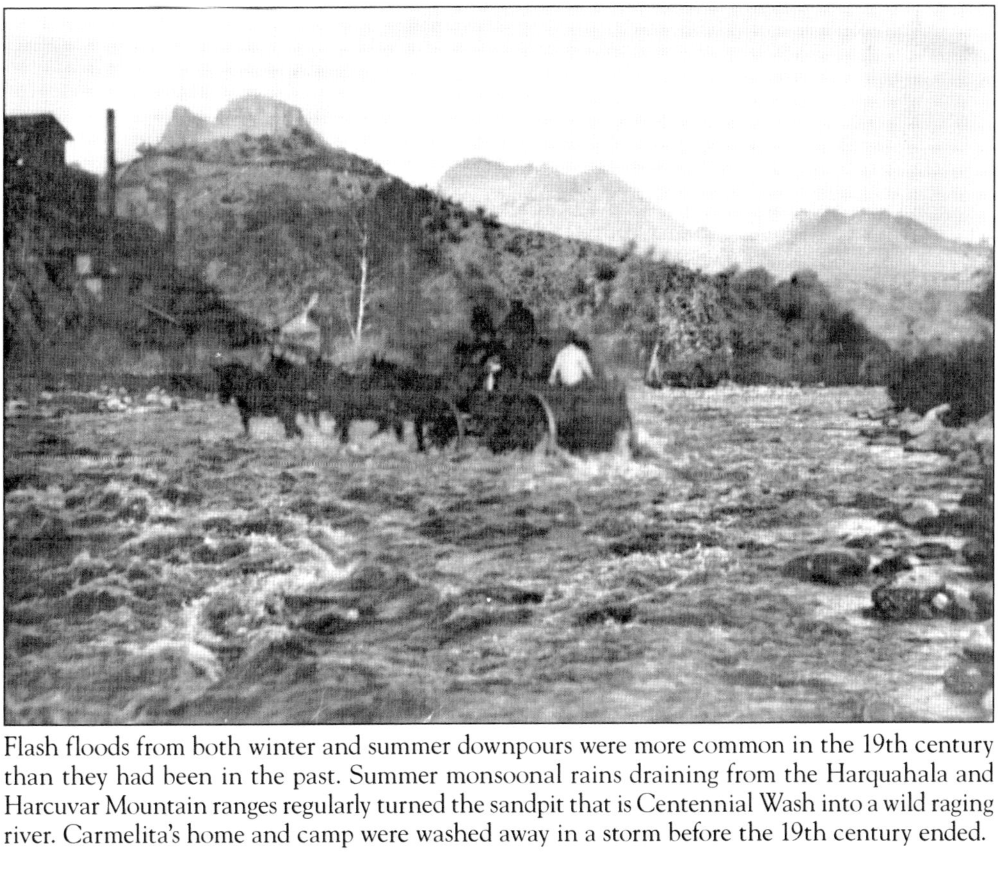

Flash floods from both winter and summer downpours were more common in the 19th century than they had been in the past. Summer monsoonal rains draining from the Harquahala and Harcuvar Mountain ranges regularly turned the sandpit that is Centennial Wash into a wild raging river. Carmelita's home and camp were washed away in a storm before the 19th century ended.

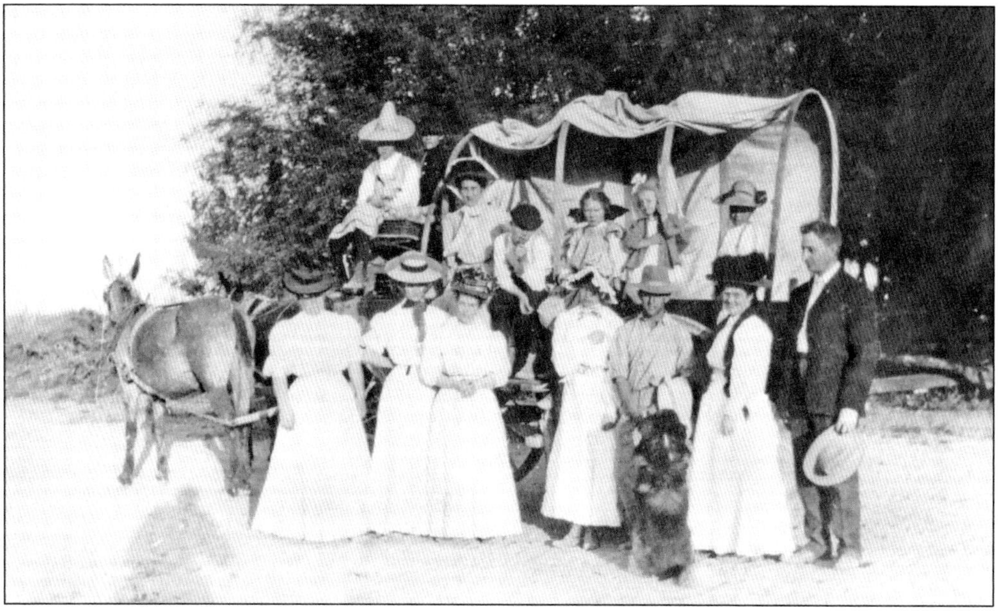

In her memoir, *Desert Memories*, Sadie Martin writes about the close relationship the Martins shared with the Reids. Sadie Martin often walked the 5 miles from the San Marcos Mine to visit Mary Reid at her ranch. Upon moving to Harrisburg, Sadie Martin organized school picnics at the Reids'. Sadie Martin (third from the left) stands in front of the wagon.

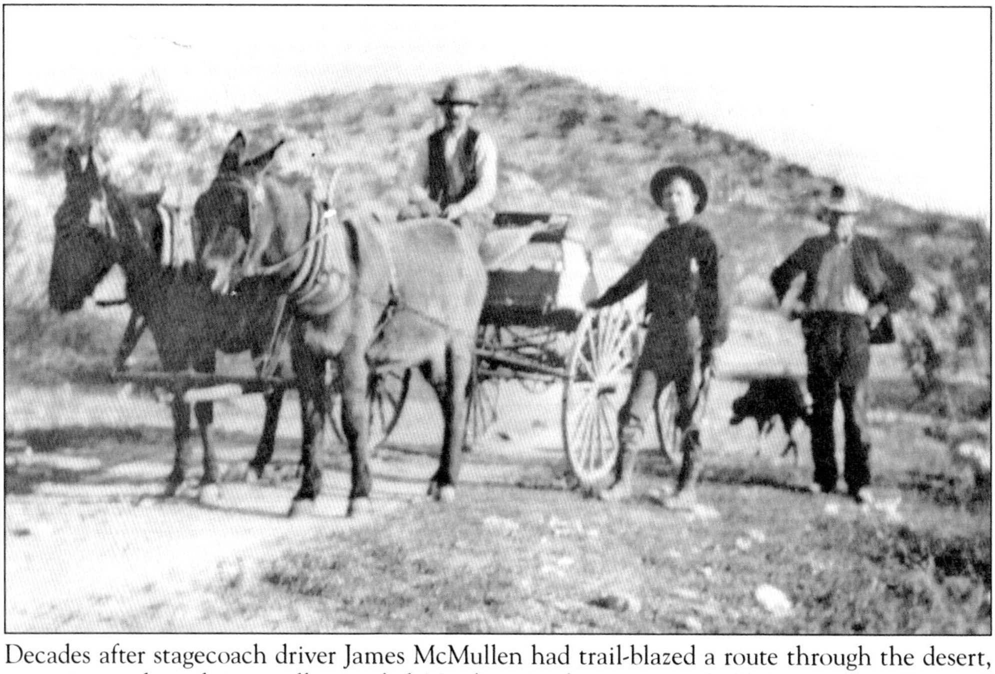

Decades after stagecoach driver James McMullen had trail-blazed a route through the desert, primitive road conditions still prevailed. Newly arrived pioneers and old-time miners all agreed that better roads would reduce their isolation, expand commerce, and improve the quality of their lives. The road issue, present from the earliest days of settlement, would remain a recurring theme in shaping the lives of residents in the valley for generations.

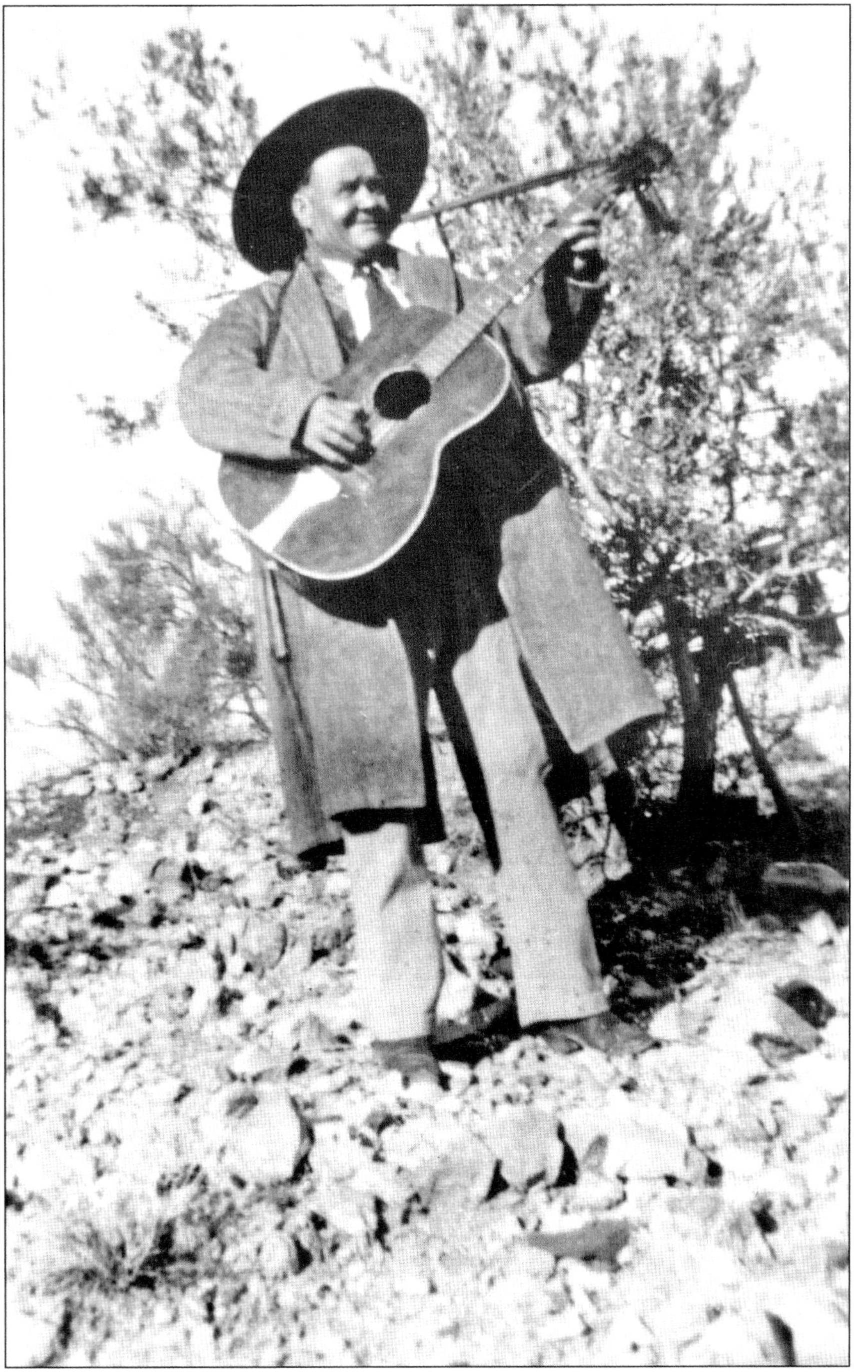

Musical entertainment could turn a long lonely desert night into an event. Saturday evening entertainment and dances were weekly features of life in Harrisburg during its heyday. As the camp declined, so did the opportunities for regular entertainment. Roland Nichols was an itinerant cowboy who worked the ranches and farms for a day's pay. In the evenings after dinner, he would pick up his guitar and sing. One young girl, now in her 90s, still fondly recalls his generosity for his gift to her of her first guitar.

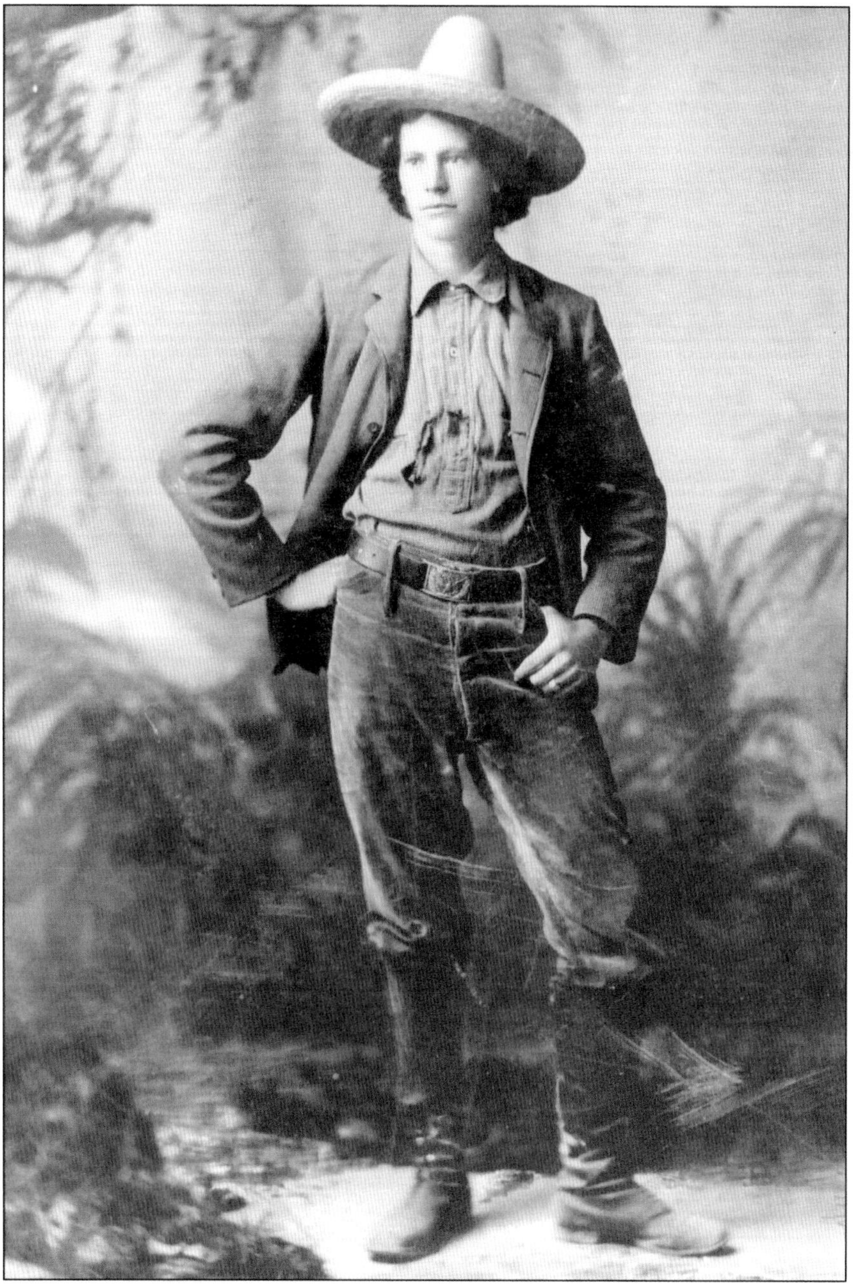

The first recorded Dick Wick Hall sighting in the Great Arizona Outback recalls his entertaining appearance at a Halloween party in Harrisburg in 1903. Hall openly shared his wit and engaging personality and was the "life of the party." However, it is doubtful that he was as open about his "certain knowledge" that the Santa Fe Railroad would soon begin laying track in the McMullen Valley. Born in March 1877 in Creston, Iowa, on what he called the coldest day of the 19th century, this young man came to the Southwest with a zest for life and inclinations toward satiric embellishment. DeForest Hall was too large a personality to be shackled to one name, identity, profession, or hometown. During a stint as a journalist, he found a mentor in Henry Wickenburg. He honored Wickenburg by transforming himself into Dick "Wick" Hall. (AHS Tucson.)

Two

The Mythmaker Envisions a Desert Paradise

Having come West an idealistic adventurer and friend to the Hopi, Dick Wick Hall was transformed by his experiences in the Arizona Territory. By the time he arrived in the McMullen Valley, he was a former political operative and journalist with ambition.

During 1904, with his brother, Ernest, and investor Charles Pratt, Hall purchased land to establish a town site. With a compelling vision, he named his town "Salome—Where She Danced." In one of Hall's satiric tales, he claimed he culled the name from Pratt's wife, Grace Salome.

However, at the time of the town's founding, all emerging femme fatales were being called Salome. "Salomania" was an international phenomenon, awakening passions on two continents. As he was a congenital mythmaker, it is entirely plausible Hall would choose to provide his remote desert town with a name that implied a little "spice."

Hall's mythmaking began in the service of promoting his town. His stories—informed by imagination and illustrated by his artist/buddy Claude Putnam ("Putt")—painted a pastiche of colorful characters. When the *Saturday Evening Post* began republishing Hall's yarns, America fell in love with the cavalcade of dreamers, optimists, and visionaries who lived their lives in Hall's desert paradise.

Fame was fleeting. When Dick Wick Hall died suddenly in 1926, Salome's 15 minutes of fame came to an end. The paved road he fought for remained an unrealized aspiration. His town lay stunted and stagnant. On the day Dick Wick Hall died, some wrote Salome's obituary as well. Current residents would deem those death notices as premature.

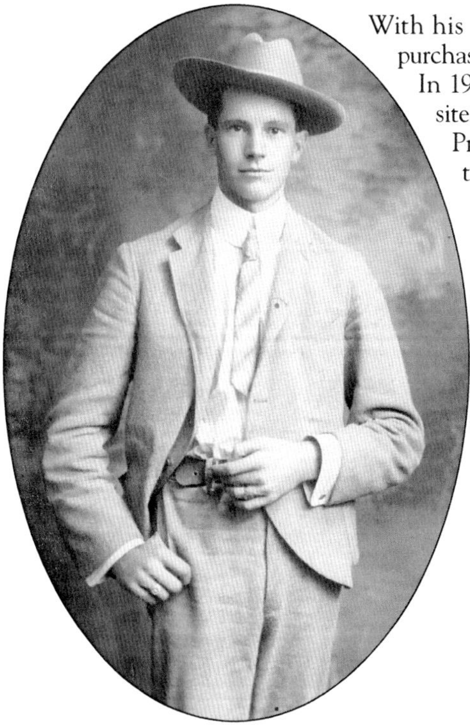

With his brother, Ernest, and investor Charles Pratt, Dick purchased land for a town adjacent to the Santa Fe Railroad. In 1905, they began building and marking off housing sites. Dick and Ernest remained to oversee construction. Pratt went off to sell their land. Reports filtered back that Pratt had been arrested on swindling charges in Cleveland. Undeterred, the Hall brothers pressed on. (AHS Tucson.)

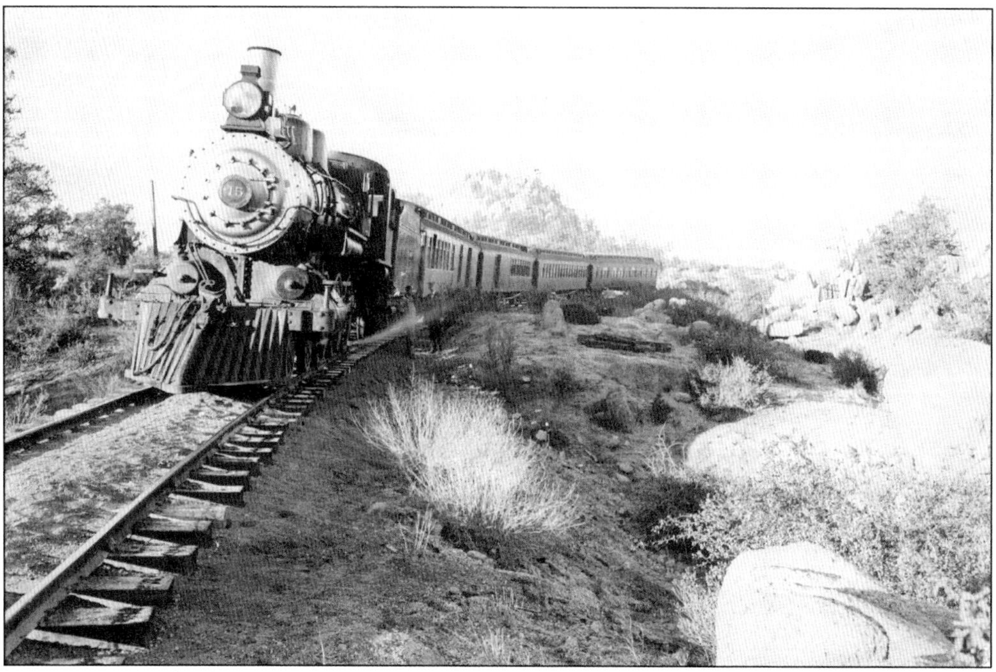

Experience taught that the arrival of the railroad would change everything. When the Santa Fe laid track a half-mile from the proposed route, the Hall brothers were surprised. But as Dick wanted his town next to the railroad, they had little choice but to pick up and move the town. So began 20 years of the improvisation and creativity Hall would need to survive. (Sharlot Hall Museum.)

E. S. Jones, an English immigrant, joined his old friend Dick Wick Hall in Salome. Initially Jones ran a general store, supplying the needs of the railroad builders. Eventually he built a boardinghouse, the Blue Rock Inne, and an automotive repair business. Fueled by Hall's never-ending schemes to promote the town, Jones's entrepreneurial dreams never ceased.

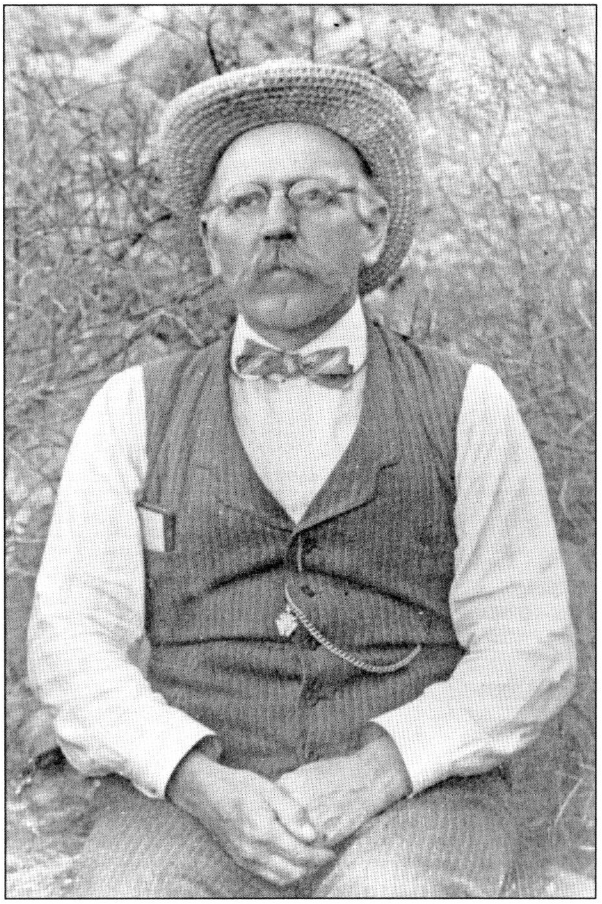

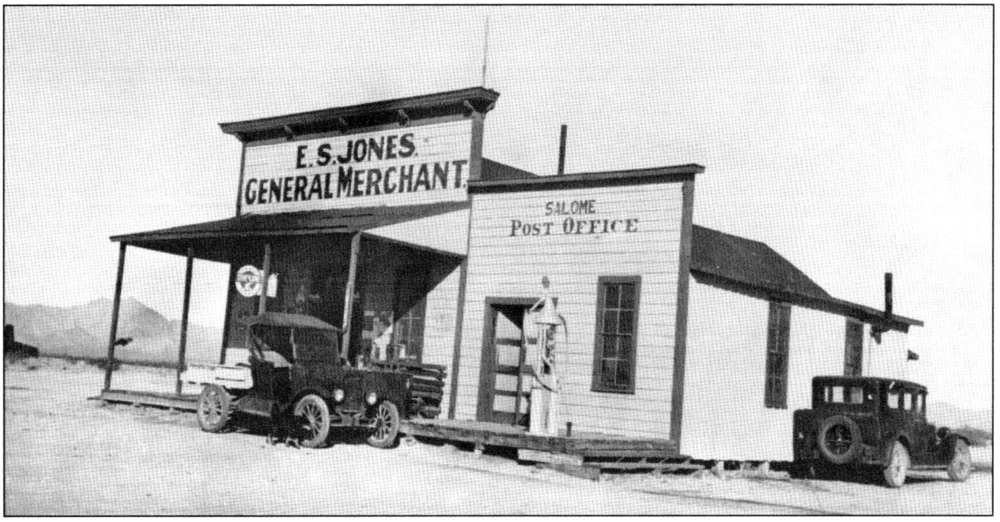

For the first decade of business in Salome, Jones ran the operation for Brayton Commercial. By the date of this photograph, 1916, Jones had bought out Brayton and was running his own shop. The gasoline pump indicates that the road traffic between Wickenburg and California had begun to pick up.

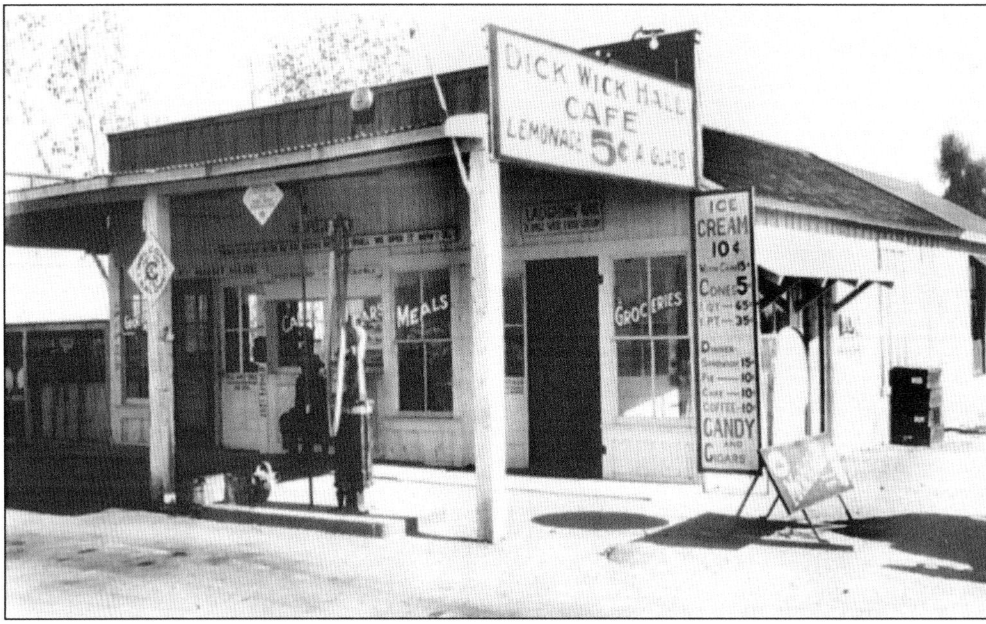

Fifteen years after he began, Dick Wick Hall's mines were not the glory holes he had hoped for. As talented and creative as he was, Dick Wick Hall's greatest gift was resilience. Dick bought a gas station and promoted it with ingenious road signage and the newspaper he called the *Salome Sun*, which became the launch pad for "a frog, who couldn't swim;" a 23-mile-long golf course; and a cast of characters like the Reptyle Kid and Chloride Kate, whose exploits he recounted, often in rhyme. The *Saturday Evening Post* began reprinting his stories, catapulting Dick and Salome to nationwide fame.

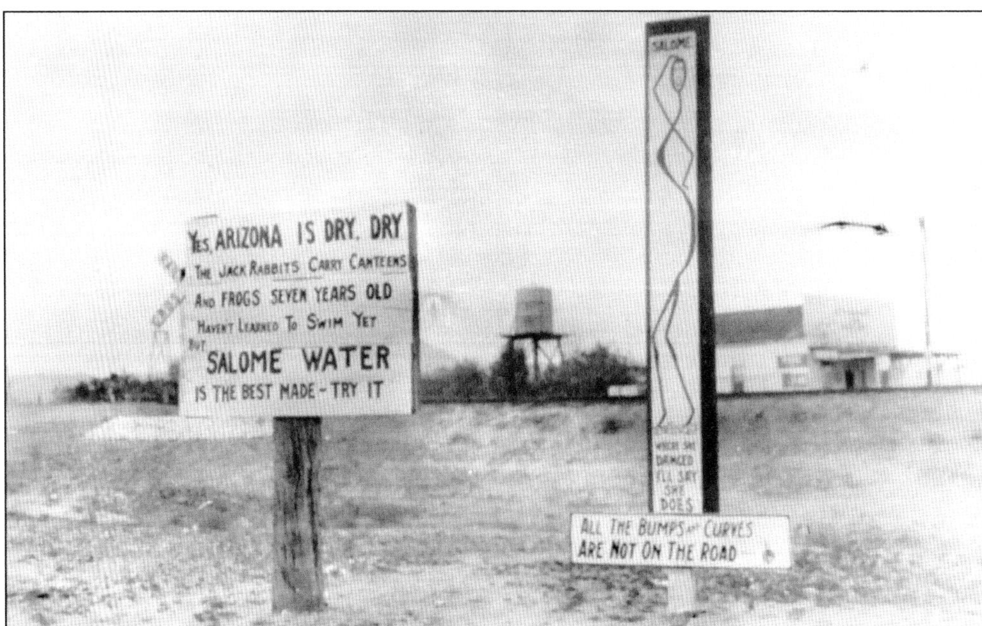

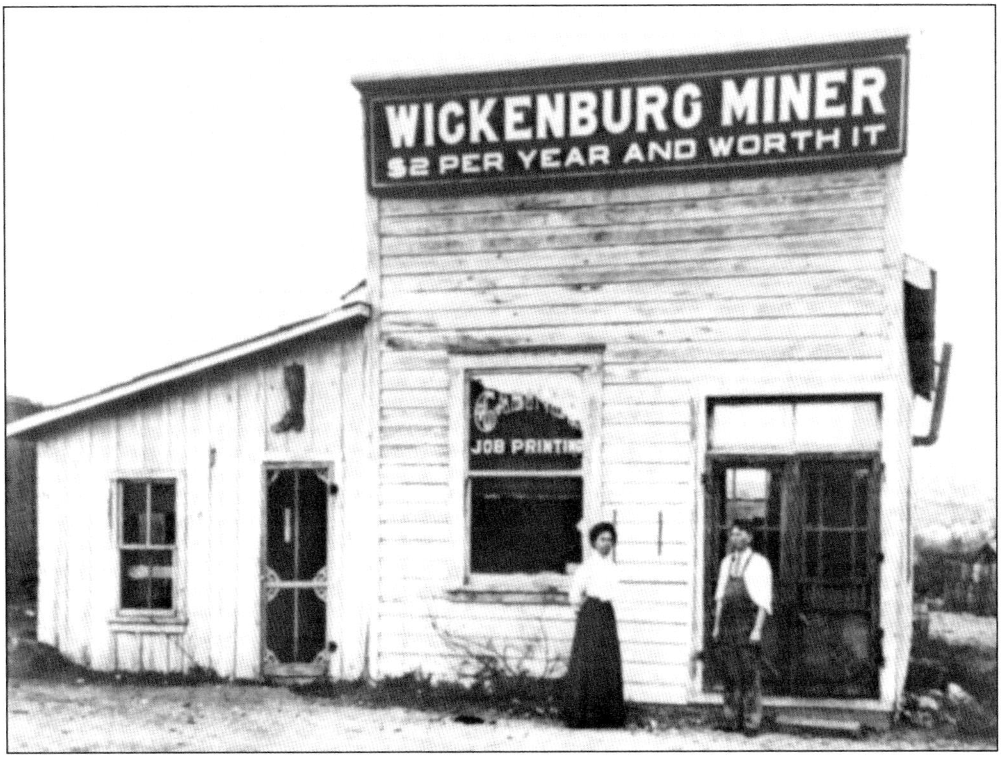

In 1903, Angela Hammer, a divorced mother and trained typesetter, bought the *Wickenburg Miner* newspaper. Becoming its publisher as well as its reporter, advertising manager, and editorial columnist, Angie saw the economic growth the railroad brought to the McMullen Valley as an opportunity to boost circulation and advertising rates. She devised a plan to sell her newspaper in Wenden, Salome, Bouse, and Swansea. Her "desert syndicate" would print a customized front page with local news and advertising. Weekly, Angie rode the train and was met by her local stringers. Newspapers were removed from the train as she hurriedly collected tidbits, rumors, and gossip suitable for publication before reboarding for the next town. Below, the stationmaster at Wenden Depot is caught in a jovial mood. During this time, only one train with passengers was on this route. (Above, University of Arizona Press.)

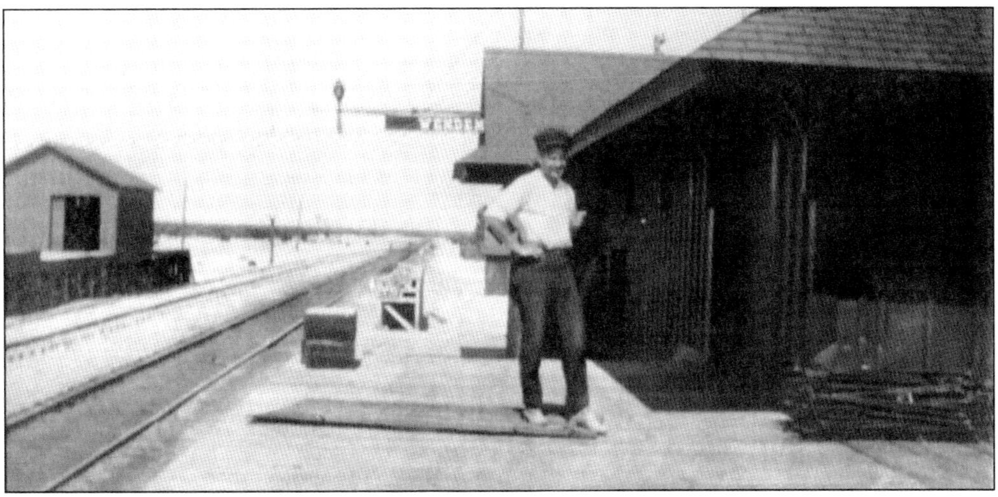

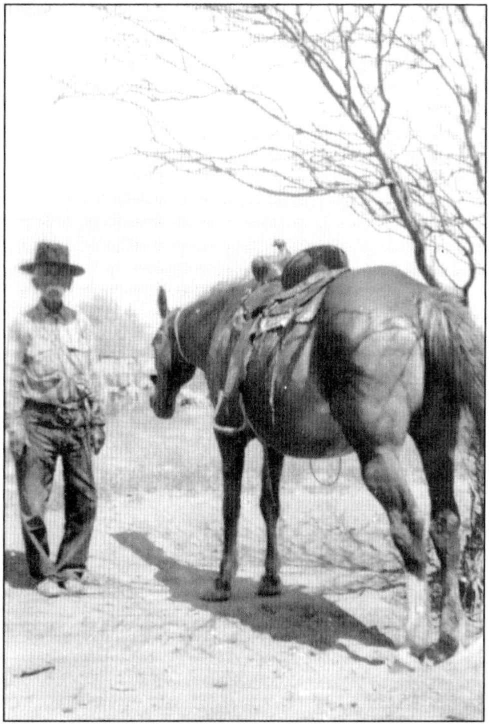

Remembered fondly by older residents of Wenden, Pete Nevarez was an early miner who hand dug a productive well. Pete's well's reputation came from supplying fresh water for horses and unlimited amounts of clean, potable water. Pete lived many years, sharing fond memories of the miners long gone and their adventurous nights in the mining camps of Harrisburg and Harqua Hala.

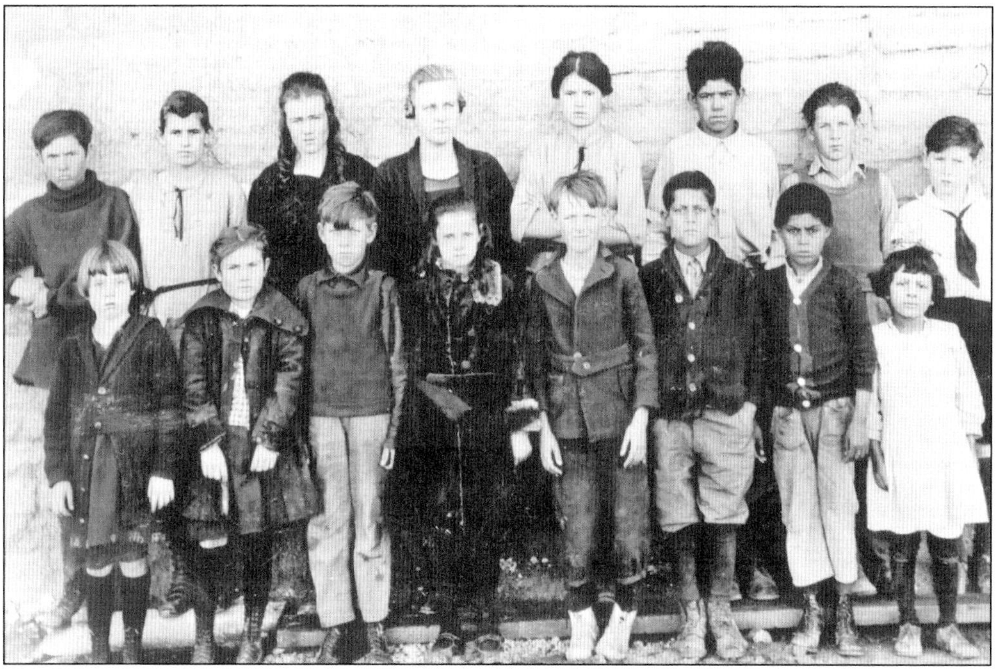

Students of Salome Elementary School are pictured standing outside the Bluebird saloon in 1923. A classroom by day, the Bluebird was a desert bar at night. In 1928, a school building was constructed. Evelyn Watkins, E. S. Jones's daughter and Salome's first teacher, stands in the second row. Among those identified are (first row) second from left, Nell Brown and, fifth from left, Hayden Brown; (second row) far left, Ted Brown and, third from left, Annie Brown.

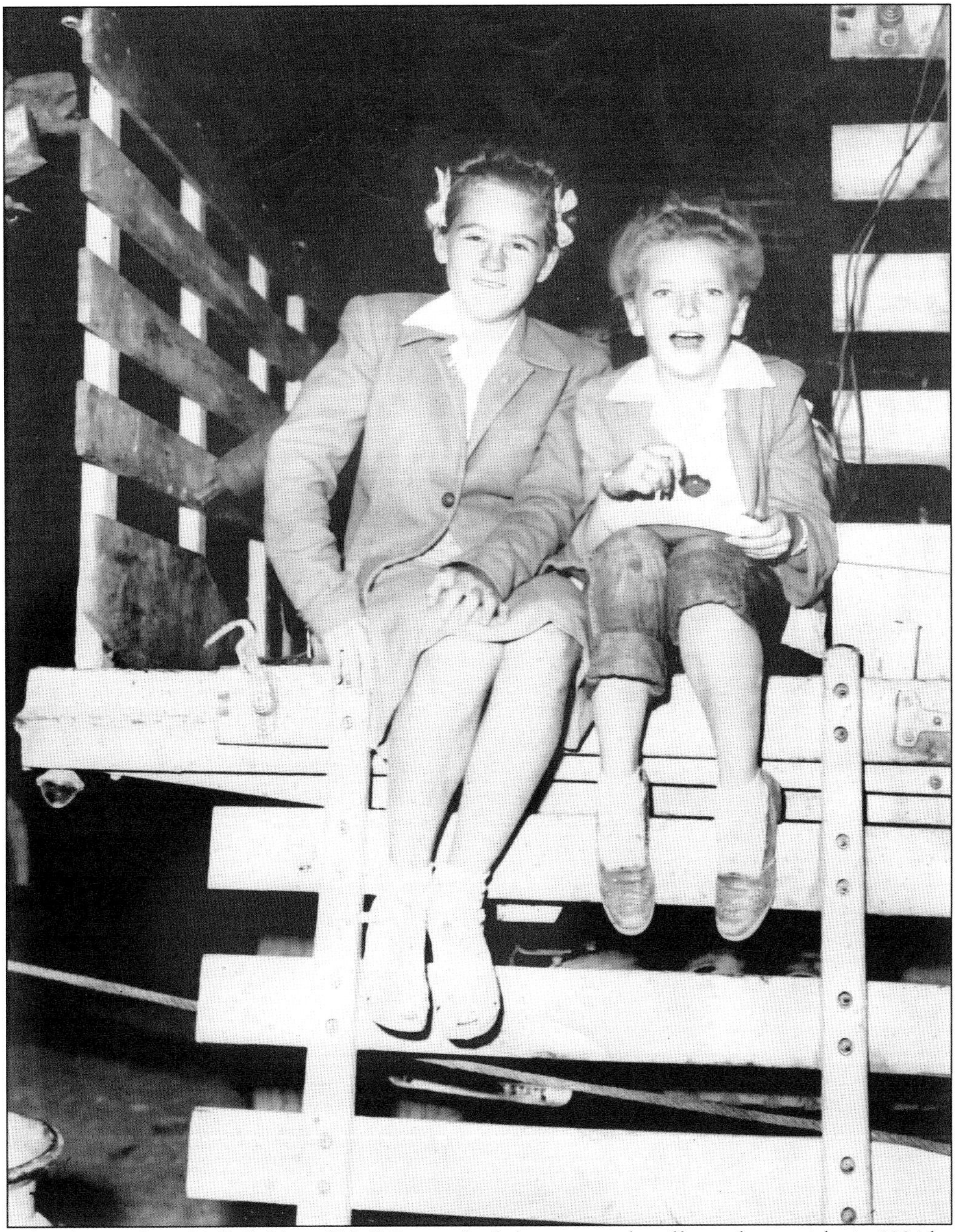

Schoolmates Jane Hall (left) and Nell Brown (right) were caught off guard one night in 1924 by a photographer's flashbulb. Nell can't recall the night 84 years ago as clearly as she would like. However, she does believe she and Jane were having a very engaging conversation and the food that night was particularly tasty.

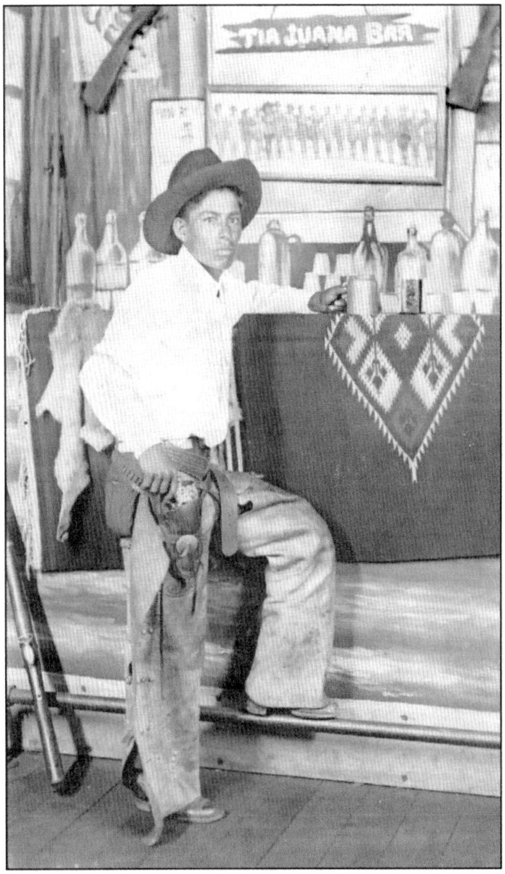

The smartly outfitted young caballero, obviously too young to be served in a real saloon, was raised outside of Bouse. Ray Montijo would begin his career with the highway department working on the Parker Bridge and remain employed for many decades. He would marry Marcella Esquerra, whose family had founded the renowned Planet Ranch near the Bill Williams River in 1844. They would become Armando "Mo" Montijo's parents. (Montijo family.)

The burgeoning movement of emigrants from eastern cities and rural expanses of Europe provide the Great Arizona Outback residents with ancestors from a wide variety of backgrounds. Pictured making their way west are members of the Randall family from Norway. Their descendant K. K. Randall would operate the Randall Brothers garage for many years beginning in the 1950s. (Montijo family.)

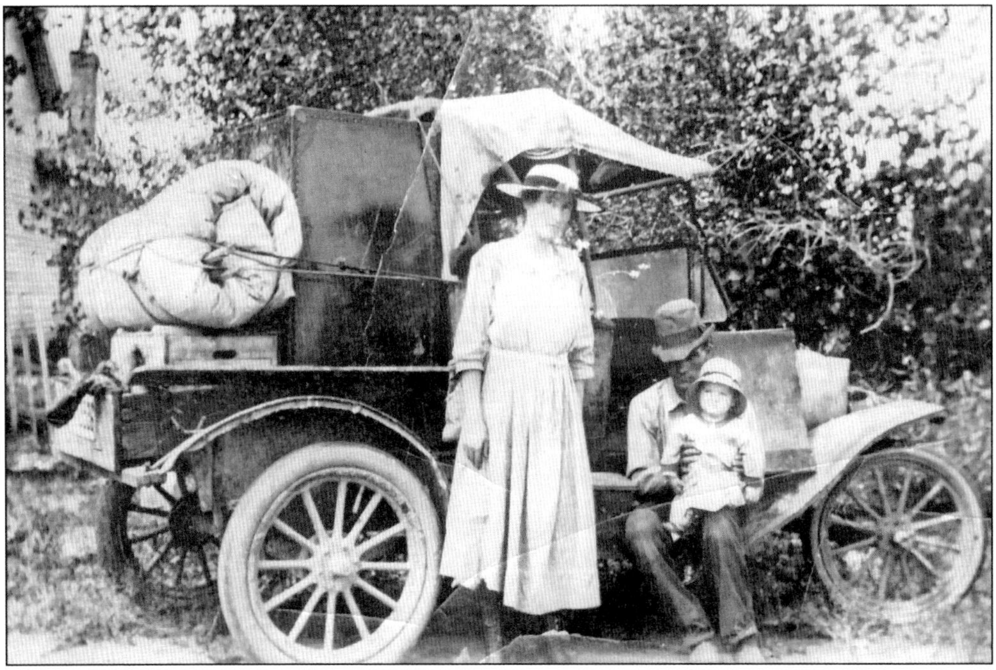

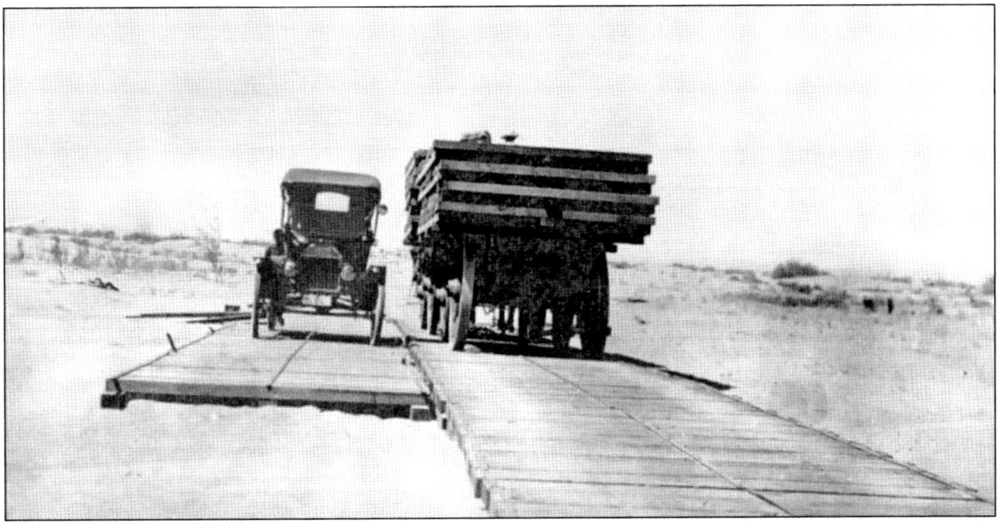

To his last breath, Hall would proselytize about the need for a good, decent, and paved road through the McMullen Valley. He believed the development the town deserved would not be possible without it. Most of his battles were with Yuma County and their highway department. Although Hall belittled the antiquated, infamous wooden plank road (pictured), it was a source of pride for the officials in Yuma. (AHS Tucson.)

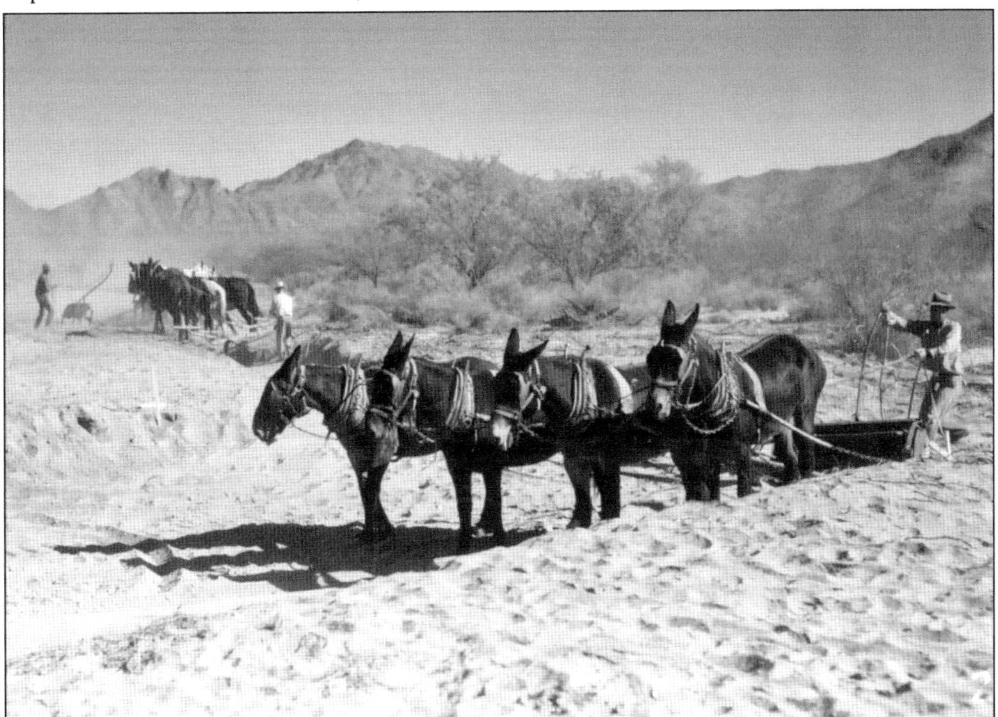

In his travels around the West, Dick Wick Hall saw that roads were being built everywhere but Yuma County. He wrote friendly and vituperative letters, trying everything to stimulate action on the road issue. But only when he attained national prominence did Yuma County begin answering his letters. They never built the road Hall wanted. The state did, but Dick Wick Hall never lived to see it. (AHS Tucson.)

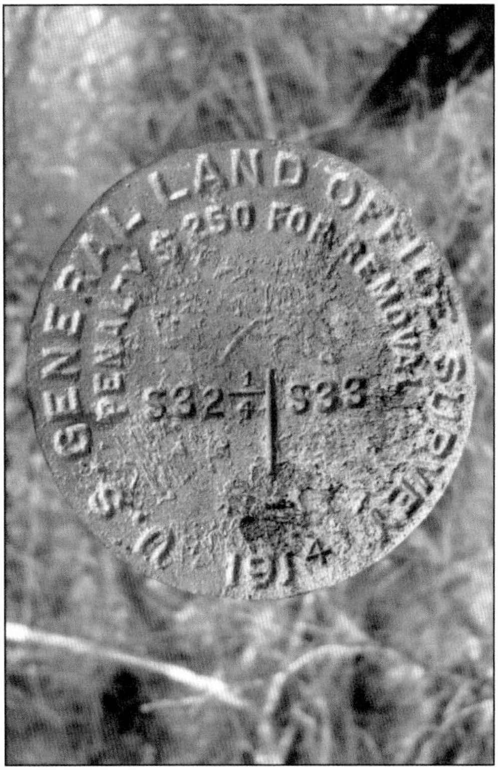

This U.S. General Land Office Survey pin was recently found in the foothills of the Harcuvars. Nearby, an aged and deformed golf ball was discovered. Some old-timers conclude that the pin marked part of Dick Wick Hall's 23-mile Greasewood Golf Course. The land once owned by Dick's sidekick and one-time cook Chloride Kate will soon be home to the Rattle Ranch Retreat, an institute for creative arts.

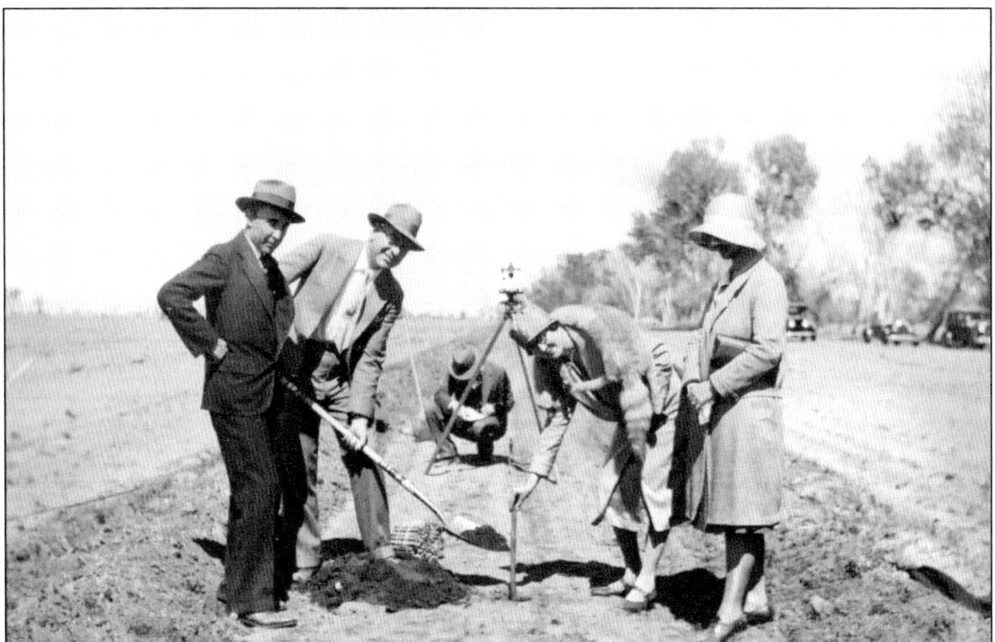

Despite growing national fame, Dick Wick Hall's struggles to make ends meet were never ending. Pictured in the mid-1920s in a publicity shot promoting one of his many projects, Hall (holding the shovel) would never be rich but always remained indomitable. (AHS Tucson.)

Hall once wrote, "This valley, about 15 miles wide and 40 miles long, lying between the Harquahala and Harcuvar Mountains, appealed to me strangely the first time I came to it. Not only its abundant warmth but the wonderful peace and quiet of it which only a dweller of the desert can understand and appreciate. It is where I get acquainted with myself and maybe find something which every man in his own soul is consciously or unconsciously searching for." This serious statement was by the man who invented "the frog who couldn't swim." Dick Wick Hall was drawn here by *Salome Sun* artist and collaborator C. G. "Putt" Putnam. Below is the Sunkist Trail map, from a c. 1930 tourist magazine that picked up Hall's mantle urging travelers to drive through the McMullen Valley.

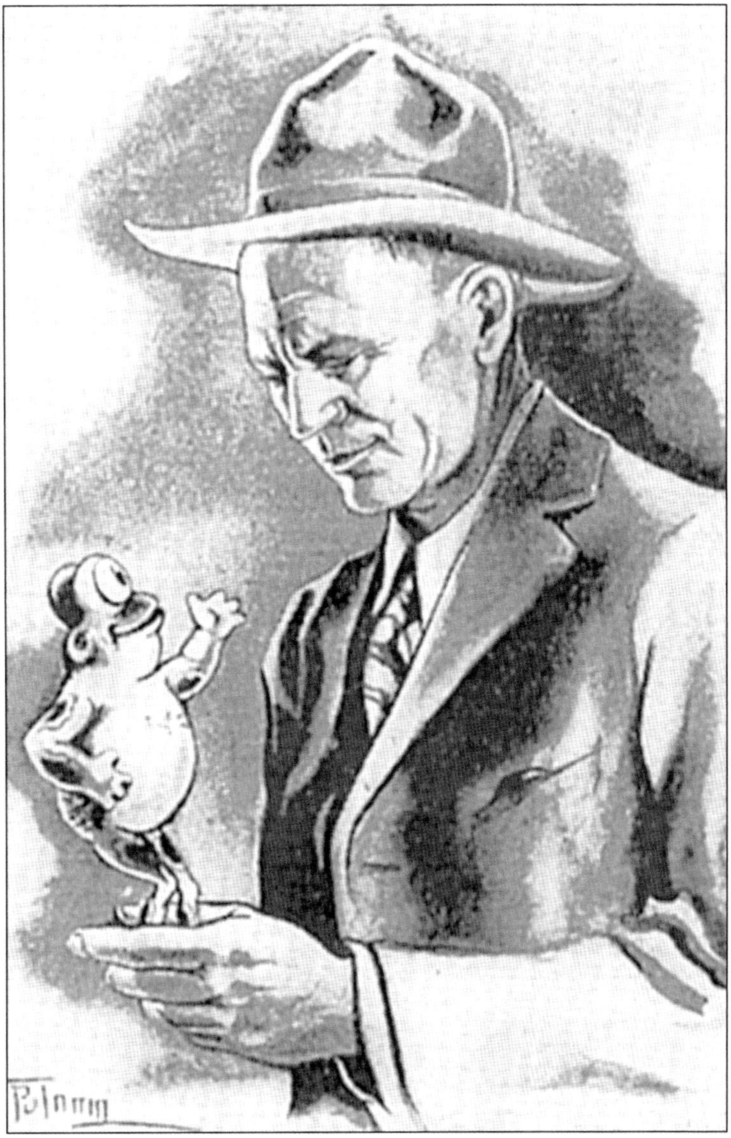

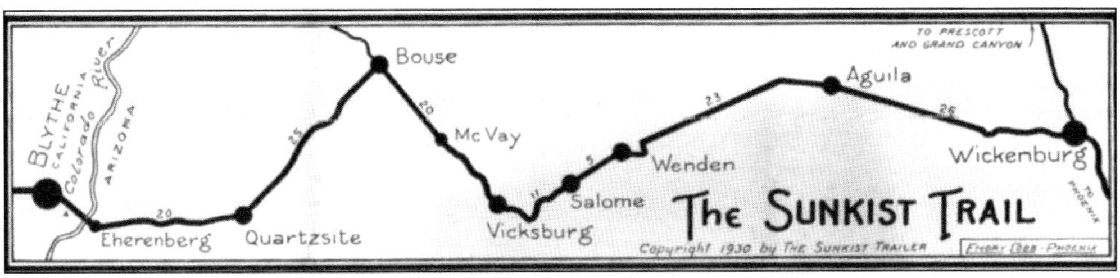

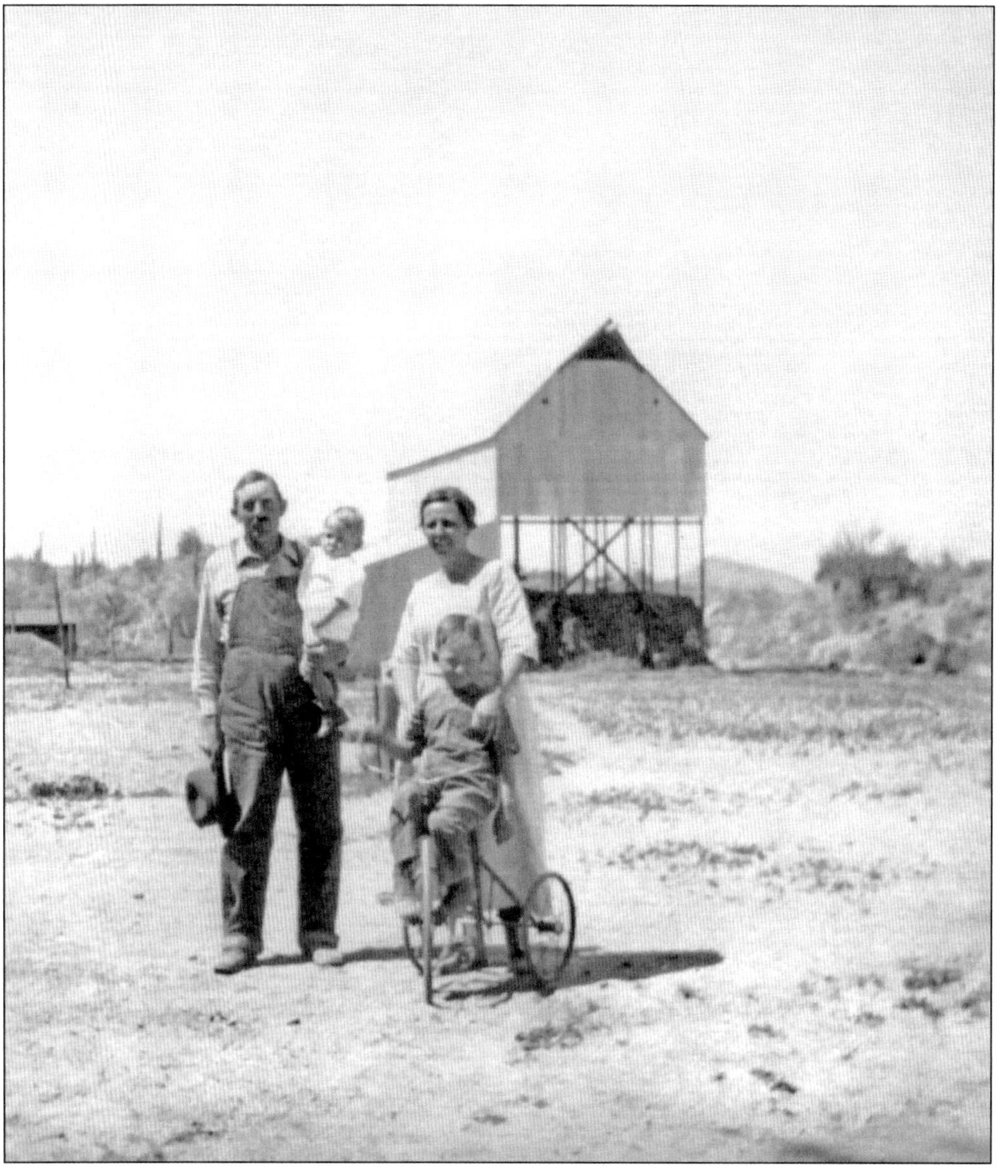

August Nord remains a prodigious figure remembered for turning the desert into a lush oasis of green fields and orchards surrounded by a tall grove of eucalyptus trees. His extensive cattle enterprise ranged across thousands of acres. The Swedish immigrant arrived in 1905 to work in the mines but quickly returned to his first love: farming. He served as a Yuma County supervisor and proved to be a tower of integrity throughout his life. Nord is pictured in 1922 holding his son Donald, with his wife, Kitty, and son Jack on his tricycle. The Nord Ranch was renowned for Kitty's gracious hospitality. Their youngest son, Albert, born in 1926 and not pictured, resides locally with his wife, Irene Walker Nord. (Nord family.)

Three

Wenden Ores, the Universe Soars, and a Diva's Encores

Founded as Wendendale one year after Salome in 1905 by Otis E. Young, the community initially served as the commercial center for the mines located in the nearby foothills to the north and south. Spanish families via Mexico, sons of European operatic divas, and California land barons laid out and developed extensive ranches and farms.

By 1907, the early mining camps were becoming ghost towns. However, around Wendendale, 5 to 10 miles north, numerous small mines were steadily producing sufficient gold for the Wells Fargo Company to open an office. The town was quietly growing faster than noisier Salome when a distant postmaster decided it would be more efficient for the post office if the name were shortened to Wenden. Despite local objections, the shortened version stood.

In 1919, the U.S. government's scientific agency, the Smithsonian Institute, chose Harquahala Peak above Wenden as the site of their most advanced solar observatory, as it offered the clearest skies and most opportune climatic conditions for year-round observation of the universe. The nation's top scientists braved primitive conditions and communications to gather data unavailable elsewhere. The ability to view the Milky Way remains one of the McMullen Valley's most valuable assets.

Wenden was not immune to the economic disaster that devastated the nation in the early 1930s, but its miners continued prospecting, its ranchers raised cattle, and local farmers still put seeds into the ground. Things would continue as they always had in Wenden, in quiet isolation. In 1935, many of the old miners returned to Harrisburg to bury one of their own, Bill Bear. After the funeral, they withdrew to a saloon, recognizing that an era was ending.

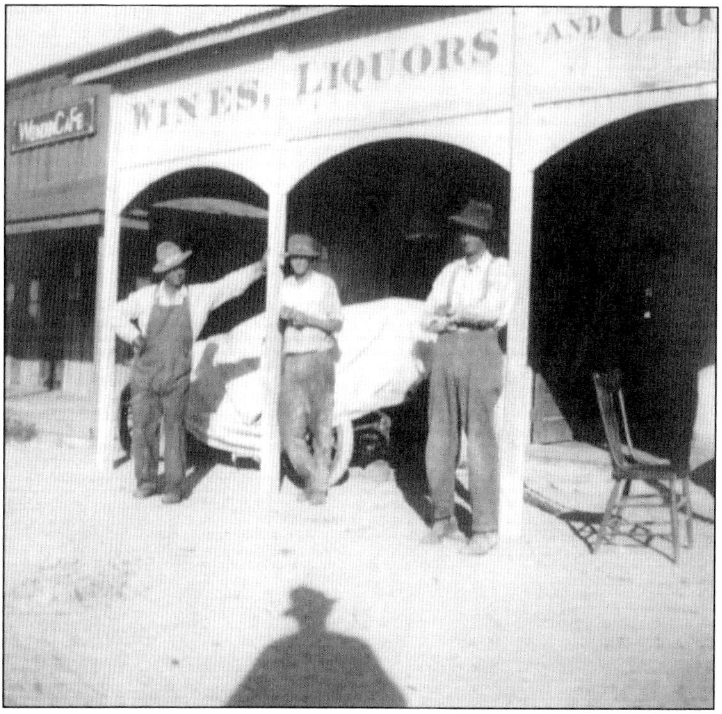

A day in Wenden was a day for business and some pleasure. The three unidentified men at left stand in front of one of the Wenden business establishments dedicated to providing general merchandise and spirits to help facilitate such pursuits. The adjacent Wenden Café is remembered for serving plain fare, with beans and rice that were usually warm and meat that was sometimes identifiable.

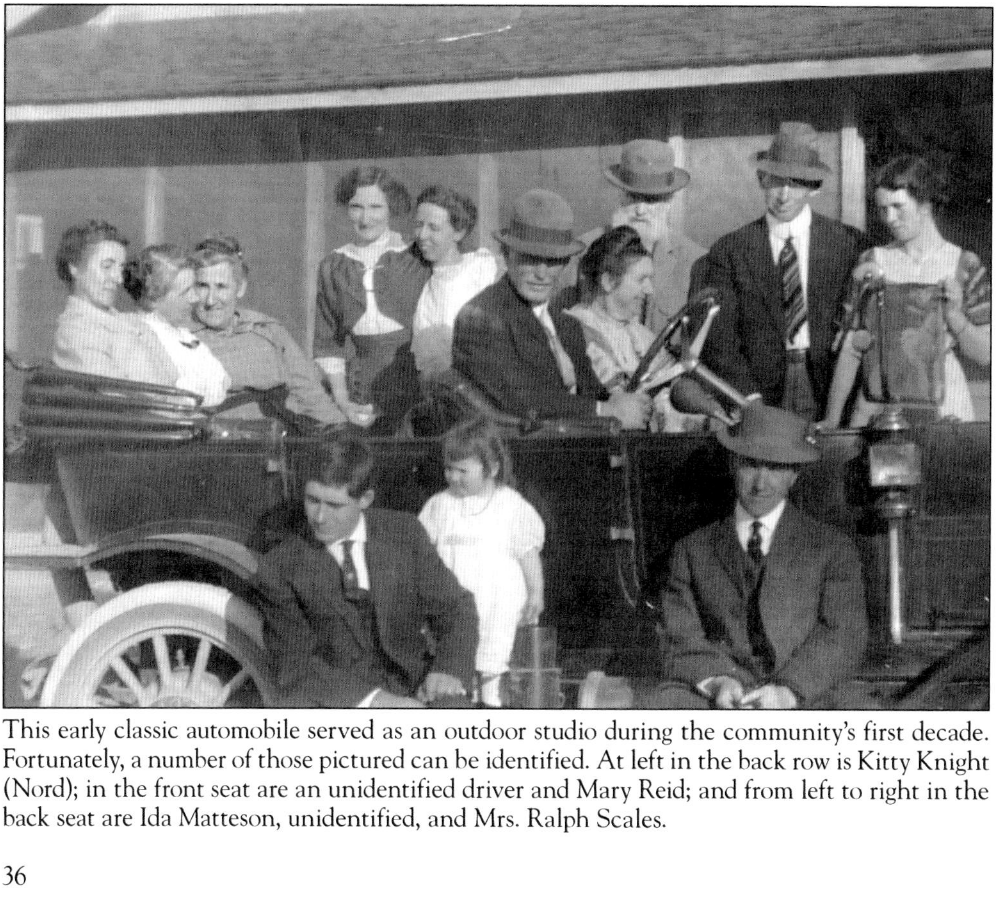

This early classic automobile served as an outdoor studio during the community's first decade. Fortunately, a number of those pictured can be identified. At left in the back row is Kitty Knight (Nord); in the front seat are an unidentified driver and Mary Reid; and from left to right in the back seat are Ida Matteson, unidentified, and Mrs. Ralph Scales.

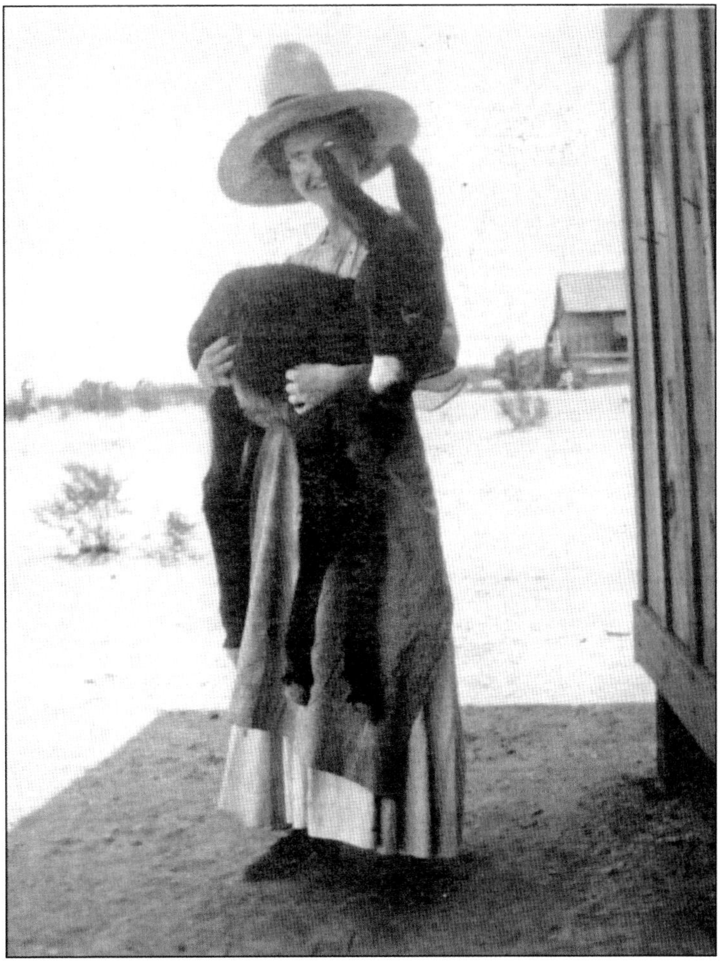

Five miles east of Salome, Wendendale dates its beginnings to 1905. The Santa Fe rail depot prompted the early establishment of a Wells Fargo office in 1907. Within only a few years, J. E. Matteson and other merchants came to open businesses that would make available everything prospectors might need. In addition to practical requirements like personal and professional supplies, hard rock miners needed to have some fun. This is perhaps one explanation as to why Ida Matteson agreed to be photographed in 1910 holding this baby burro.

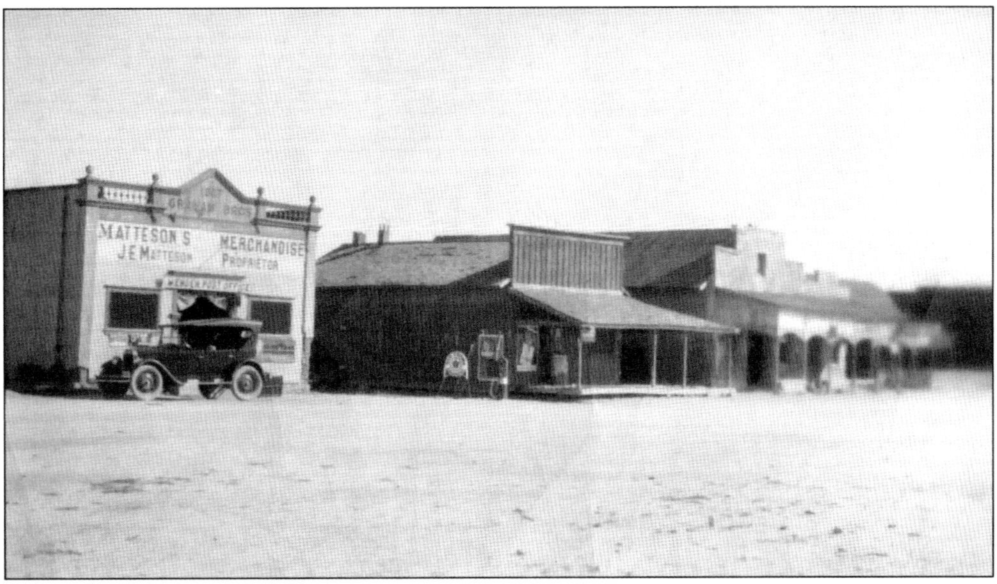

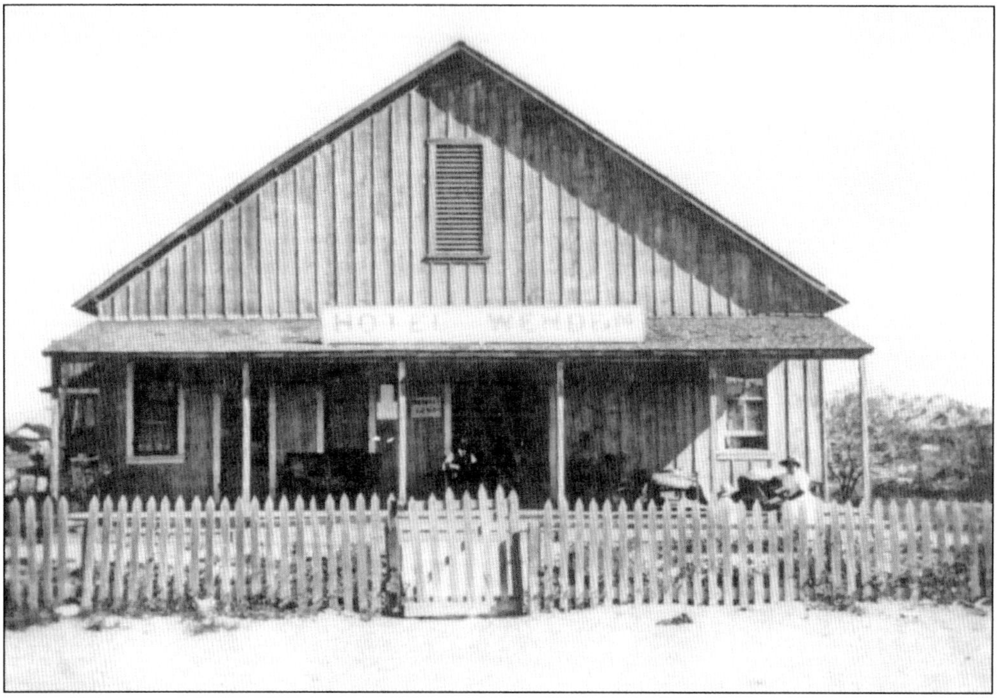

Mining records indicate that the years 1907–1908 were filled with numerous miners discovering small caches of valuable rock. The flurry of activity in Wenden resulted in a fresh flow of cash that prompted rapid growth. The Wenden Hotel (pictured above) opened to host peddlers and merchants who came to exploit the expanding pool of customers. The proprietress, a Mrs. Moss, is seated on the porch.

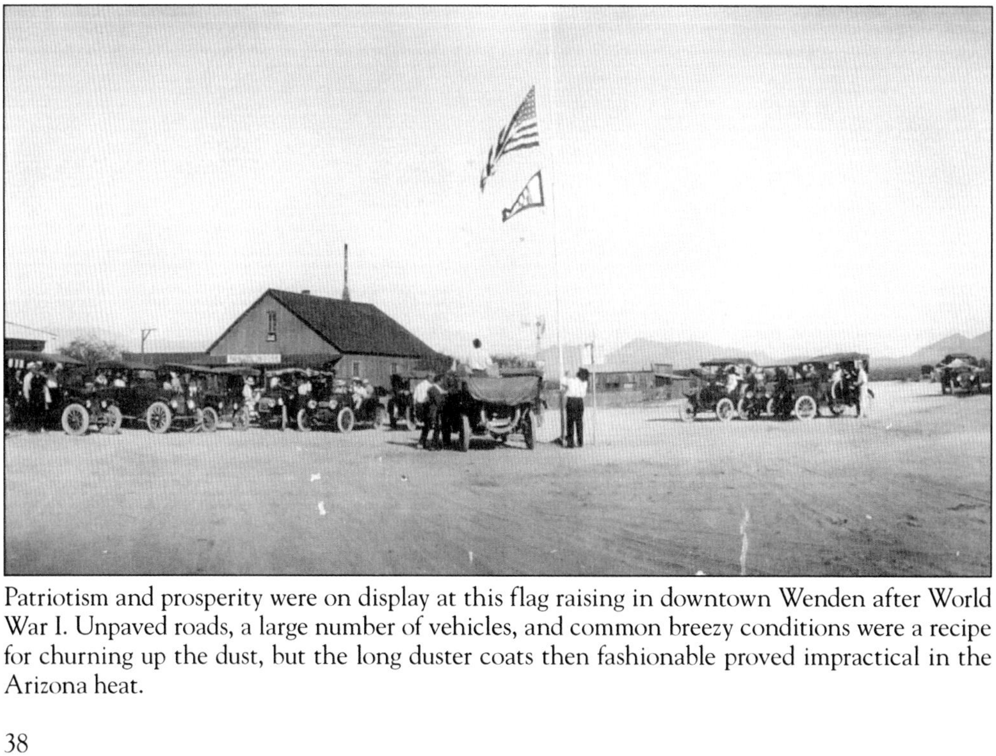

Patriotism and prosperity were on display at this flag raising in downtown Wenden after World War I. Unpaved roads, a large number of vehicles, and common breezy conditions were a recipe for churning up the dust, but the long duster coats then fashionable proved impractical in the Arizona heat.

The stage is set below for one of the most unusual cultural events to ever take place in Wenden—a Red Cross benefit performance in 1917 by Madame Ernestine Schumann-Heink, a world-renowned contralto. Several years earlier, the Metropolitan Opera singer had purchased a nearby ranch for her asthmatic son, Fred. With planks of wood placed on barrels, adjacent to a building and a pasture, the concert began at dusk. Cows returning home to their trough were also coming closer to the concert. By the time headlights from parked cars were turned on to illuminate the stage, harmonizing bovine voices had joined Madame Schumann-Heink in song. According to her personal account of the event, "Far more distracting was the large black beetle that flew inside the back of my dress." Madam Schumann-Heink is pictured at right at the time of her American debut in 1896.

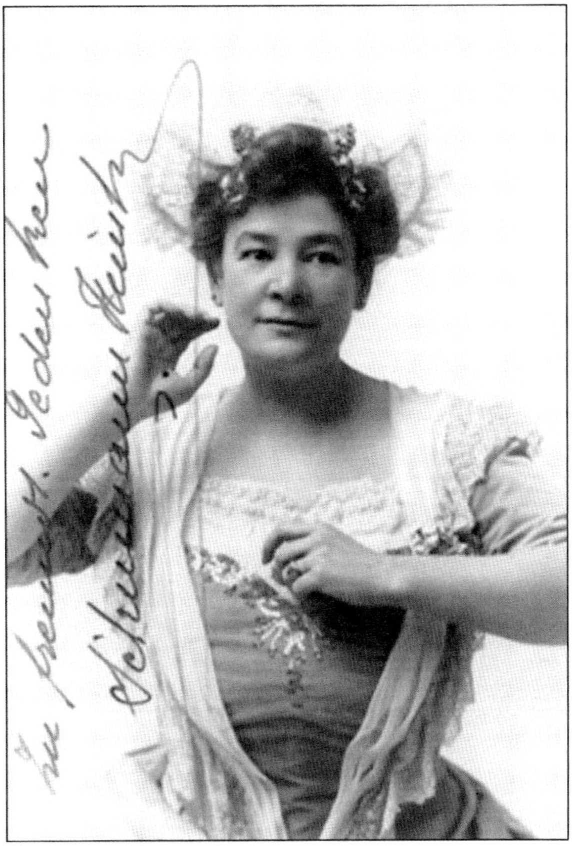

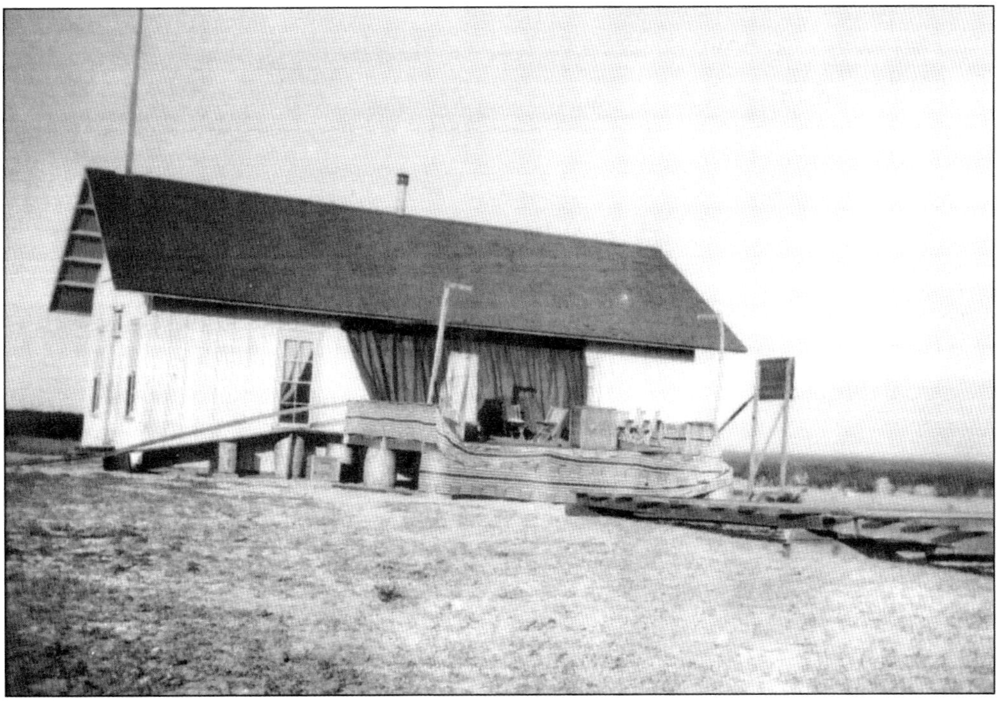

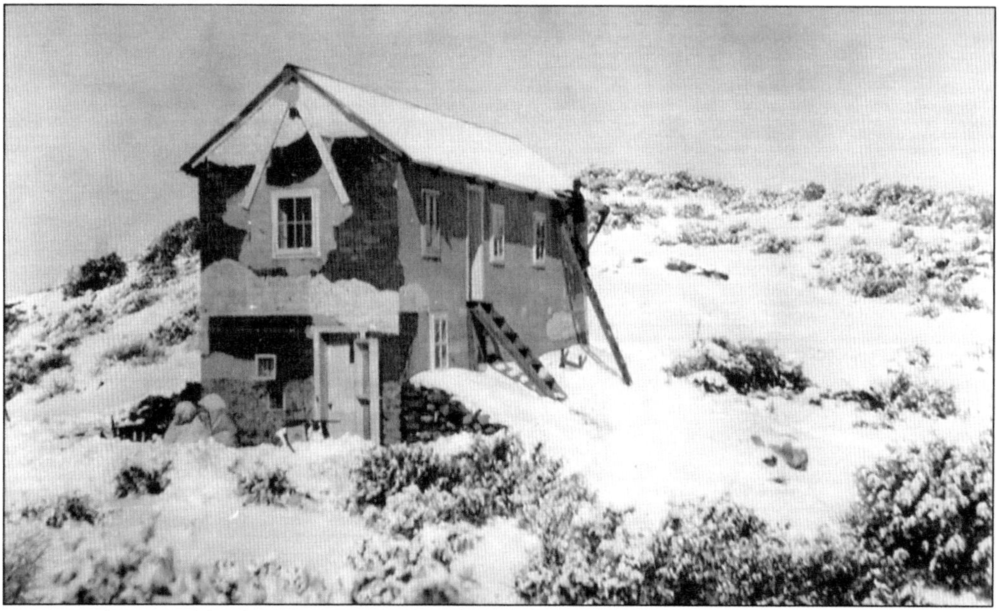

In 1920, after a worldwide search, the Smithsonian Institute chose Harquahala Peak above Wenden as the site for its most advanced solar observatory. After securing the surface rights from miner Charles Ellison, who had claims at the mile-high peak, lead scientist Charles Abbot contracted with locals from Wenden to build facilities, transport delicate instruments, and provide supplies. The 12-mile trek, the last 5 nearly vertical, took three hours. Communications were dependent on Morse code and heliograph mirrors, as radio had not yet been introduced to the area. Living conditions were primitive. However, the solar-constant measurements secured at the highest point above the McMullen Valley increased scientific understanding of the universe immeasurably. The harsh winter conditions above undermined the field station before construction was completed. Note the tie rod braces used to straighten the south wall. Below, the field station was photographed in 1924. (Both Smithsonian Institution.)

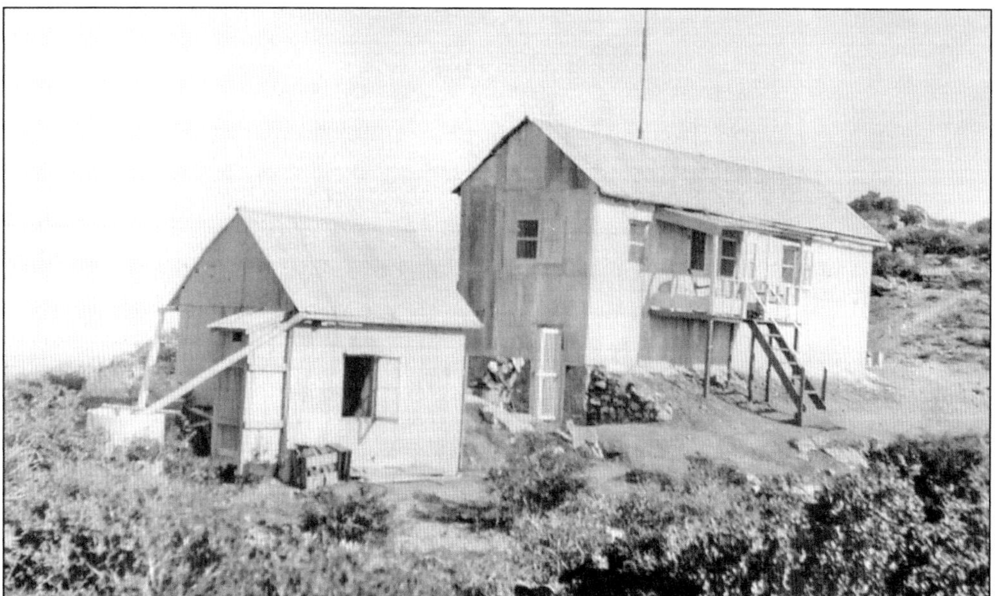

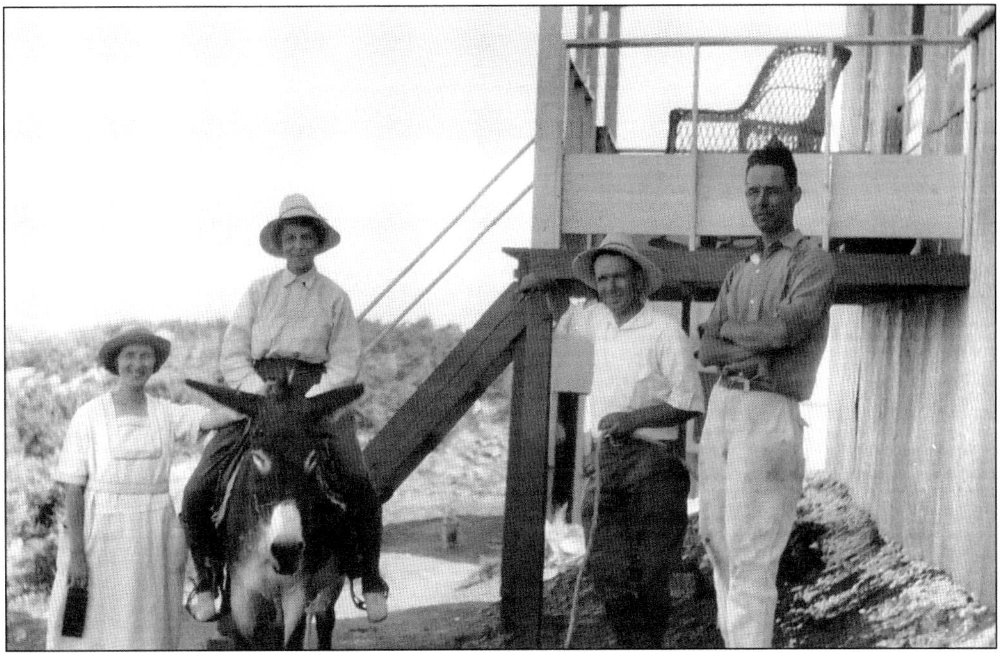

After one year, Abbot was satisfied with the data collection but troubled by furious spring winds and winter snows. Newly married Alfred Moore was chosen as his resident replacement. Moore accepted after his bride, Chella, agreed to share his remote scientific assignment. As the only woman, Chella Moore's presence had a civilizing effect. Her garden yielded vegetables that supplemented the men's all tinned-food diet. Chella's correspondent Lillian Abbot accompanied her husband, Charles, when he returned for a visit. Taken in 1922, the photograph above shows, from left to right, Lillian Abbot, Chella Moore, Albert Moore, and Fred Greeley. Below are Alfred Moore's Ford truck and a garage built at the foot of the vertical trail for hauling supplies and easing Chella Moore's trips to Wenden. These days, the Bureau of Land Management administers the site as part of a natural wildlife reserve. (Both Smithsonian Institution.)

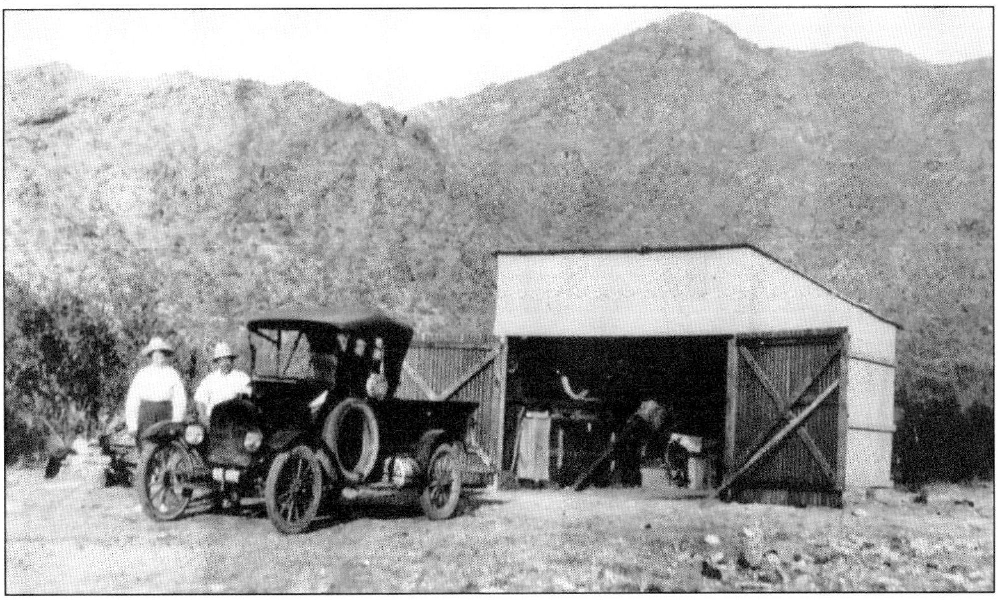

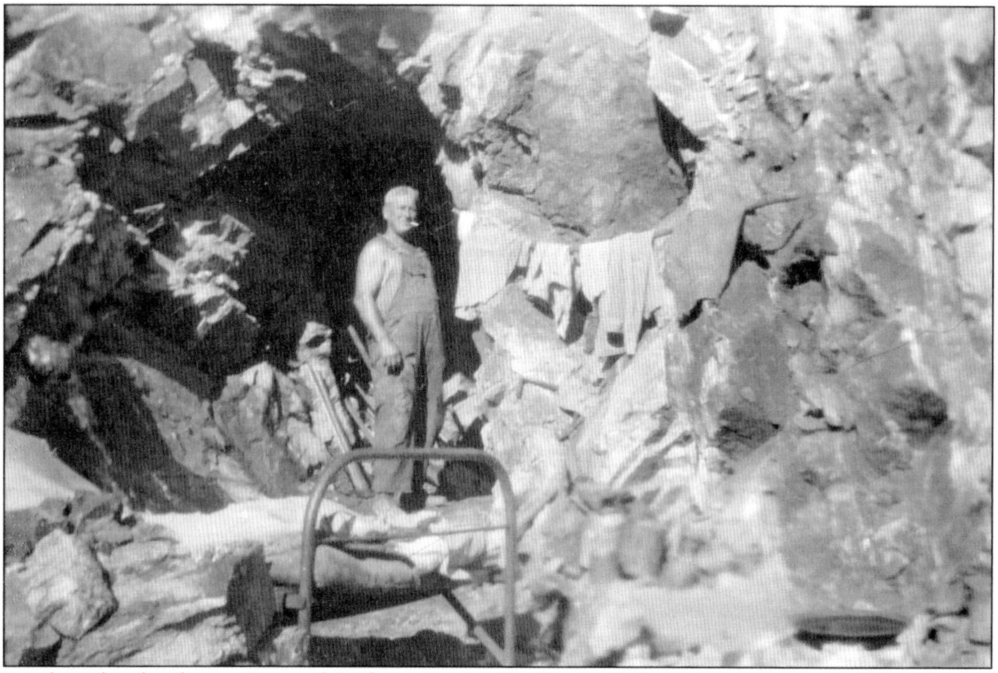

It is laundry day for a miner at his claim site in the Harquahalas in approximately 1915. If water were unavailable, it would have to be hauled great distances. Scarcity made recycling and reuse the credo. (Rohrig family.)

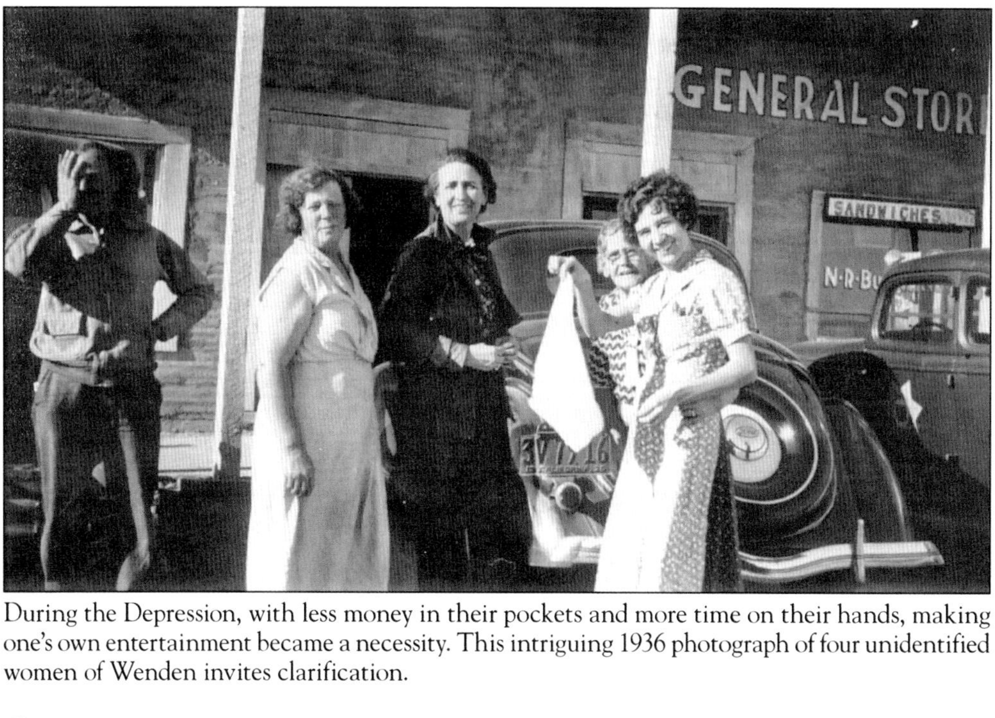

During the Depression, with less money in their pockets and more time on their hands, making one's own entertainment became a necessity. This intriguing 1936 photograph of four unidentified women of Wenden invites clarification.

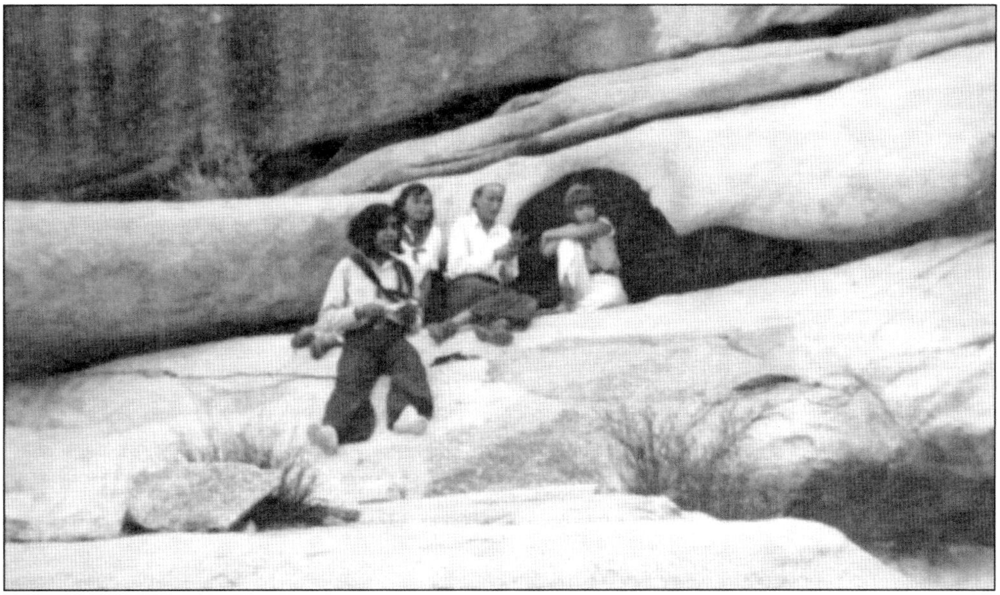

In 1930, Stella Orosco of Wenden (front left) and friends hiked to the pools at Indian Springs. Located in the northwestern corner of the valley, close to the convergence of the Granite Wash and Harcuvar Mountains, the springs have continued as a favorite destination for hikes, picnics, and Easter breakfasts for generations. (Rohrig family.)

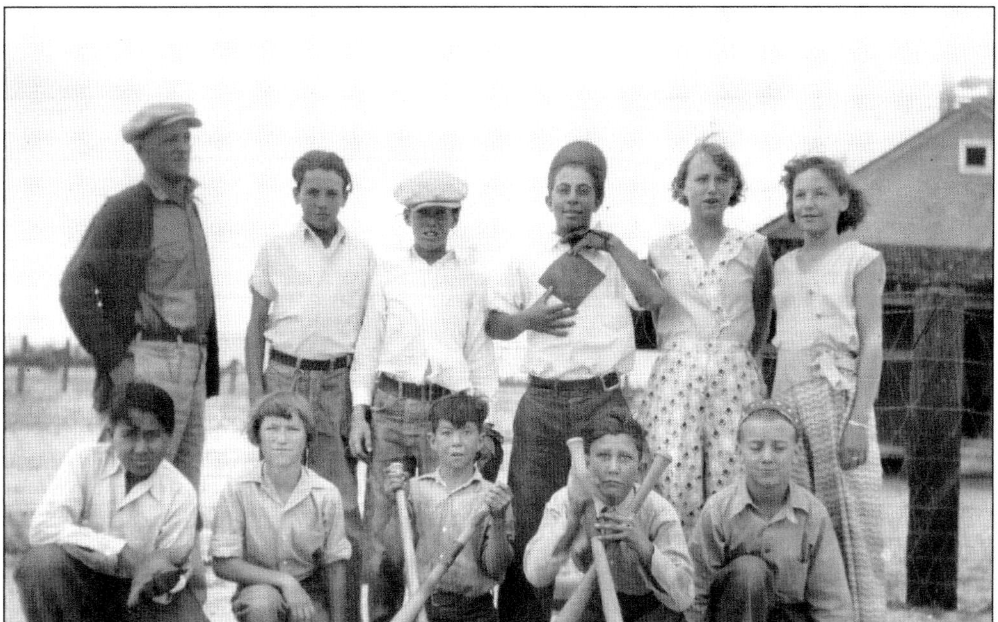

In 1931, this unisex team of boys and girls were the Wenden baseball champions. Contemporaneous photographs from the Wenden school indicated that other boys were available to play; they simply did not make the team. (Rohrig family.)

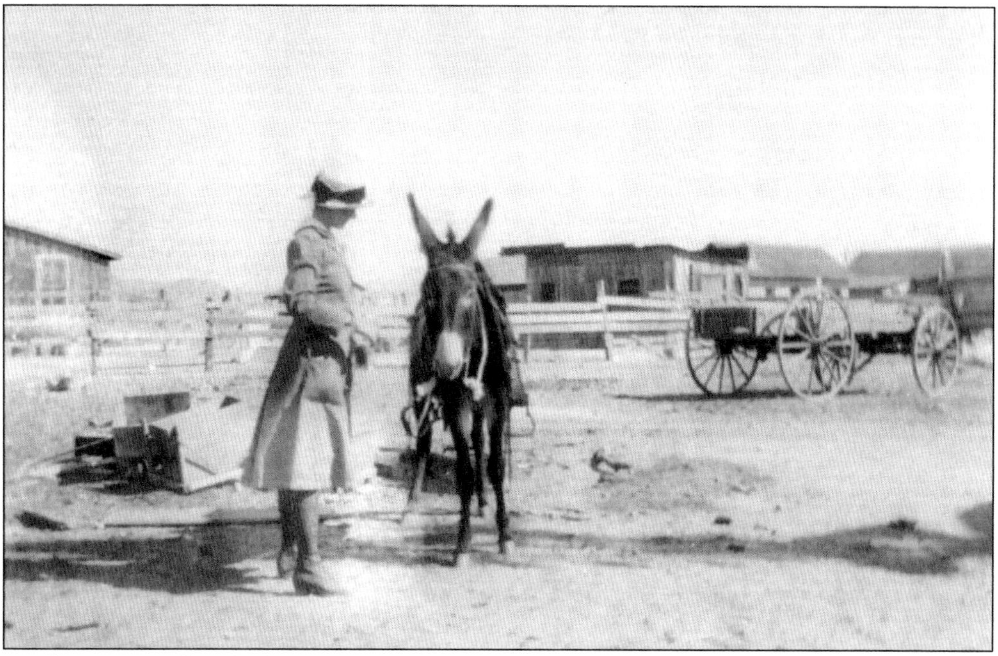

As the 1920s ended, finding investors for mining ventures had become more of a challenge. Agents were hired to sell investors on the "lucrative adventure" of owning shares in a gold mine. Wealthy Easterners with stylish lady friends were brought out from their winter homes in Phoenix on inspection tours.

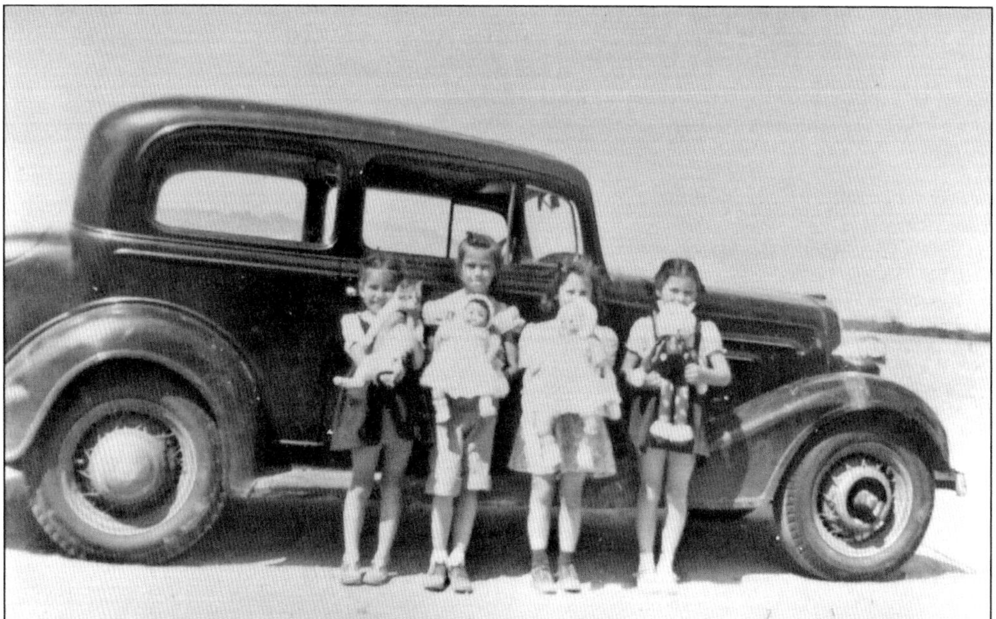

The Santa Fe Railroad tracks have always separated neighborhoods in Wenden. But it has never been one of those towns where which side of the tracks you lived on mattered much. The Orosco cousins played with all the neighbor kids. Pictured from left to right are Donna Orosco, Betty Getty, Nellie Atchley, and Frances Trainor. (Frances Baird.)

Viola Orosco, pictured in 1929, was a member of the large and respected Orosco family, one of the first Latino families to settle in Wenden. A natural teacher, Viola is remembered as an inspiration to her students. She taught for 40 years. A beloved educator, she would be honored with induction into the Arizona Teachers Hall of Fame. A monument in honor of her achievements graces the school to this day. (Rohrig family.)

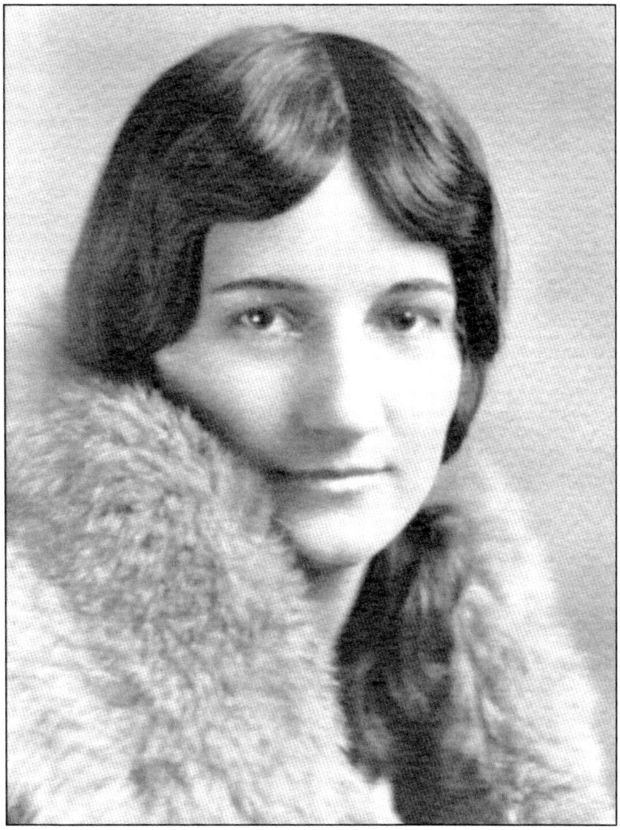

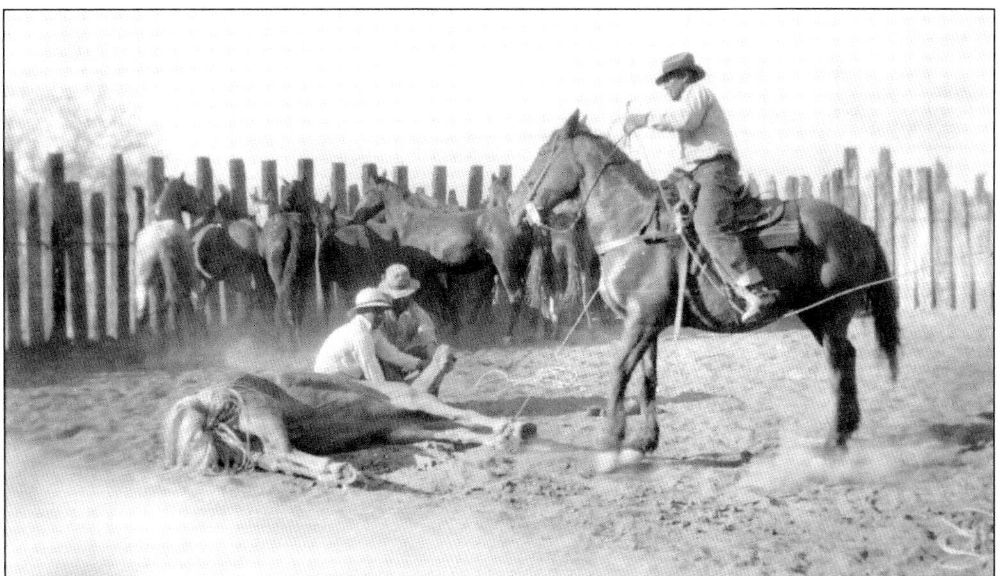

A photograph shows people branding horses at the Orosco ranch outside of Wenden in 1935. The family ranch raised cattle and horses and farmed as well. The reputation of their outstanding watermelons has stood the test of time. Elias Orosco (on horseback) was also known as "Smokey" for his fiery temper. (Rohrig family.)

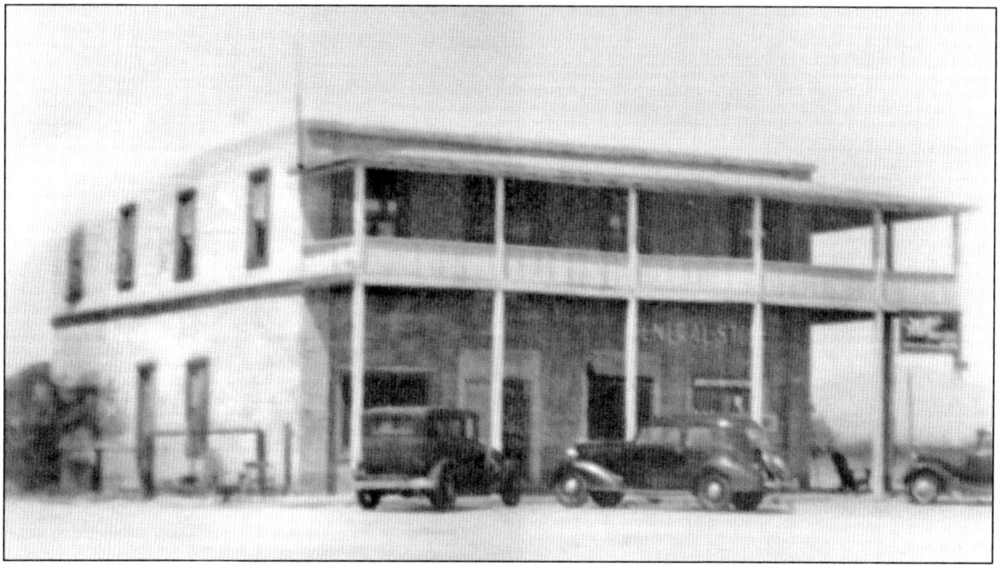

Pictured is the southwest corner of the Main Highway and East Second Street in Wenden as seen over the past 90 years. The photograph above shows the building after its construction some time before 1920. The second-floor balcony provided the boardinghouse residents with fresh air and a clear view of the railroad tracks. It is reported that several female residents never opened their curtains to take in the view. The photograph below dates from the mid-1930s. Whether the balcony was destroyed by fire or a planned removal remains lost.

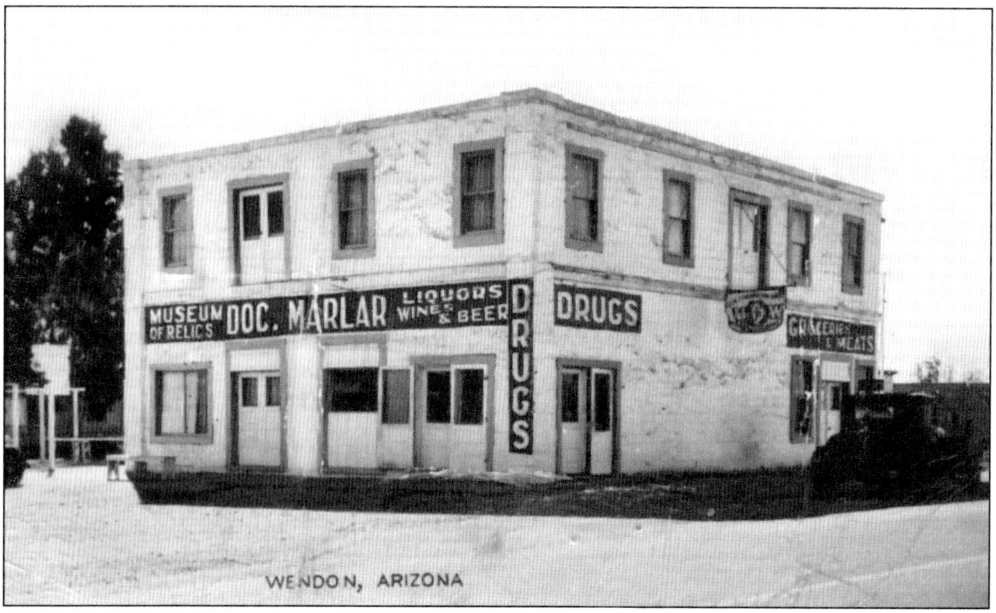

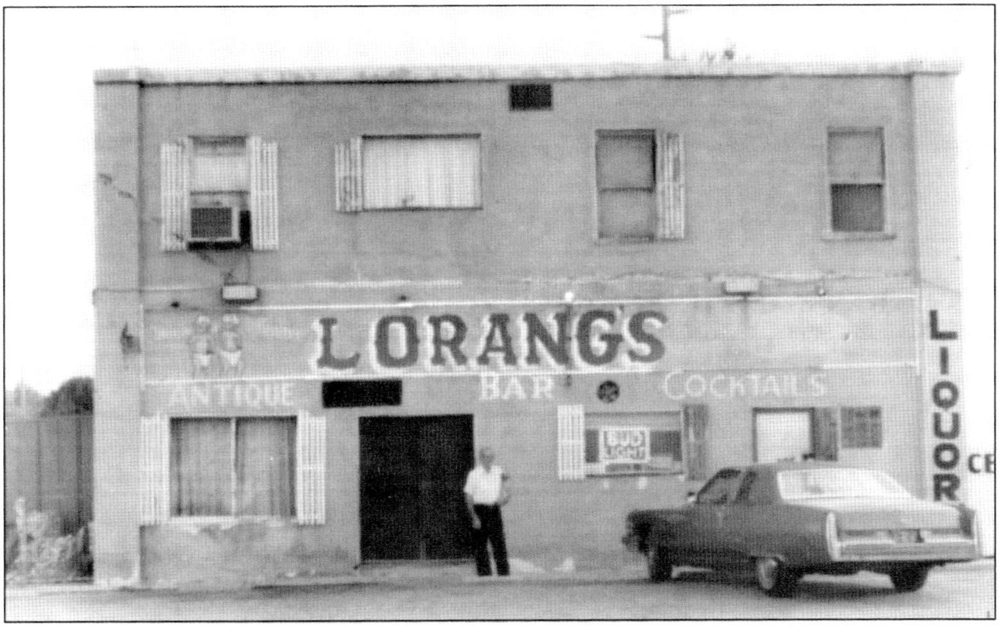

Jimmy Lorang took over the boardinghouse in the 1940s, turning the establishment into a saloon. Since it was the closest bar to the back gate of the U.S. Army's Camp Bouse, thirsty soldiers appeared day and night in quest of cold beer. Wild tales of the servicemen's invasion of Wenden abound. A favorite stunt of the young soldiers was to ply the local dogs with beer. Drunk, wandering dogs became a common sight until the residents urged the practice be stopped. Once the troops shipped out, quiet returned to the town bar. After Lorang's death, the ownership changed hands several times. It is now a bar and restaurant currently known as Rees' Outback, owned by Sam Rees, grandson of Salome's first fire chief, Tom Davis.

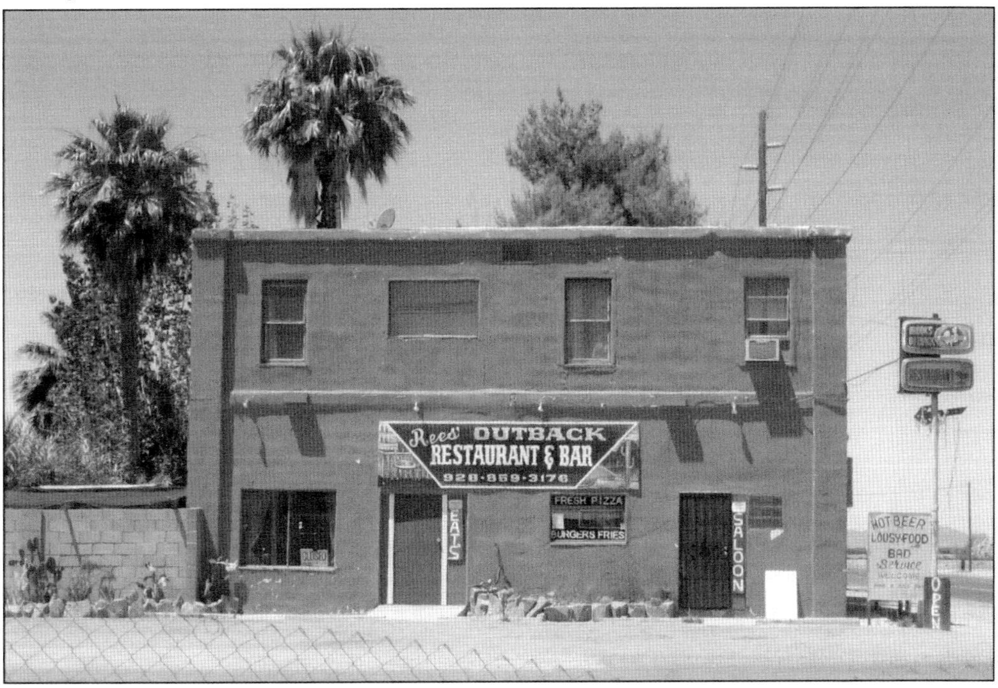

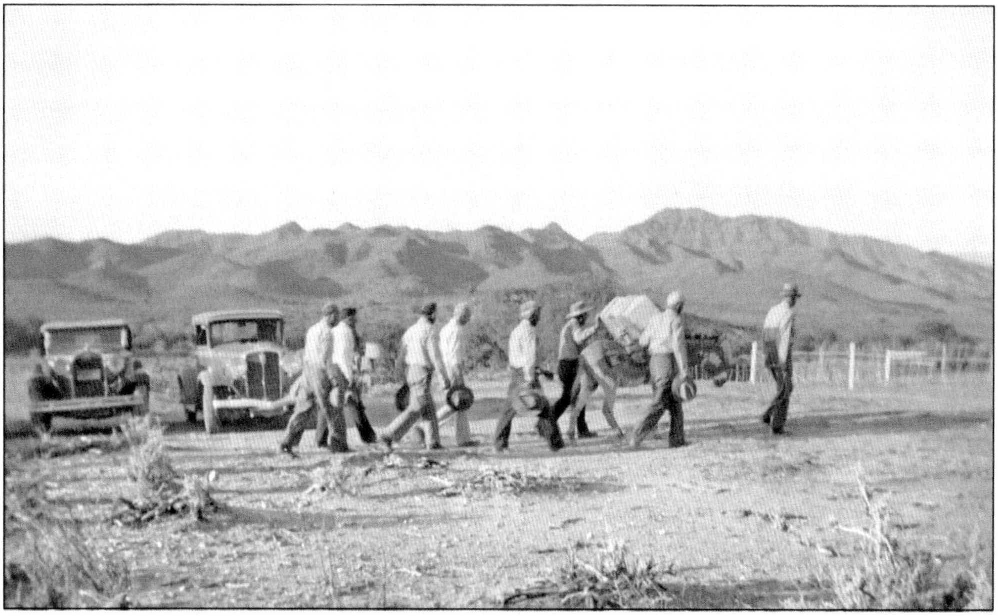

By the mid-1930s, few of the original miners at Harrisburg and Harqua Hala remained. The only evidence of their lives was poorly marked graves in the nearly forgotten, untended Harrisburg Cemetery. Among them was Mary Beard, wife of Harrisburg cofounder Bill Beard, who had promised to join her. In 1935, Sadie Martin learned that Bill had died and was buried alone in Yuma. Aware of the Beards' desire to be together, and of the cemetery's disrepair, Martin coordinated the rehabilitation of Harrisburg Cemetery and the transfer of Bill Beard's remains. Above, Bill Beard's proper funeral was held as part of the rededication of the Harrisburg Cemetery. Below, an unidentified miner attends the funeral. Reuniting Bill and Mary Beard at Harrisburg for eternity was recognized as the end of an era. (Both Rohrig family.)

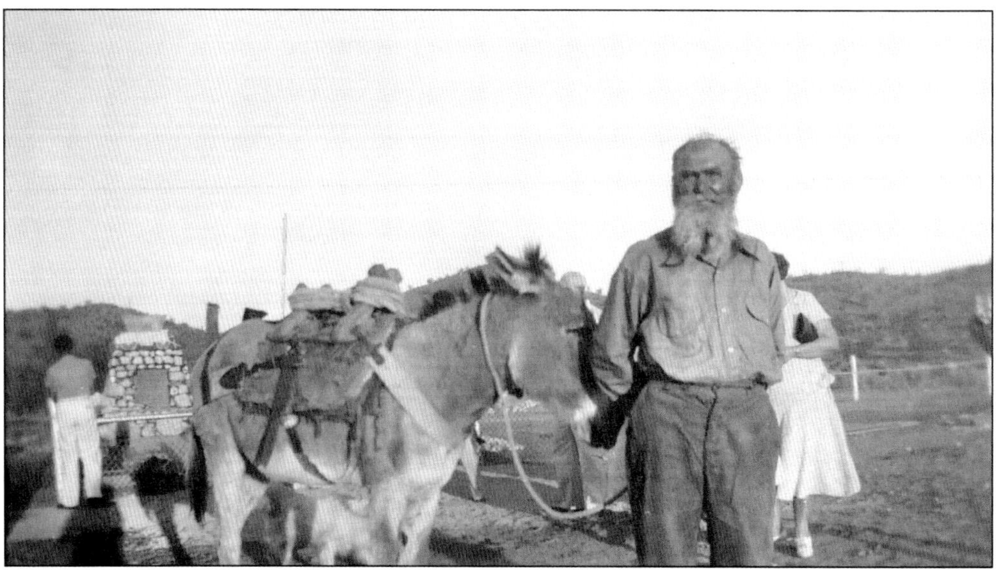

Four

Vicars, Vice, and Visionaries

The Depression of the 1930s encouraged one last gasp of the Wild Wild West to flourish in the McMullen Valley. There were brothels, gambling joints, and mining scams as well as good, solid families, church services, and the civic-minded ladies of ViSaWen (Vicksburg-Salome-Wenden) Women's Club.

Twenty-five years after the founding of Salome, the first church building was opened. There was a congregation eager to support its reverend and his good works. Under the leadership of the energetic Rev. E. T. Simpson, his church would open the first hospital in Salome, directed by Alexander "Doc" Armstrong. Unfortunately, the state would close the facility, insisting that his affectionate moniker was not as valid as a certified medical license.

Dollie Wiley was a famous madam from Prescott whose life had been made into a Hollywood film. She was almost on her way to respectability when she married George Wiley, a former bootlegger, and moved to Salome.

Legitimate businessman Russell Sheffler manufactured, distributed, and serviced "vending machines" (slot machines). With his partner and brother Bill, he sought to find new markets when their offshore venues were closed down. Upon finding Van's "famed café" in Salome, they found a prime location for their vision. Had the dice rolled their way, the tables might have turned: Salome and the McMullen Valley would be a world-renowned gaming resort and the village of Las Vegas a little-known hamlet.

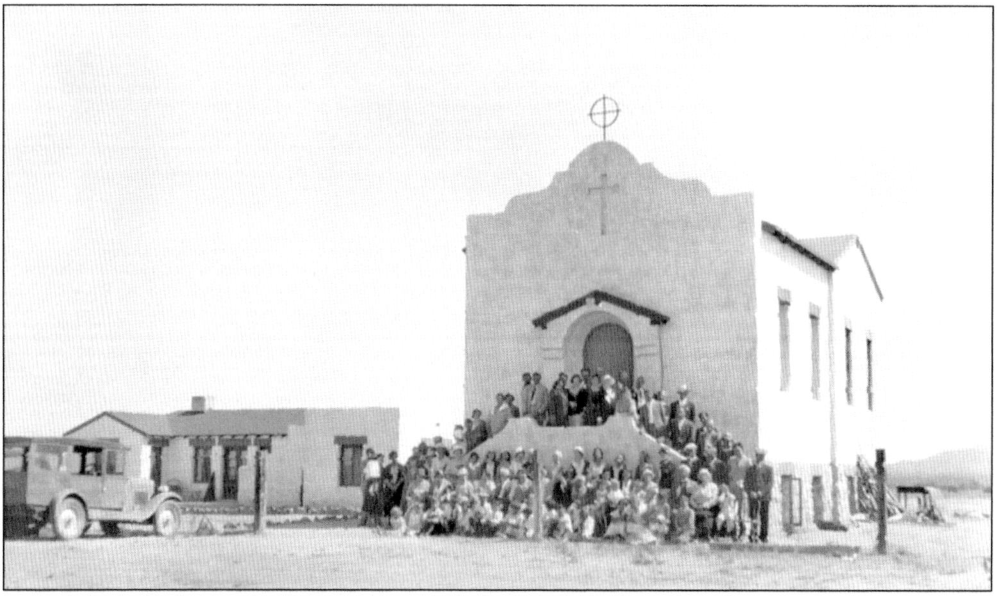

Parishioners join Rev. E. T. Simpson in front of the All Saints Episcopal Church soon after its completion. The church was very active in the community in the early 1930s. Seminary graduates under Simpson's guidance also held services near Vicksburg, in Quartzsite, and in the Harquahala Valley.

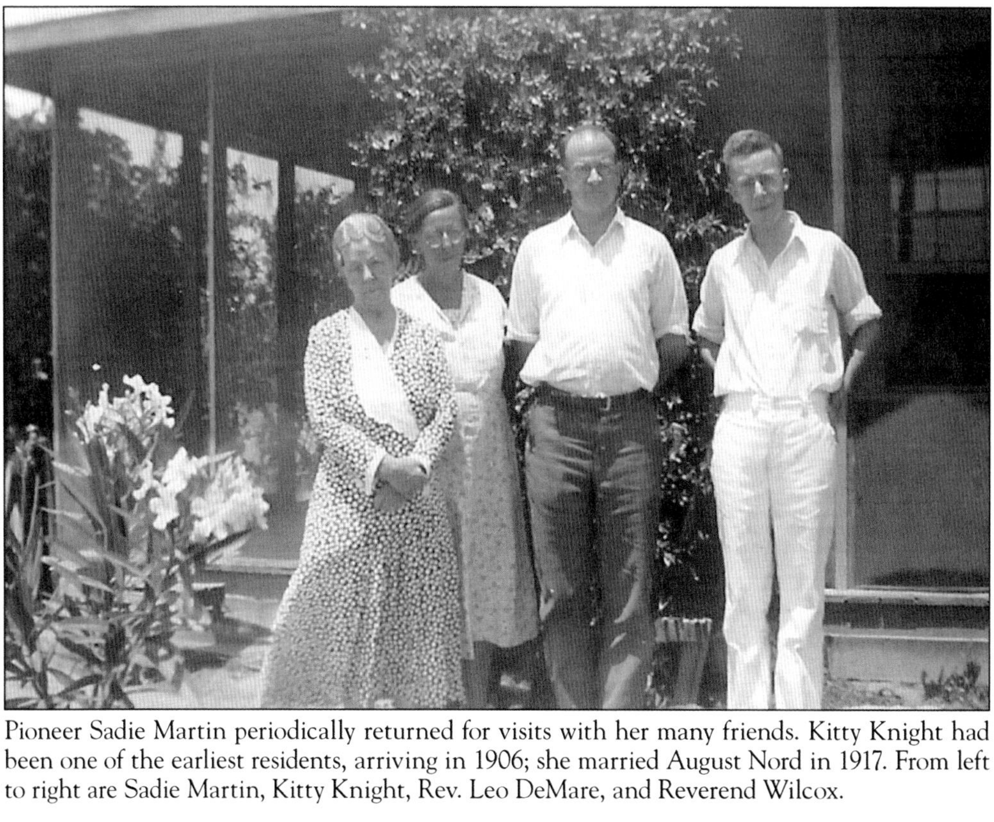

Pioneer Sadie Martin periodically returned for visits with her many friends. Kitty Knight had been one of the earliest residents, arriving in 1906; she married August Nord in 1917. From left to right are Sadie Martin, Kitty Knight, Rev. Leo DeMare, and Reverend Wilcox.

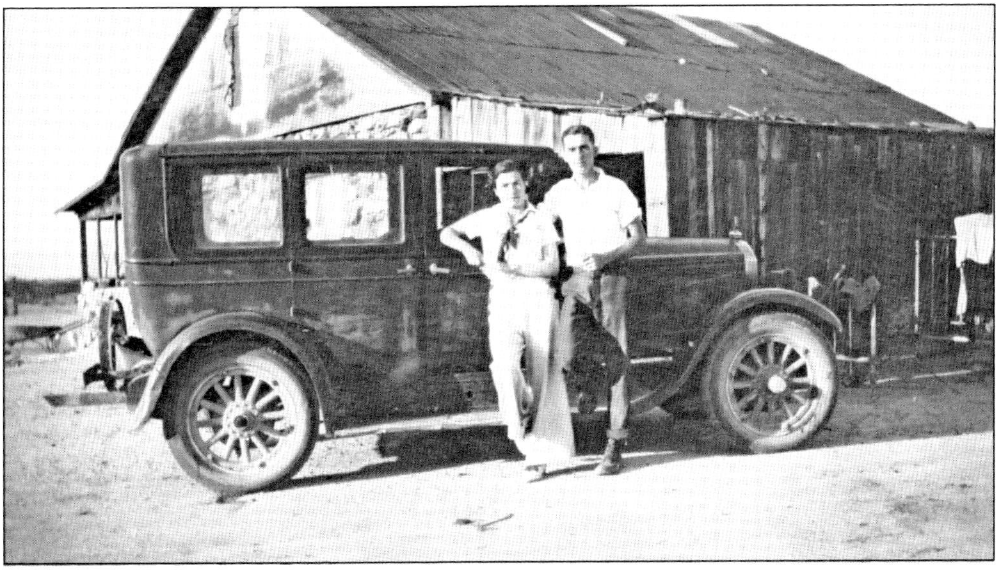

Seen previously as a little girl on the back of a truck, Nell Brown grew up by 1935 and found a beau. Nell is pictured at Easter with Bill Simcox, the man she would marry. Her father, F. J. Brown, had come from Texas in 1915 to establish a 30-acre farm, one of the first in the McMullen Valley. The family's famed stone house can be seen in the background. (Nell Brown.)

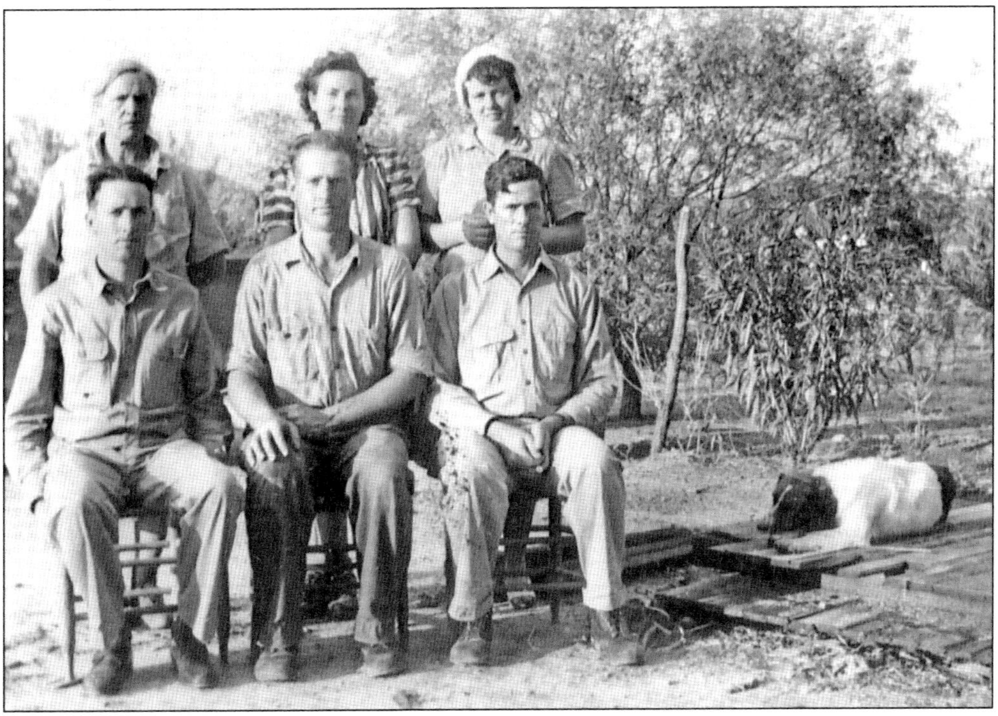

If a burro was found in the swimming pool at Shefflers or a comment made that was so witty everyone repeated it, one of the Browns was likely responsible. For over 80 years, members of the Brown family have been lively, colorful, and winsome members of the community. From left to right in this 1942 photograph are (first row) Ted, Hayden, and Art; (second row) Sonny, Nell, and Annie Brown. (Nell Brown.)

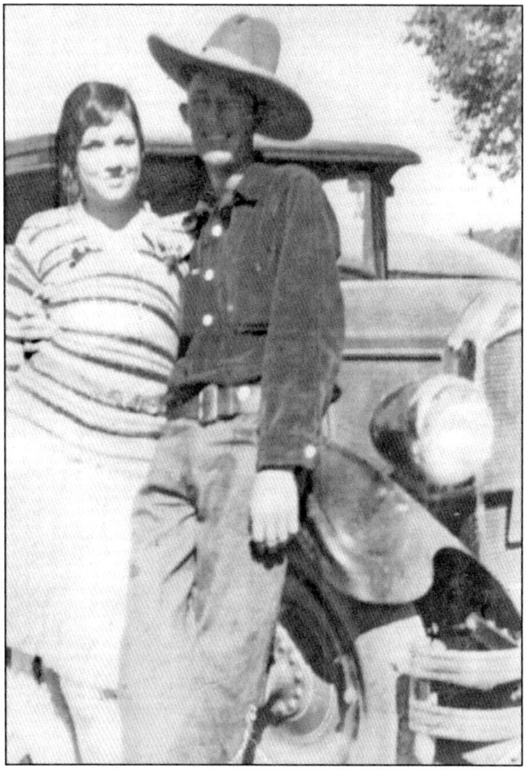

Jack Wilbanks was an authentic cowboy. A superb rider and roper, his facility with a bullwhip was legendary. Arriving in 1931 with a herd of cattle, he created a ranch in the beautiful wilderness near the Kofa mine. Wilbanks built a stone cabin for his daughters and wife, Martha. Though plagued by water problems, he still grew a small orchard of apples and peaches. (Brian De Ganahl.)

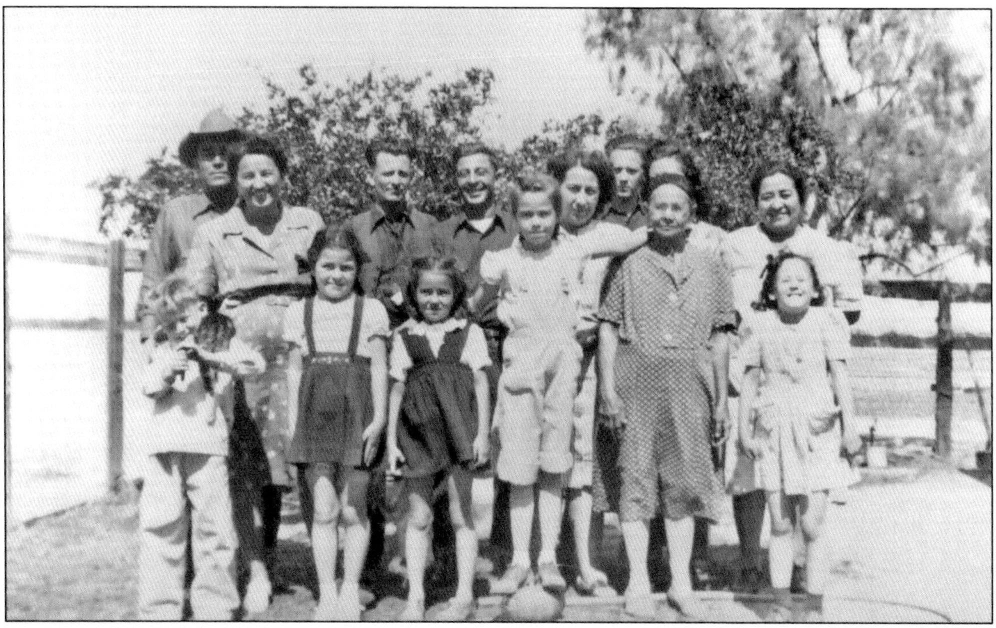

Family and friends helped each other survive the Depression years. Several of the Oroscos posed with family members before the Second World War. From left to right are (first row) Wiley Atchley, Frances Trainor, Donna Orosco, Betty Orosco, Grandma (Frances) Orosco, and Nellie Atchley; (second row) Elias and Viola Orosco, Keith Atchley, Alonzo Orosco, Betty Getty, Wayne Atchley, unidentified, and Amy Trainor. (Rohrig family.)

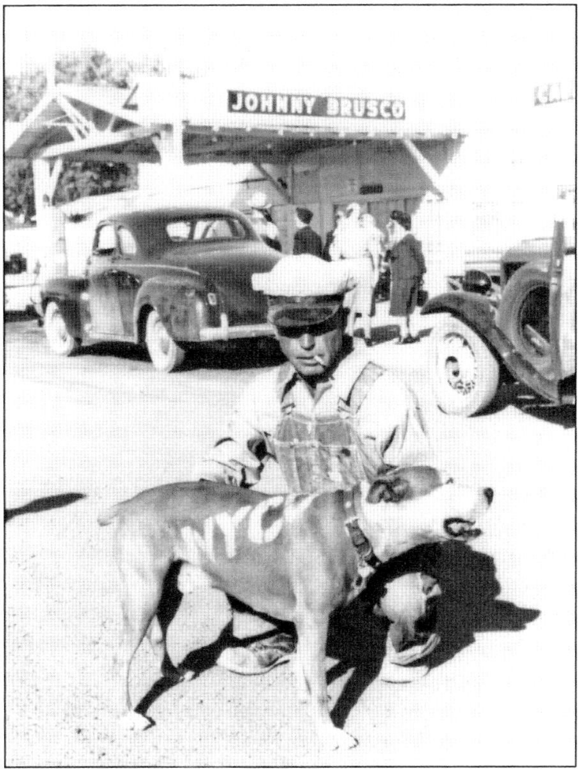

Johnny Brusco's service station was a fixture in Salome for years. His central business location on Route 60 made his place a popular stop. An unidentified local character poses with a dog promoting North Yuma County, which was the commonly known name for the area in days past. (Wolfe family.)

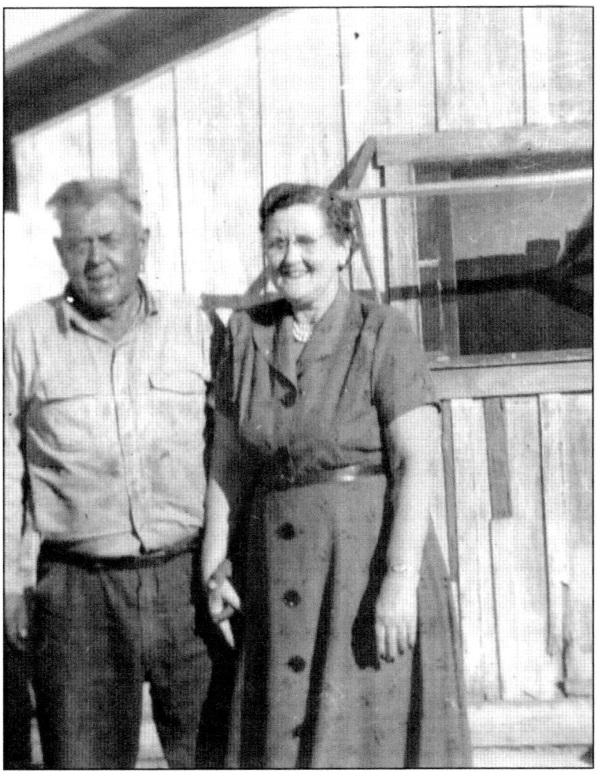

Tom Saunders arrived in 1929 from California when still a young man and used to hard work. Tom found farming in Wenden filled with challenges, especially as his large tract of land was exposed to the periodic flooding of the Centennial Wash. Later in life, his sister, Muriel Youell, joined him at his large spread. They were photographed together in the 1950s. (Jeanne Youell.)

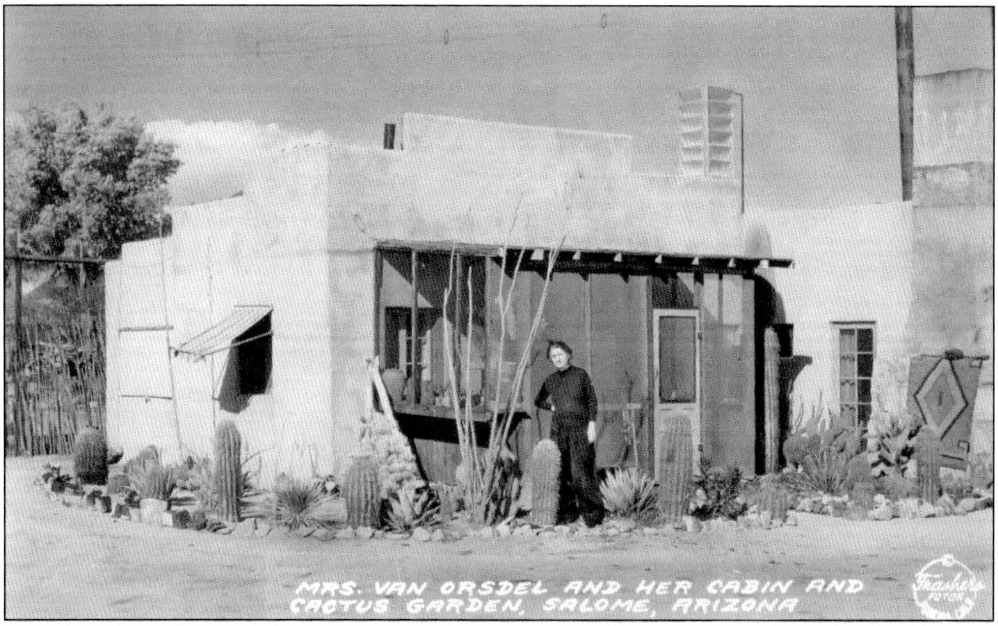

Addie Lee Van Orsdel (Mrs. Van) brought her ailing husband, Joseph, to Salome in 1927. She appeared to channel the spirit of Dick Wick Hall. Mrs. Van built a gas station and café, passionately promoting her businesses and the charms of Salome. Her business thrived. She often invited tourists to view her famed cactus garden. Van's became a landmark. (Pomona Public Library, Pomona, California.)

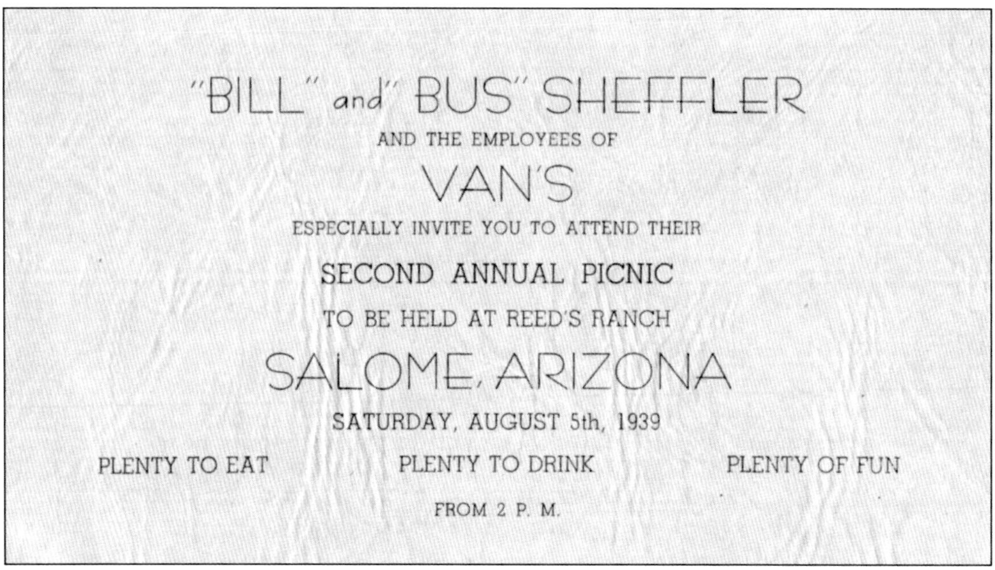
"BILL" and "BUS" SHEFFLER

AND THE EMPLOYEES OF

VAN'S

ESPECIALLY INVITE YOU TO ATTEND THEIR

SECOND ANNUAL PICNIC

TO BE HELD AT REED'S RANCH

SALOME, ARIZONA

SATURDAY, AUGUST 5th, 1939

PLENTY TO EAT PLENTY TO DRINK PLENTY OF FUN

FROM 2 P. M.

Van's burned to the ground with the crews paving Route 60 almost in sight. Needing to borrow heavily to reopen in time for the paved highway, Mrs. Van took in investors. Vending machine magnates Russell "Bus" and Bill Sheffler were distributors of gumball machines, one-armed bandits, and other entertainment apparatus. They believed their product line of crowd favorites would be a profitable enterprise. Like their predecessors, the Shefflers had a vision.

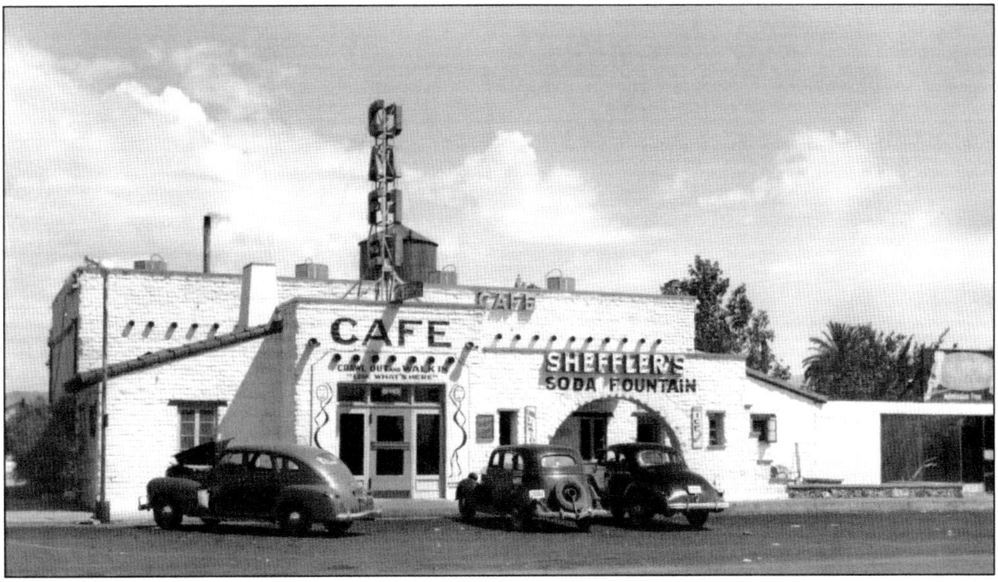

Mrs. Van retired, free of debt, to enable the Shefflers to manifest their aspirations in Salome. With the paved State Route 60-70, road traffic increased exponentially. Games of chance drew in local residents as well. The brothers built a modern motel and swimming pool. Everything built was state of the art for 1939. The idea of a destination resort in the desert with gambling was born. (Billie Farr.)

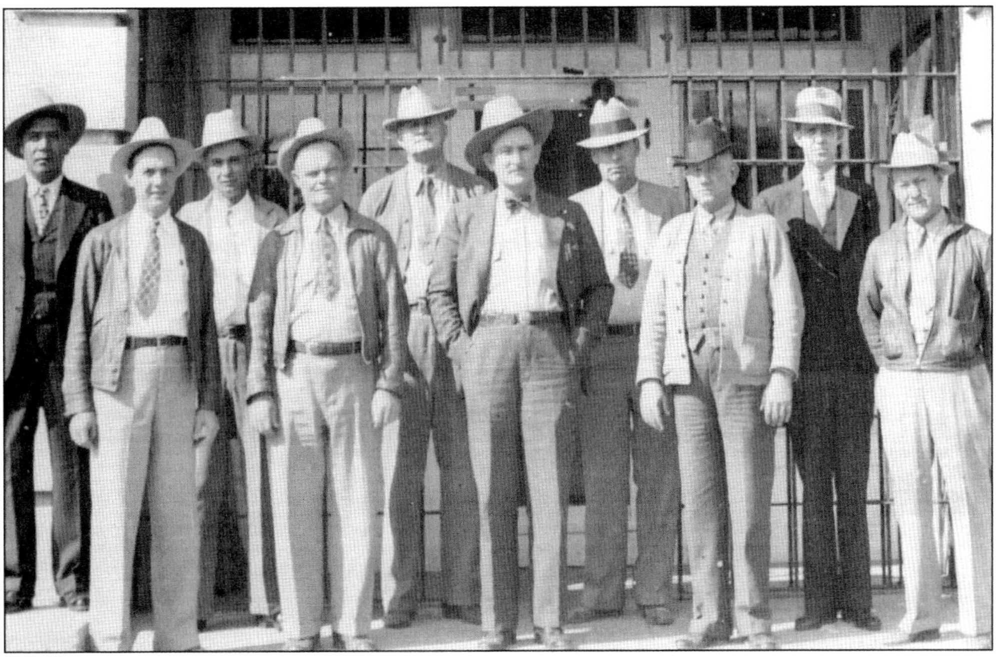

Until the early 1980s, Yuma County was larger than several states. The road from the Yuma sheriff's headquarters to Salome was an awful three-hour drive. Sheriff Pete Newman (pictured front row in the bow tie) can be seen with his entire staff of 10 men. Enforcing the law under such circumstances was difficult at best. It also did not hurt that Sheriff Newman valued the Shefflers' friendship. (AHS Yuma.)

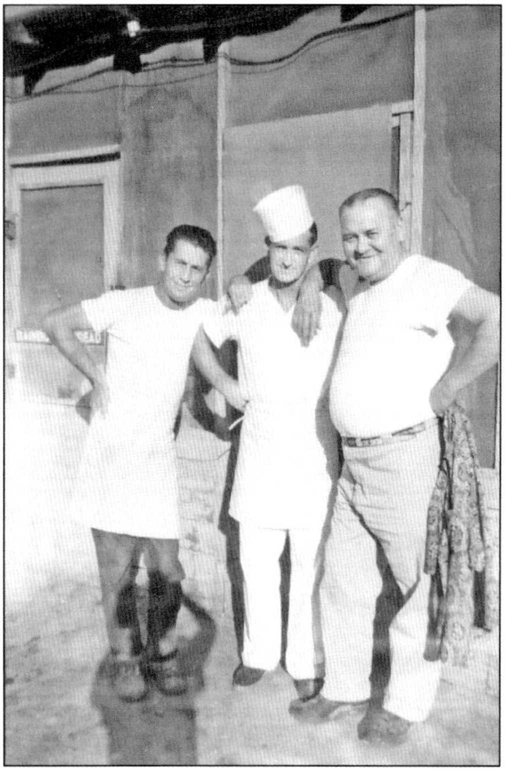

P. C. Webb, the longtime chef at Shefflers (pictured in a hat), is legendary and fondly remembered—for both the bakers' tray of "world's best" donuts and sweet rolls he left unattended at the kitchen's back door for school kids as well as his unwillingness to let any hobo go hungry. Numerous coworkers remembered that Webbie always found some way for them to earn a meal. (Amy Sweetland.)

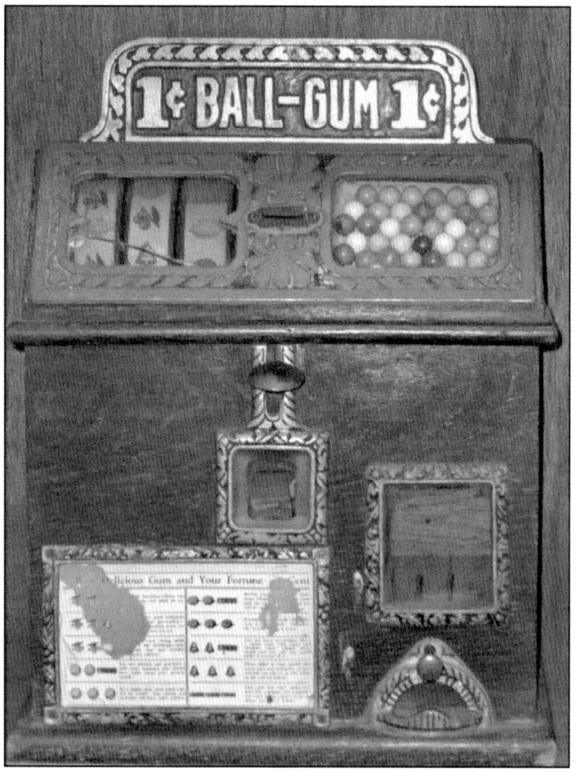

The Sheffler brothers manufactured a wide range of vending machines. The penny gumball machines pictured aren't as well remembered in Salome as the slots that delivered payouts with a high degree of regularity. (Bill Sheffler.)

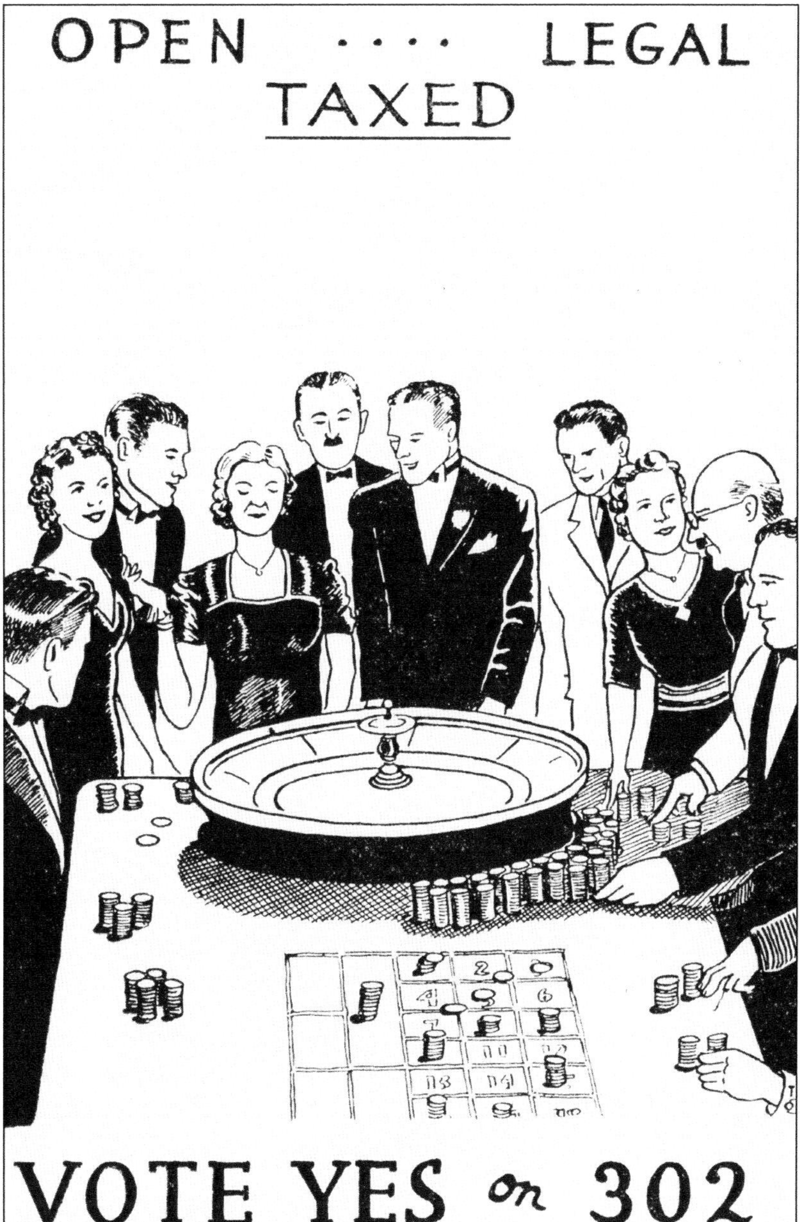

"Bus" and Bill Sheffler wanted to be engaged in legal businesses. They were entrepreneurs who manufactured, distributed, and serviced vending machines. When gambling ships were legal off California, they had supplied the slots. They observed that legal gambling drew more than nefarious characters. Upstanding professionals, movie industry people, and others with resources had happily endured travel inconveniences to reach the ships. After Nevada went legal but years before Bugsy Siegel dreamed up Las Vegas, the Shefflers envisioned Salome bursting with flashing neon, sirens heralding large payouts, and thousands of visitors. Teaming with a Phoenix attorney, they promoted a statewide initiative to legalize gambling in Arizona. Had voters in 1940 approved the Sullivan Act, Salome and the McMullen Valley might have become a world-famous resort filled with elegant casinos, lavish trade shows, and glamorous showgirls. (Bill Sheffler.)

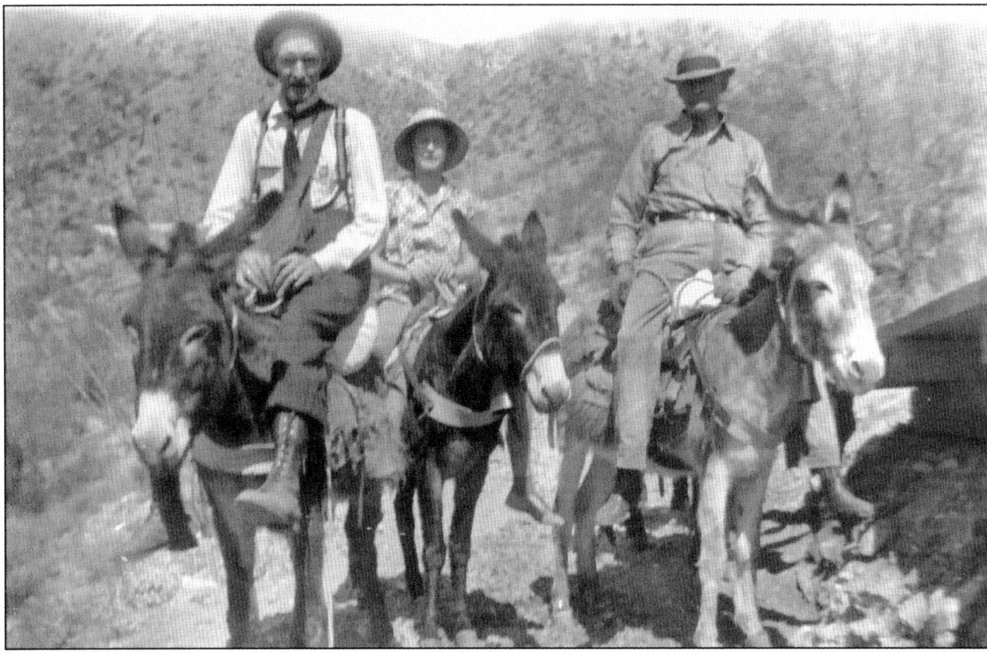

Owning a piece of a working gold mine has always been a fashionable investment. In the 1930s, Roy MacDonald engaged in the practice of bringing out investors on inspection tours. He recognized the importance of documenting the adventure in photographs. At various points on the tour, investors would be given time to get their pictures taken with bona fide working miners. Unidentified investors on the requisite mule ride to the mine are shown above. Below, miners Dawson (left) and Linnel (far right) are identified, but the young aviatrix who might have flown in for the day remains a mystery. (Both Rohrig family.)

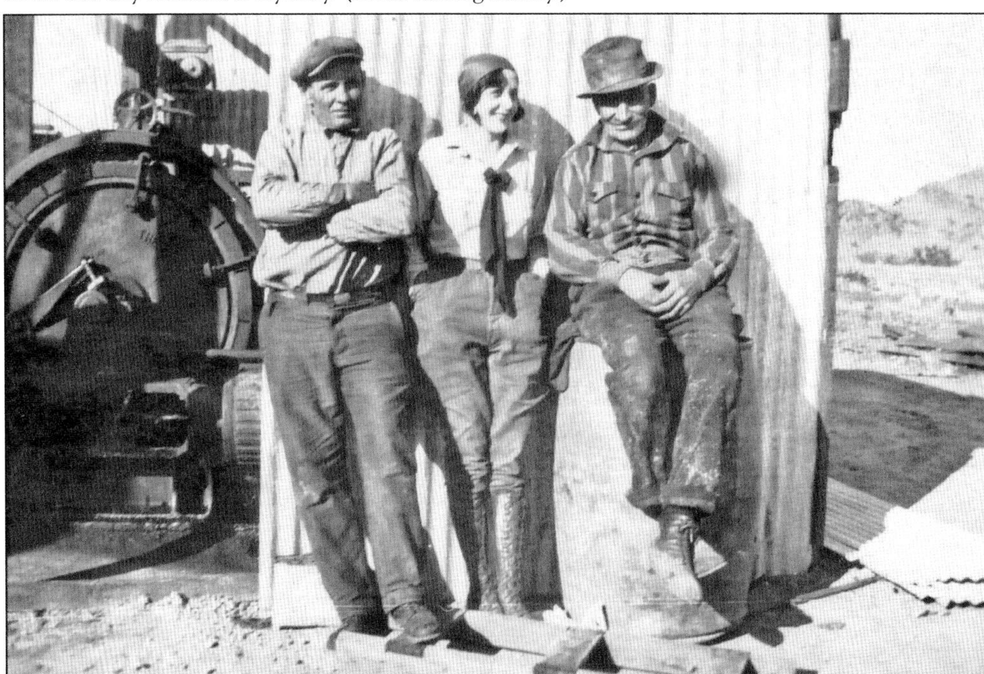

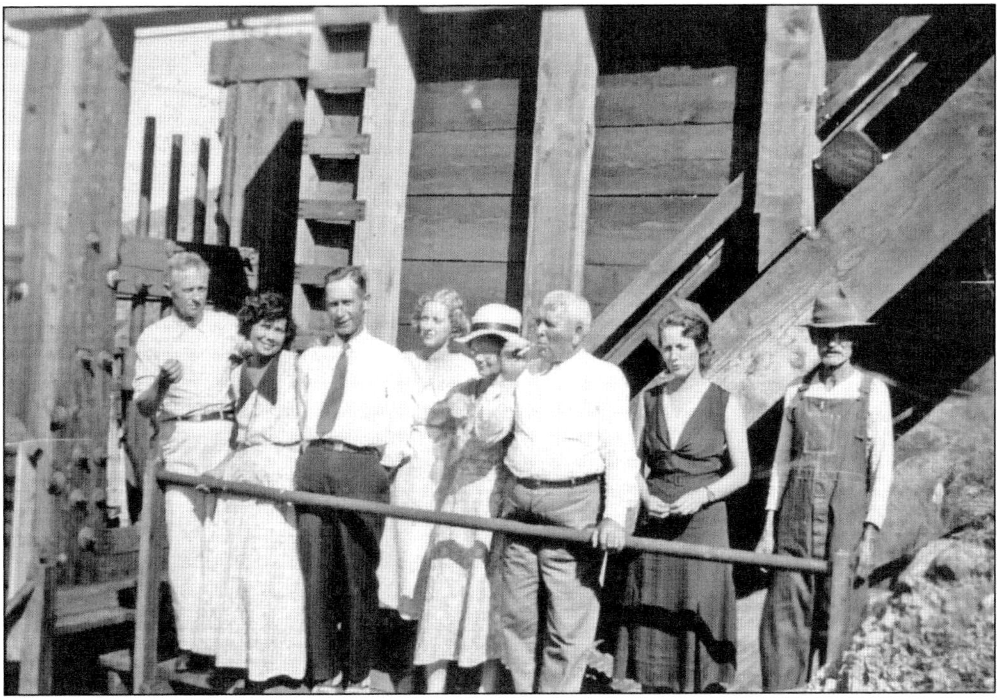

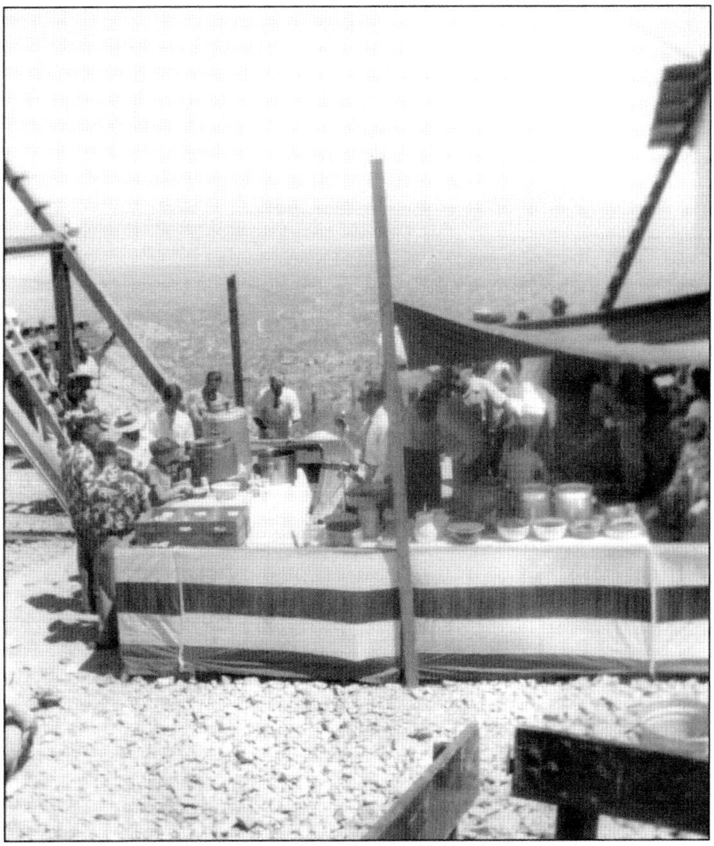

The personable MacDonald incorporated "Q and A's" into his tours, where he answered all questions and often had gold nuggets available for close inspection. Whether the gold he offered for viewing had been extracted from the site they had scrutinized remains unconfirmed. After a long hot morning exploring the mine site, investors could work up a rather large appetite. MacDonald would arrange for an extensive buffet to be available. (Both Rohrig family.)

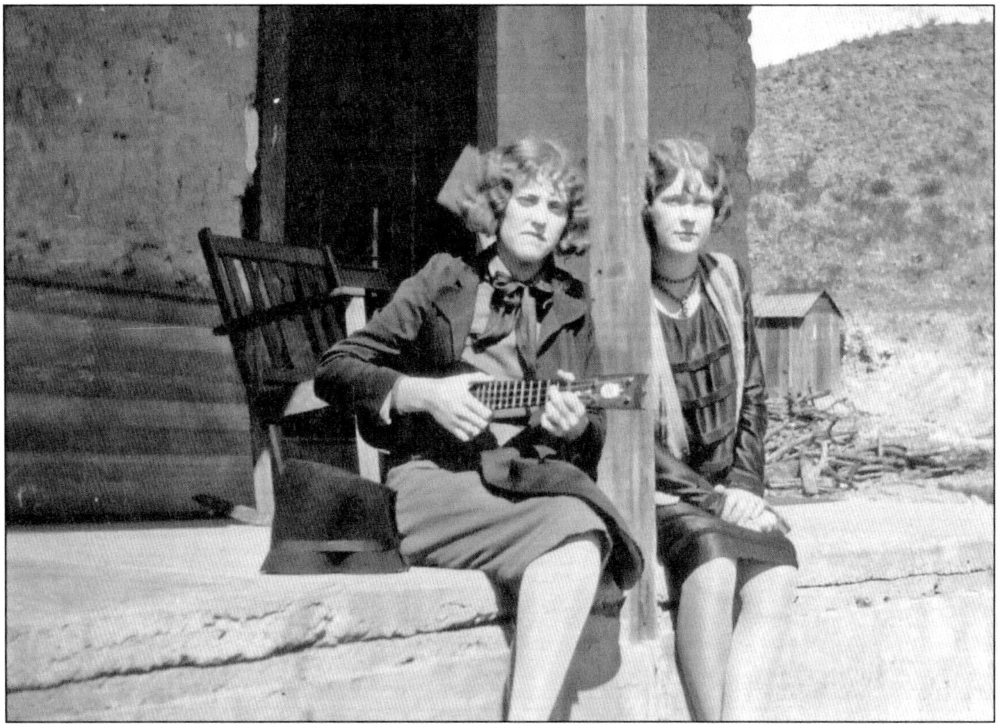

Burro rides, buffet lunches, and photographs with authentic miners weren't always enough to close the deal. Something extra was needed—something Roy's sisters, Louise (left) and Elaine (right), and gold shared in common. Tough cookies with sex appeal, these Wenden girls could shovel a truckload of ore and show some leg, especially when an investor was ready with his camera. (Both Rohrig family.)

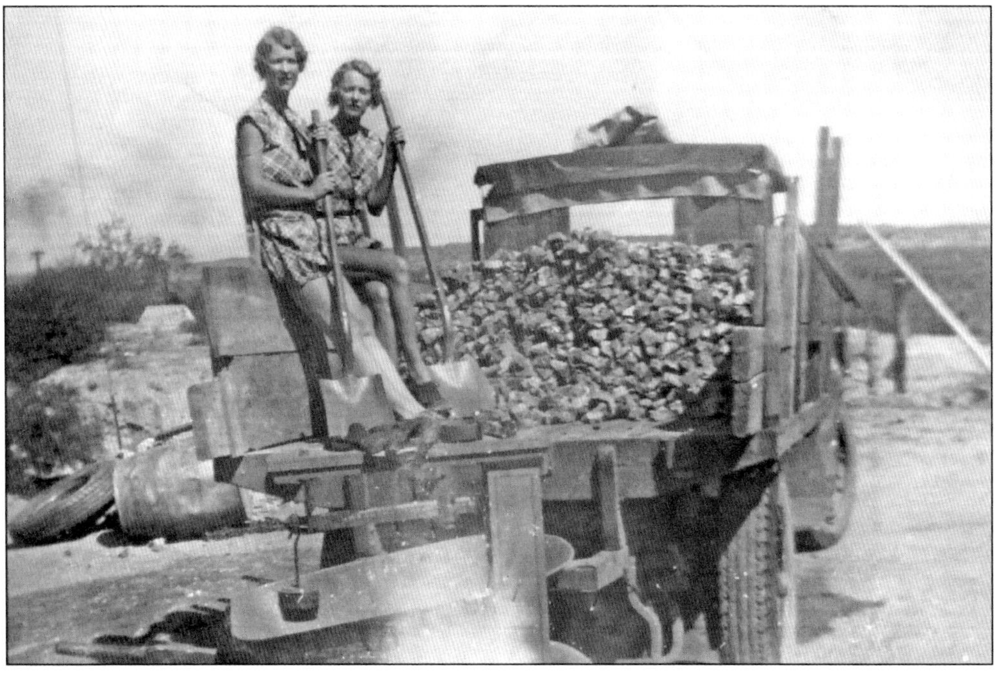

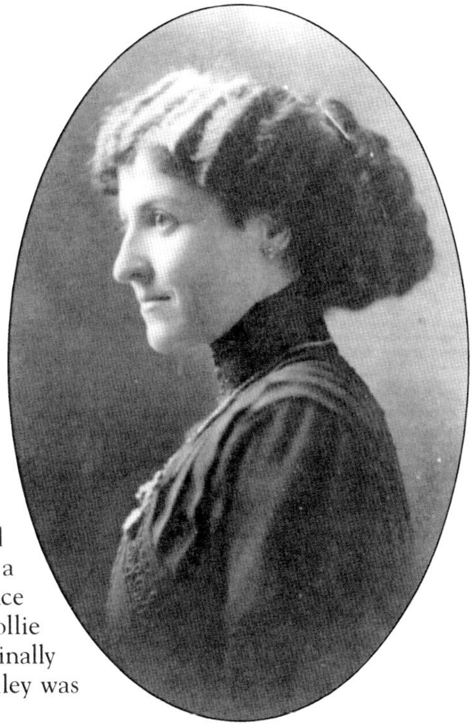

Fate brought the mythic Dollie Wiley to Salome. While a young streetwalker in Los Angeles, she was found innocent of killing her first husband. She is pictured below (front row with large hat) with coworkers and clients around 1920 before moving to Prescott, where she operated out of the Rex Arms Hotel. Dollie moved into management, beginning her climb toward respectability. In 1937, Dollie married George Wiley and moved to Salome. George ran the Texaco station and an adjacent saloon. Dollie still ran a few girls in the cabins behind the bar for pocket money. Her efforts to become a model citizen initially failed to gain her admittance to the ViSaWen Women's Club. Undeterred, Dollie simply worked harder to gain their respect. She was finally accepted, and when she died in 1962, Dollie Wiley was missed. (Both Sharlot Hall Museum.)

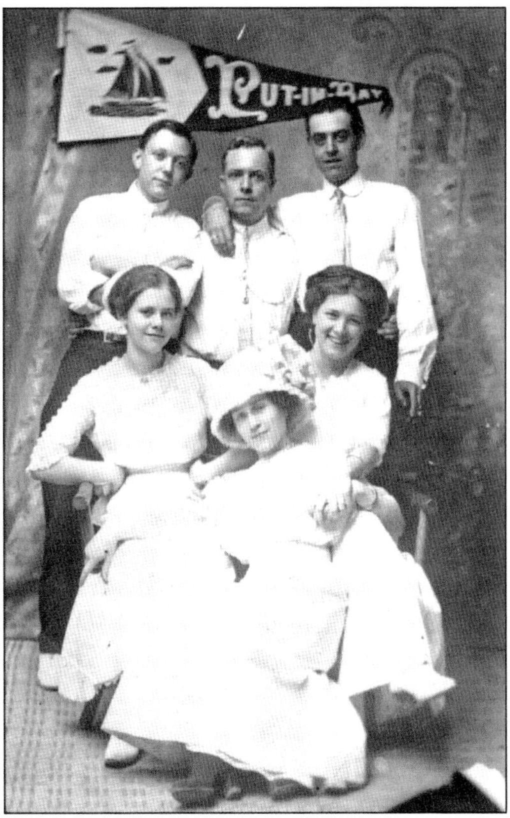

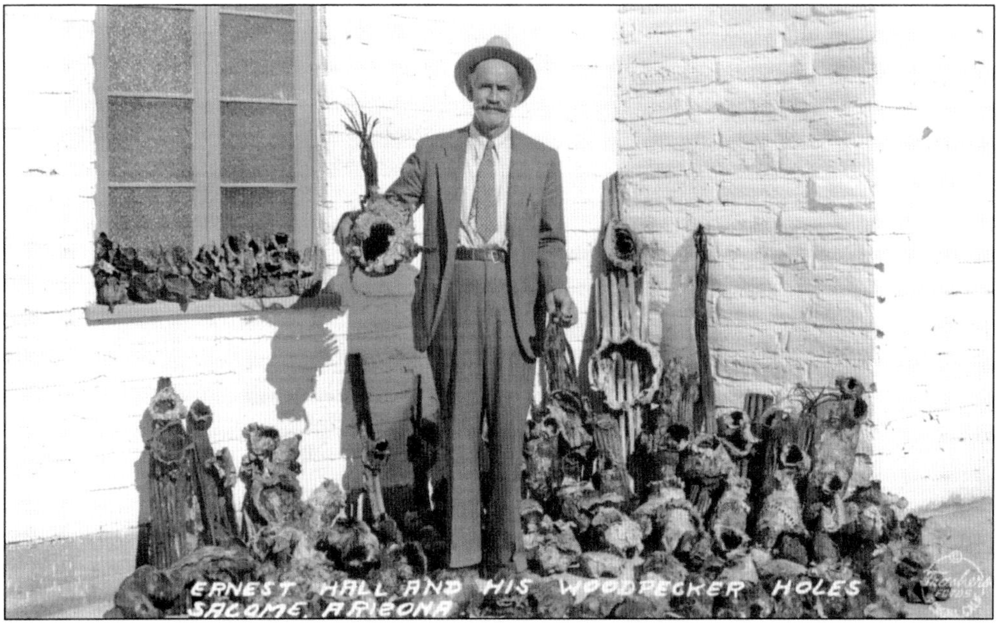

Cofounder of Salome Ernest Hall served as justice of the peace in 1906 and again in the 1950s. Having witnessed his brother Dick's buoyant attitude and undeterred resilience, Ernest believed that boundless optimism and blind confidence meant anything was possible. He is pictured in 1936 above at his roadside stand hoping to sell his priceless collection of woodpecker holes. Below, the view from Route 60 looking north up Route 72 toward Vicksburg and Bouse is seen as it was on a winter's day in 1940. Survants Restaurant, Grocery, and Service Station were the only businesses within miles. To the right just off camera were overnight cabins. (Above, Pomona Public Library, Pomona, California; below, AHS Tucson.)

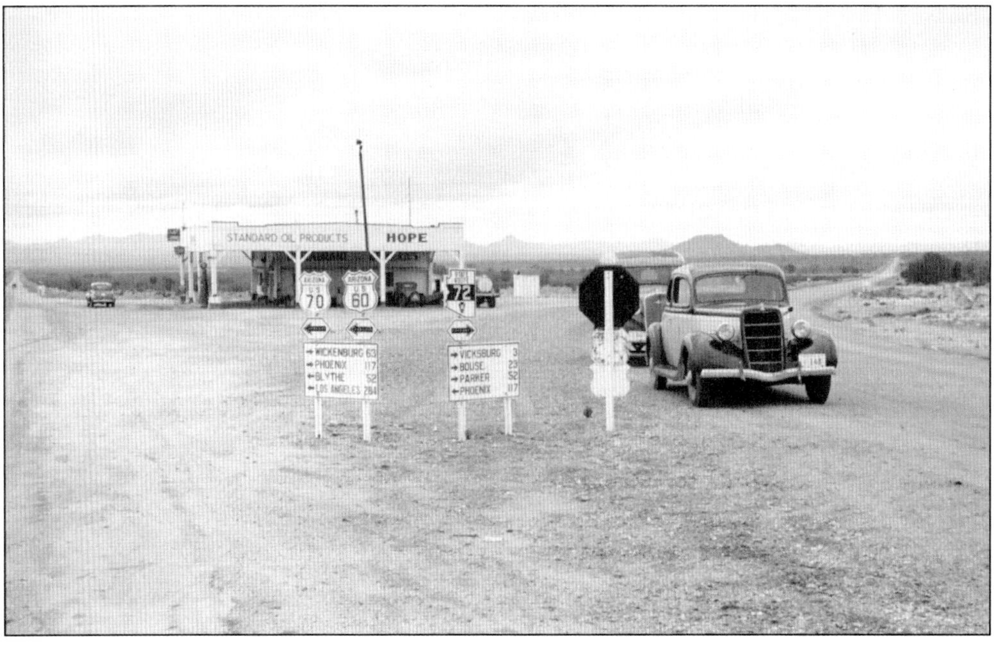

Five

PRESCRIPTION FOR PROSPERITY

When the nation went to war, small communities like those of the McMullen Valley sent their fair share of young men to serve in the armed forces. But secretly, the U.S. Army brought in over 5,000 soldiers for training and testing of a secret weapon to the adjacent Butler Valley.

Located on the northwest side of the Harcuvar Mountains, shared with the McMullen Valley, Butler Valley was home to Camp Bouse. The area was allegedly personally chosen by Gen. George S. Patton. The general, after driving around with a small staff and having seen minimal human habitation, deemed it the perfect place for secret operations. With the Arizona and California Railroad Depot located in Bouse, the army had transportation and a remote, isolated area to train crews for desert warfare.

With nearly the same secrecy that surrounded the Manhattan Project, which produced the atomic bomb, Bouse became the testing ground for a new secret weapon nicknamed "the Gizmo."

The communities of the valley hosted military personnel at their bars, brothels, and gambling facilities. After the war, local residents would tell tourists they did their part in the war effort by serving in "Patton's Playground."

As hostilities still raged overseas, the valley developed another reputation among servicemen and their families back home. With California's passage of a three-day waiting period to issue marriage licenses, Salome became a marriage mecca for servicemen and their brides from the West Coast.

After the war, the accessibility afforded by the paved highway enabled a new generation of farmers and ranchers to revitalize the valley as a commercially viable rural community. When combined with the growth of businesses servicing travelers between Phoenix and Los Angeles, the people of the valley got a taste of postwar prosperity. Military personnel and the paved highway had been the prescription that set them on the way to becoming a part of the American mainstream.

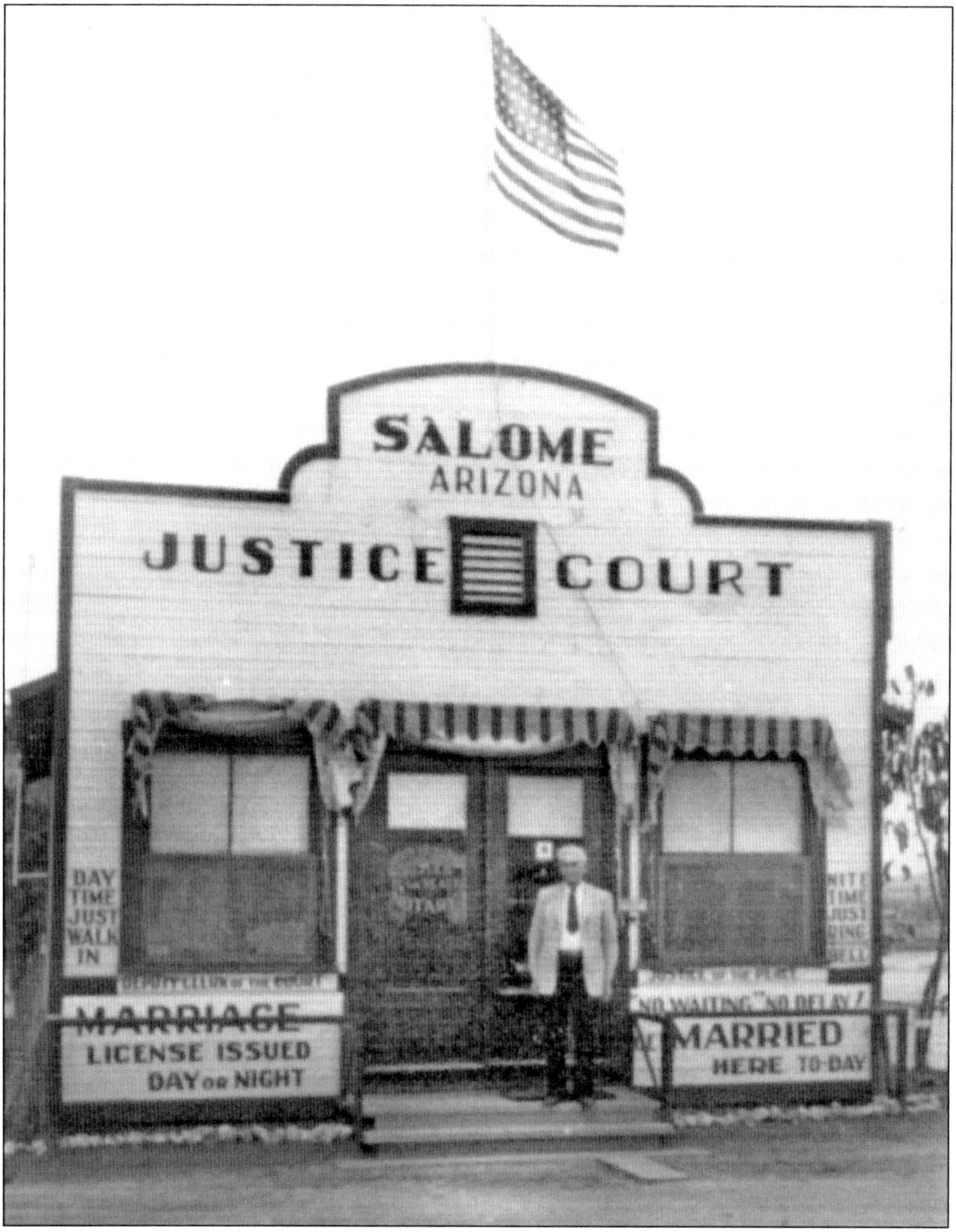

Almost 4,000 servicemen and their brides came to tie the knot in Salome before being shipped overseas. Justice of the Peace John A. Provorse, pictured on the steps, lived in the rear of the building. This made the many 3:00 a.m. ceremonies he performed more convenient.

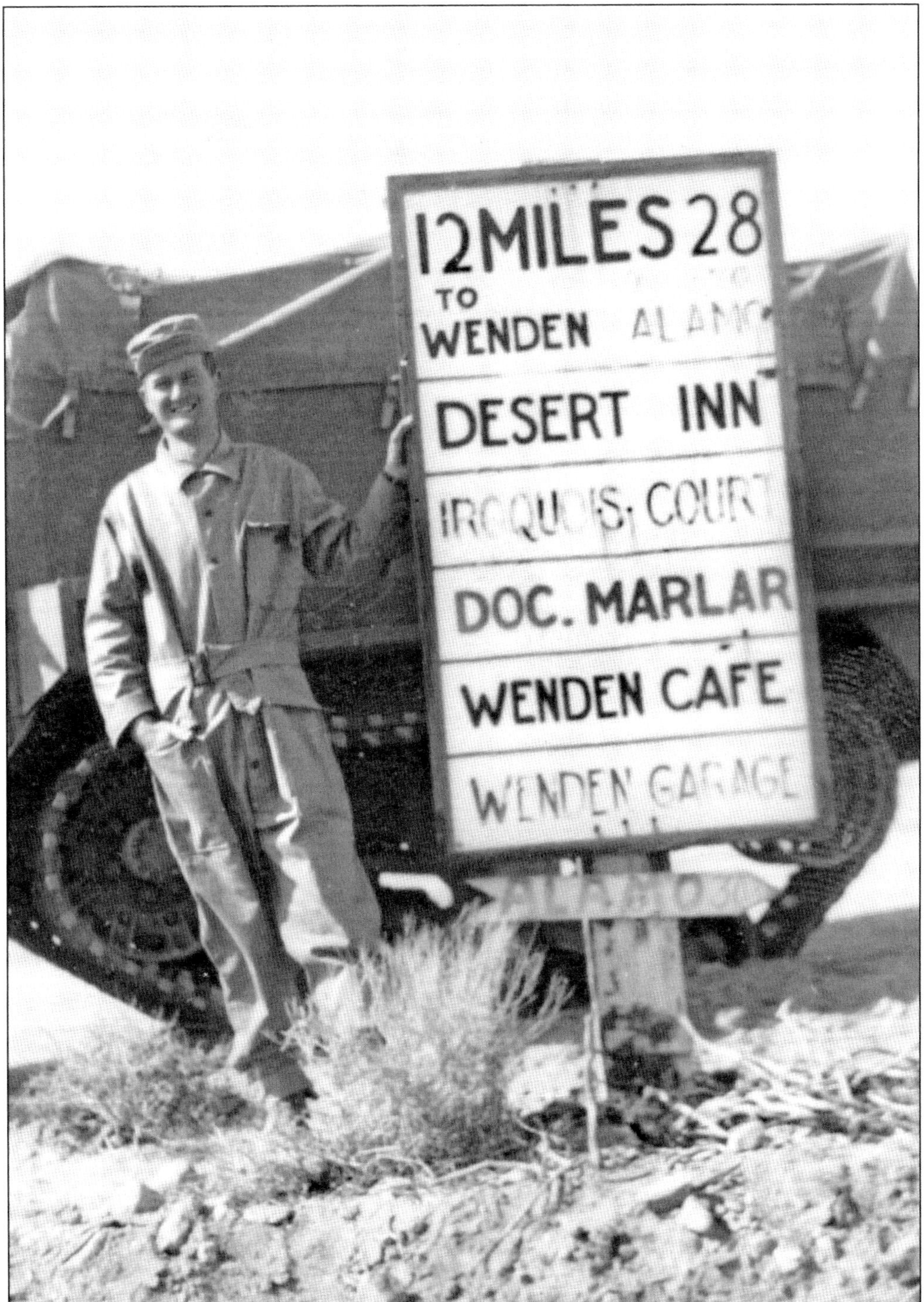

When on liberty, the soldiers of the 736th Medium Tank Battalion were under strict orders not to discuss the nature of their assignment and were required to never be in the company of less than four compatriots. As the handcrafted GI-created sign indicates, downtown Wenden businesses offering civilian food and alcoholic beverages were prime destinations. (Bouse Museum.)

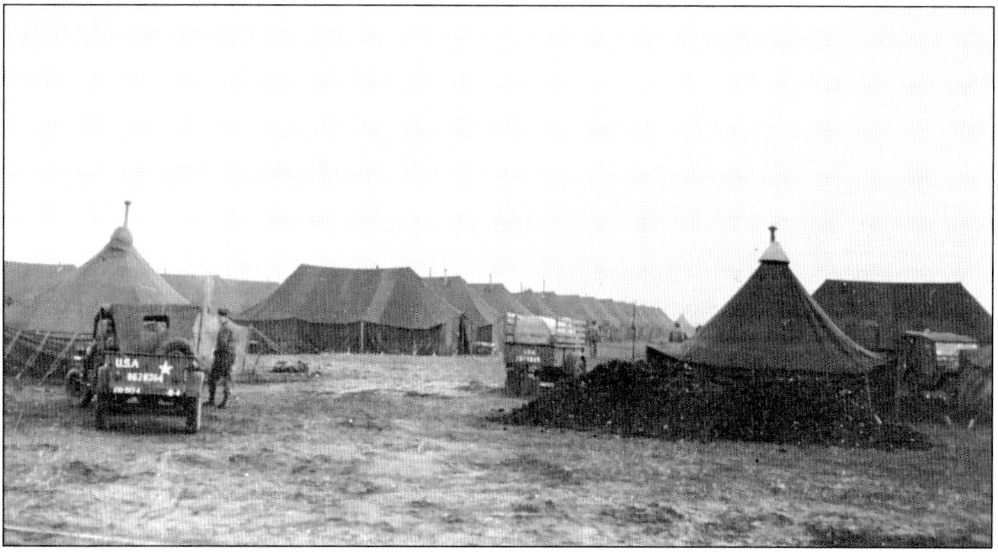

Gen. George S. Patton, preparing for the ultimate tank battle in the deserts of North Africa, chose the remote deserts of California and Arizona as training grounds. Because Patton and U.S. Army tanks became synonymous, the 736th Medium Tank Battalion bivouacked in the tents pictured at Camp Bouse have been identified as Patton's boys. (Bouse Museum.)

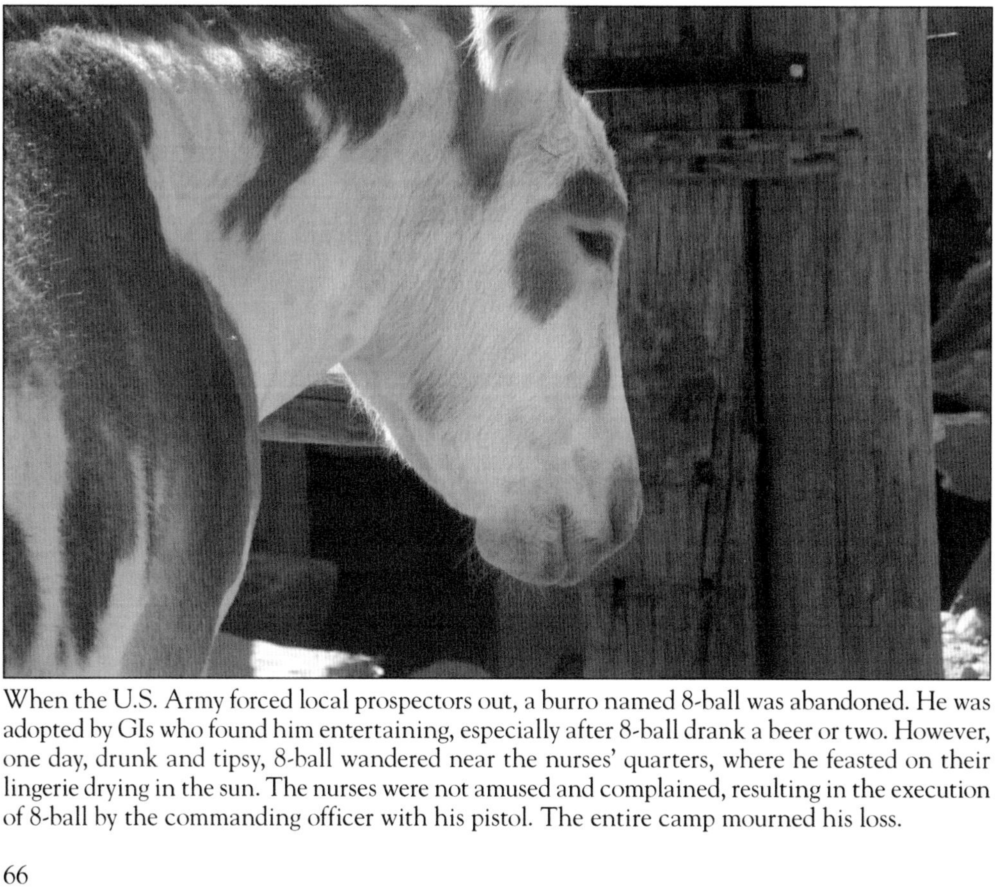

When the U.S. Army forced local prospectors out, a burro named 8-ball was abandoned. He was adopted by GIs who found him entertaining, especially after 8-ball drank a beer or two. However, one day, drunk and tipsy, 8-ball wandered near the nurses' quarters, where he feasted on their lingerie drying in the sun. The nurses were not amused and complained, resulting in the execution of 8-ball by the commanding officer with his pistol. The entire camp mourned his loss.

The camp opened in 1943, after Patton won the desert war in Africa. The army brass still needed a location to train tank crews for testing a new British-designed weapon. "The Gizmo" was the nickname for the tank-mounted laser-like 13-million-candlepower arc light, with colored shutters, intended to blind the enemy. It was intended to enable infantry and standard tanks to advance. Bouse trainees pose beneath towering saguaros. (Bouse Museum.)

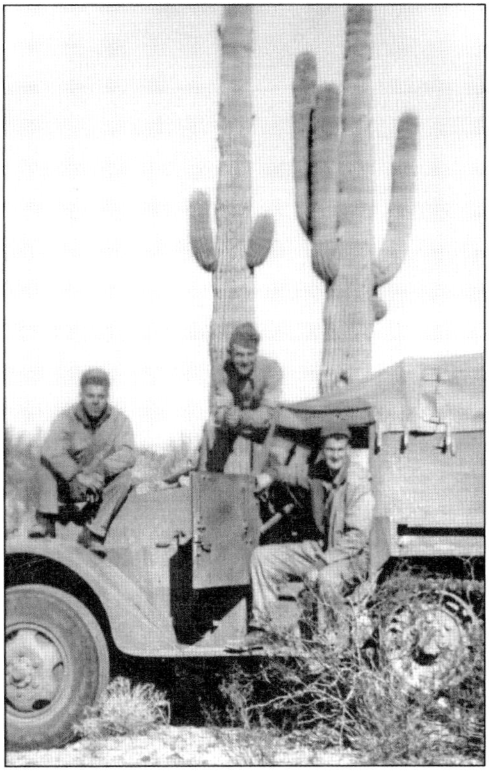

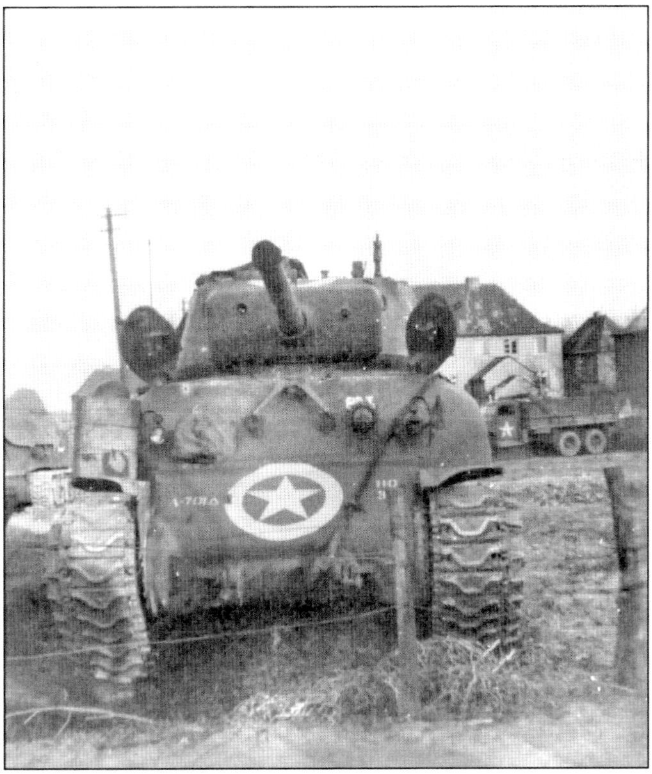

The 736th went overseas in the wet winter of 1944–1945 to fight against the Nazis in the thick forests of Northern Europe. Eisenhower assigned the 736th to serve under British command. Slowed by mud, technical difficulties, and ultimately doubts of the Canal Defence Light (CDL) tanks' effectiveness, the secret weapon was never deployed. A tank of the 736th is pictured fighting in Europe. (Bouse Museum.)

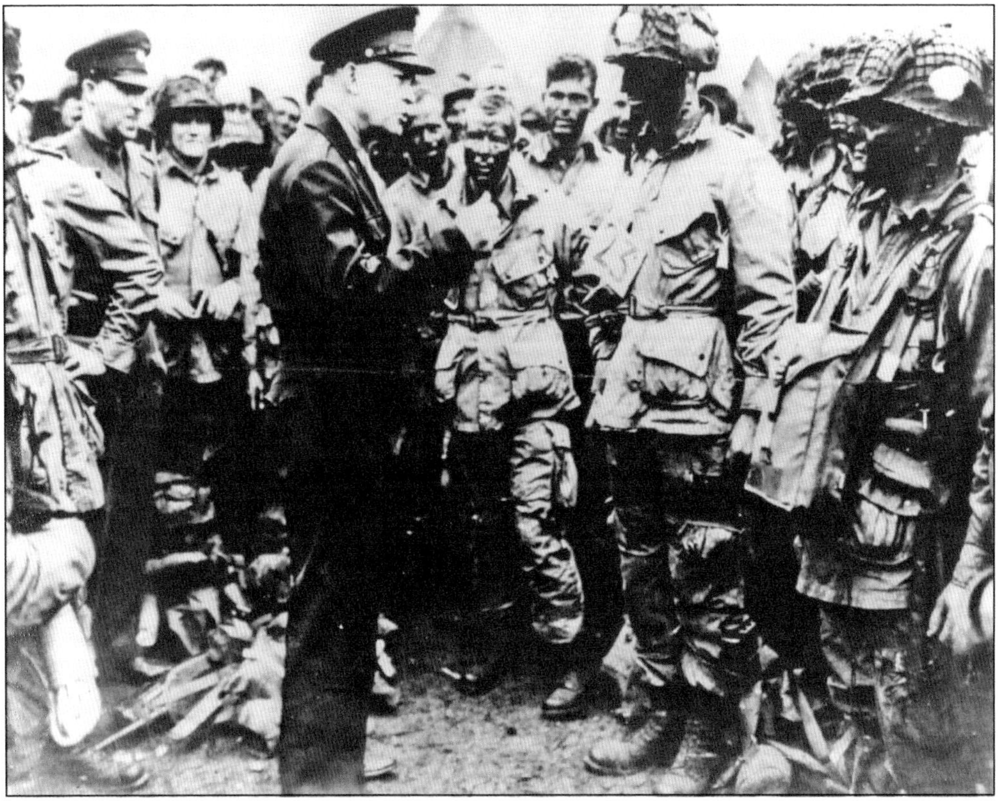

Hours before the invasion of Europe, Supreme Allied Commander Dwight Eisenhower visited troops of the 101st Airborne Division. This iconic photograph appeared on the pages of *Life* magazine. The men reportedly told the general to quit worrying. They would take care of this thing for him. On the extreme right of Eisenhower stands Ralph Farr, who would come to manage and eventually own Shefflers of Salome. (Billie Farr.)

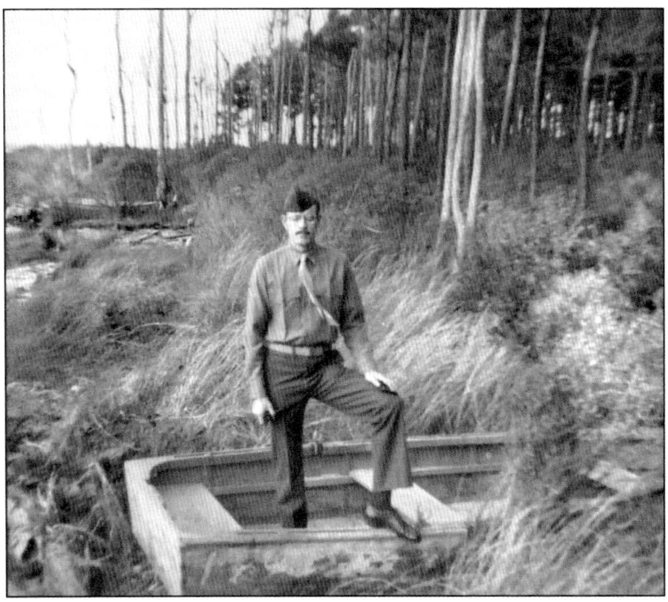

Many of the "Greatest Generation" would never return. Others who survived would return to begin new lives in new places. One such GI was Jim Youell. Jim would come as an engineer to help build the Alamo Dam with the Army Corps of Engineers. Nephew of longtime resident Tom Saunders of Wenden, Jim, with wife, Jeanne, would raise a family, fly his airplane, and operate his own airport. (Jeanne Youell.)

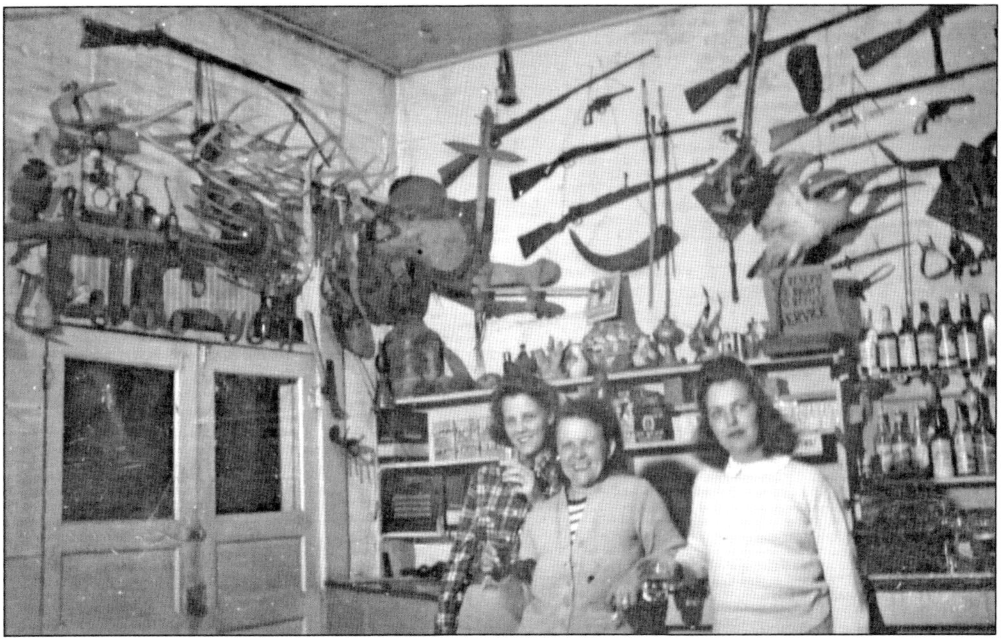

When victory and armistice finally came in spring and summer of 1945, the celebrations began. At Lorang's in Wenden, the revelry went on for months. Pictured are the unidentified bartenders/waitresses, who held their own with Camp Bouse soldiers, toasting the war's end.

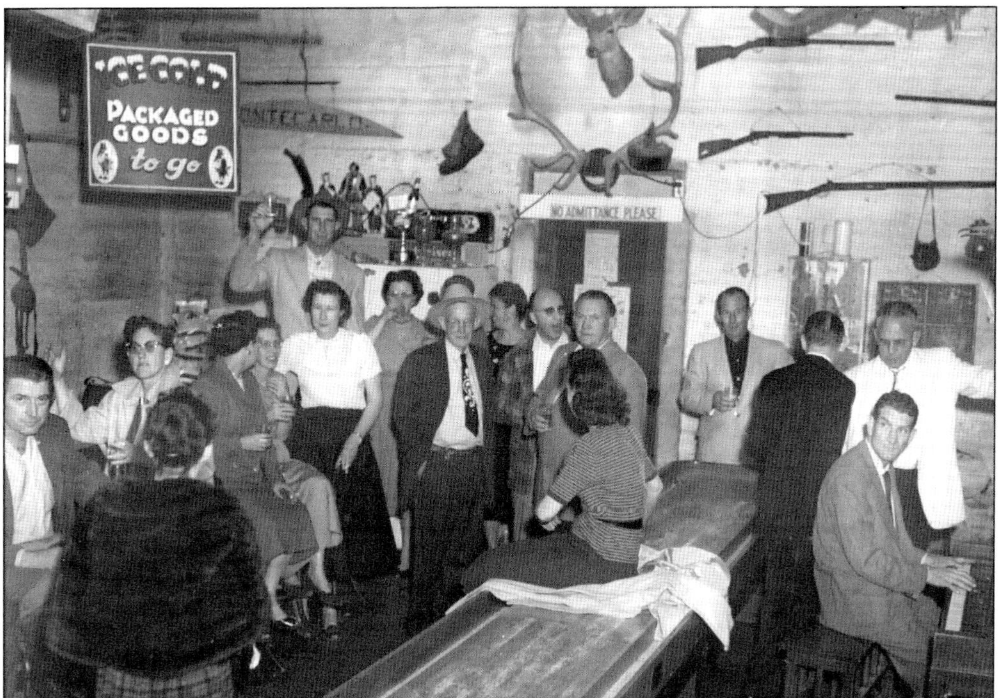

The interior of Lorang's was festooned with deer antlers, old weapons, and assorted mining implements on the walls, atmospheric reminders for locals and travelers alike of the rich past of the area. Pictured above are the saloon regulars after the Second World War. (Sam Rees.)

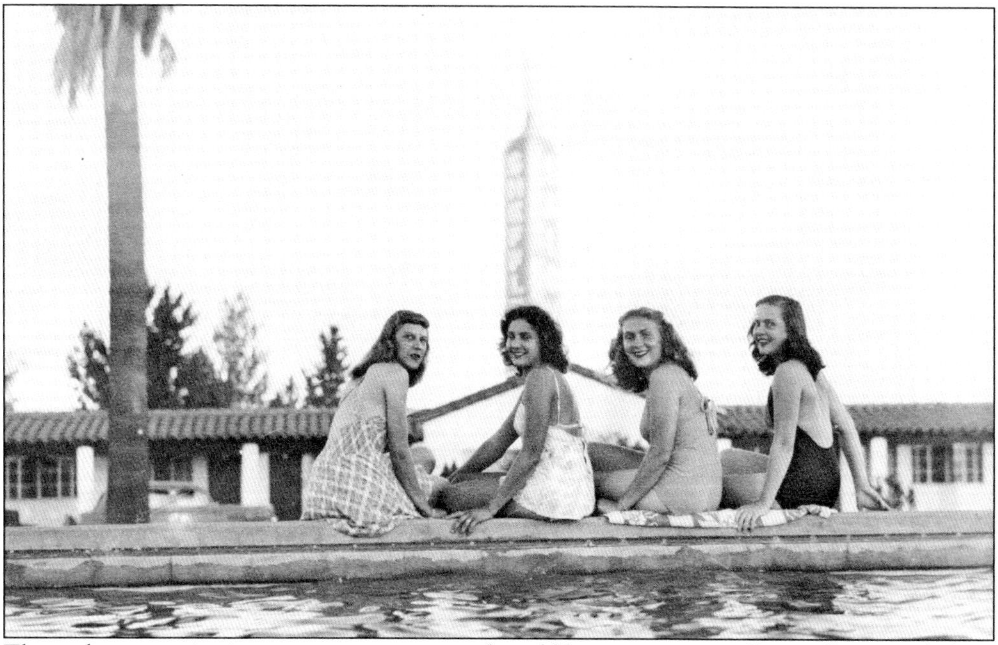

The end to gas rationing meant vacation travel could begin in earnest. Four college coeds from Valparaiso University drove across the country, experiencing the 1940s America that Jack Kerouac would capture in prose in his classic novel *On the Road*. Falling in love with life in the West, Ralph Farr, and the freedom she found in Salome, Wilma Freidel is pictured at left at the Shefflers pool with her sorority sisters from Delta Chi Epsilon. (Billie Farr.)

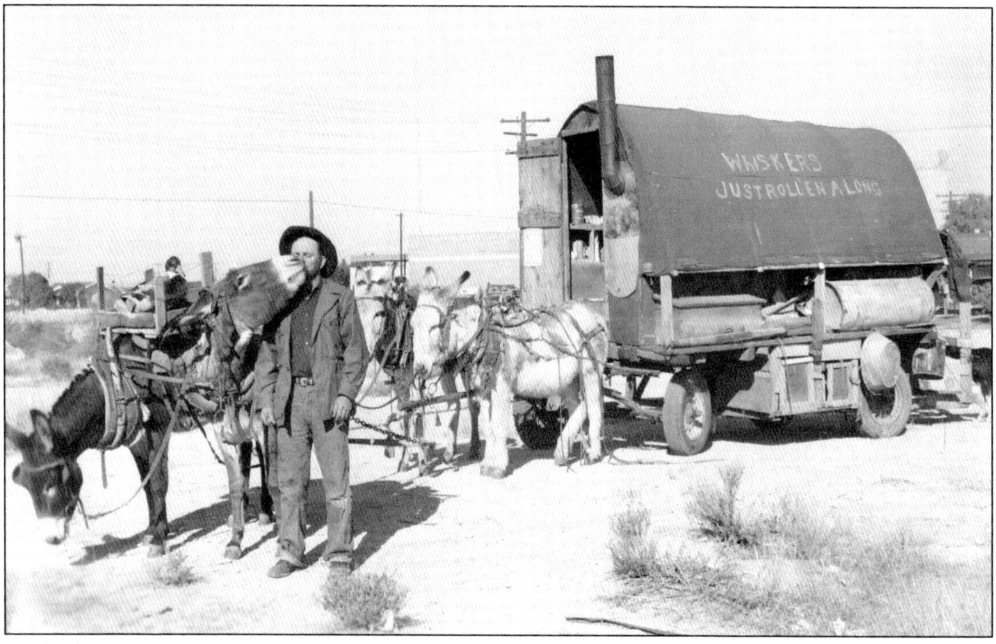

In the late 1940s, the mobile home phenomenon, which would profoundly impact the economic health of the valley, was first seen. This early hybrid traveled across Arizona. By the end of the century, the motor home and recreational vehicle culture would bring thousands of winter visitors each year. (AHS Tucson.)

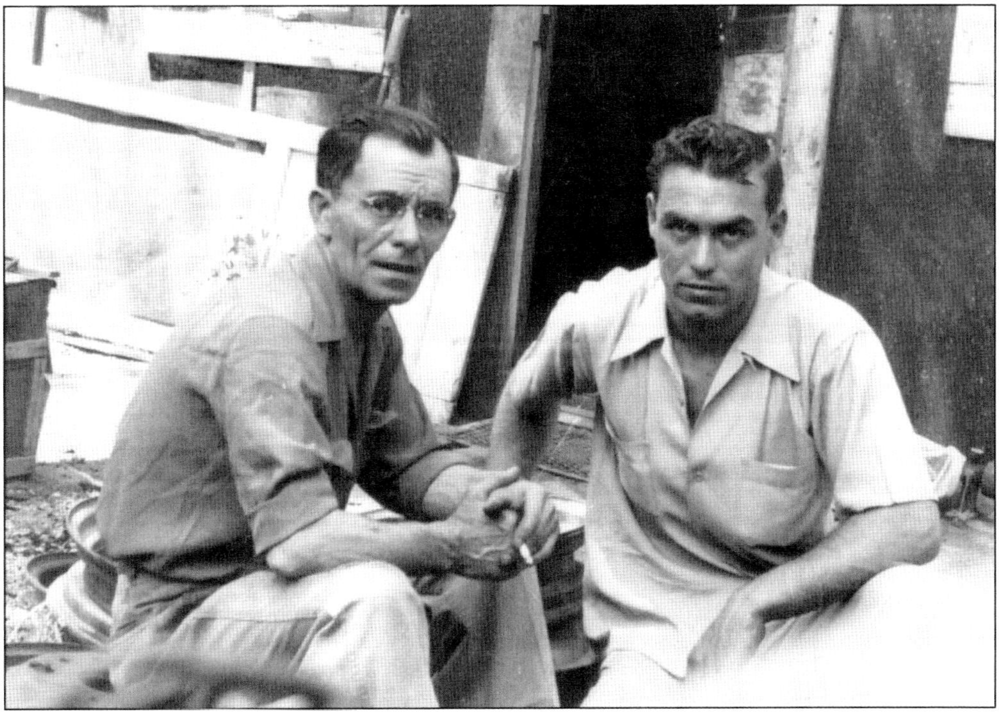

During the Second World War, strategically vital manganese deposits in the Alamo area were being extracted. Experienced miners with specialized skills were brought in, housed in cabins, and commuted each day from Wenden. Miner Alexander Rohrig (pictured on the left) arrived in 1942. After navy service, his son Lowell Rohrig joined him in Wenden. Lowell would marry Betty Orosco of the celebrated Wenden family. (Rohrig family.)

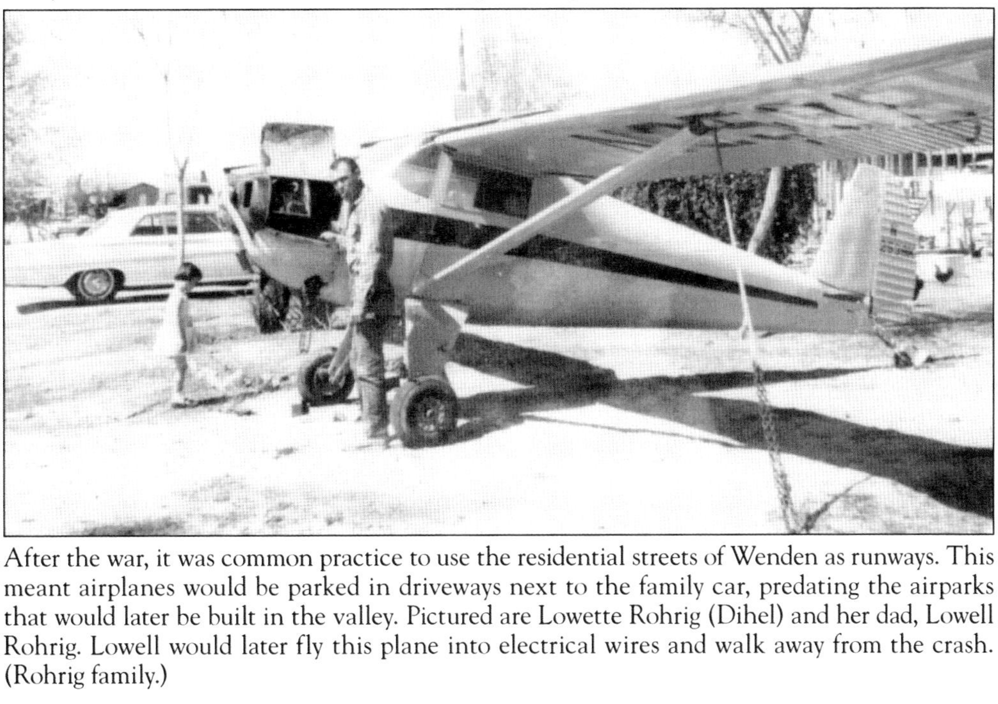

After the war, it was common practice to use the residential streets of Wenden as runways. This meant airplanes would be parked in driveways next to the family car, predating the airparks that would later be built in the valley. Pictured are Lowette Rohrig (Dihel) and her dad, Lowell Rohrig. Lowell would later fly this plane into electrical wires and walk away from the crash. (Rohrig family.)

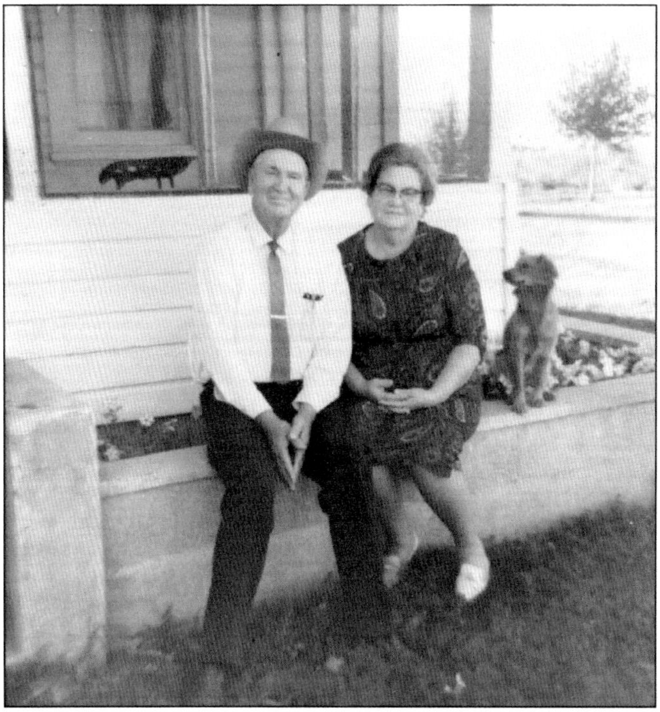

When Butler Valley reopened for civilian use, rancher Melvin Hancock came with cattle. His son Jerry expanded into farming on the McMullen Valley side of the hill. Three generations of his family would grow cotton, vegetables, and melons. Pictured in his later years is Melvin Hancock with his wife, Blanche, and their dog, Ring. (Hancock family.)

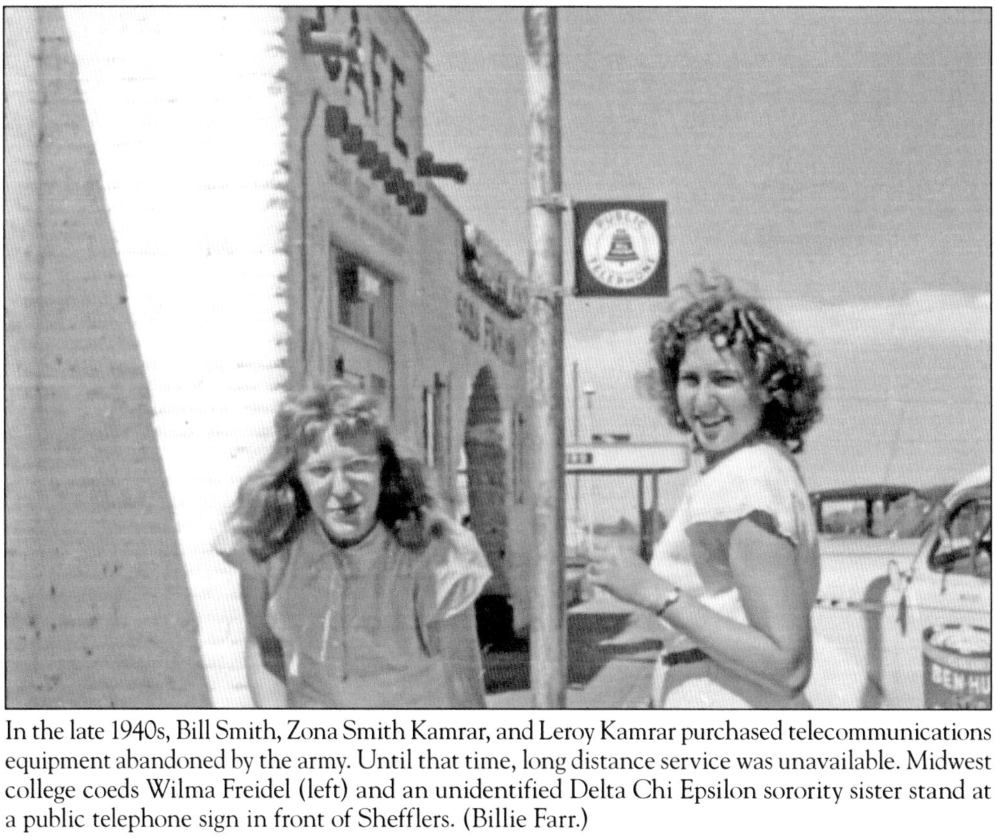

In the late 1940s, Bill Smith, Zona Smith Kamrar, and Leroy Kamrar purchased telecommunications equipment abandoned by the army. Until that time, long distance service was unavailable. Midwest college coeds Wilma Freidel (left) and an unidentified Delta Chi Epsilon sorority sister stand at a public telephone sign in front of Shefflers. (Billie Farr.)

After the war, Curt and Eunice Mork took over the Mountain Pass Truck Stop adjacent to the Richfield Maintenance Facility along Route 60. Truckers were welcome and were provided fast and courteous service. At right, Eunice Mork is pictured with her children—from left to right, Sharon, Wayne, and Donna—and, in front, Mel Mork and an unidentified neighbor child. Below, Curt Mork stands with Donna and pet burro Jack; Jack's brother, named Ass, is not pictured. (Both Mork family.)

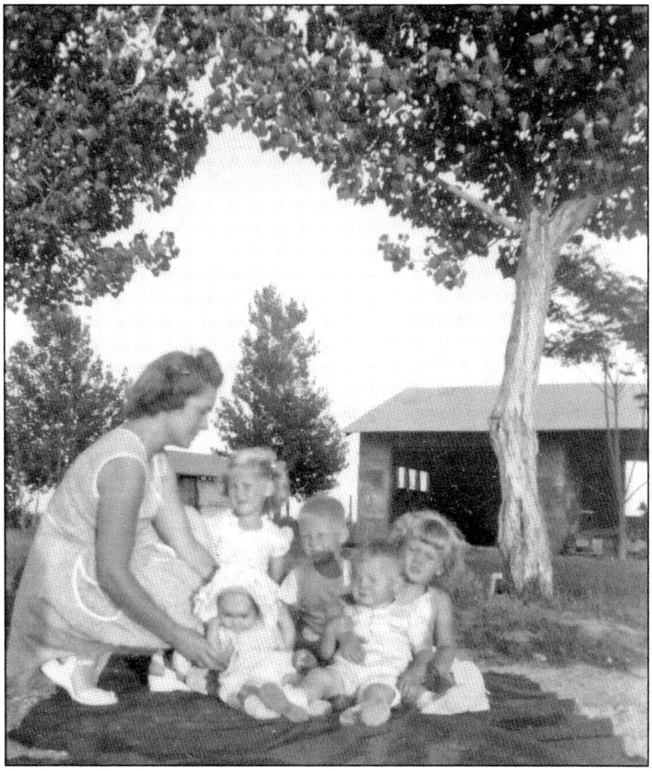

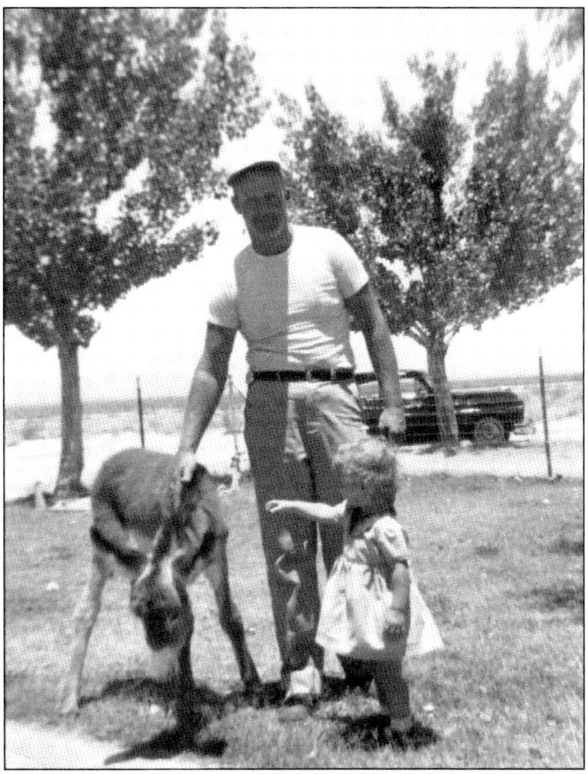

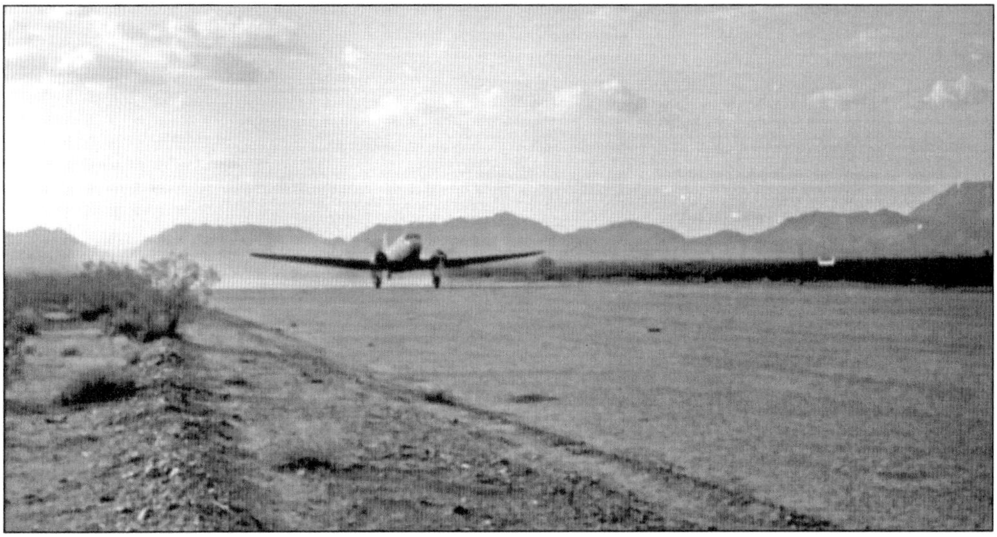

Flight training in the Army Air Corps during the war transformed thousands of wannabe pilots into flyboys. Just as homes built on golf courses gained popularity, so would airparks. Few places offered the perfect weather available in this valley. Two airparks would be built in Salome with homes constructed on adjacent runways. An airplane takes off in a 1946 Salome sunset. (Billie Farr.)

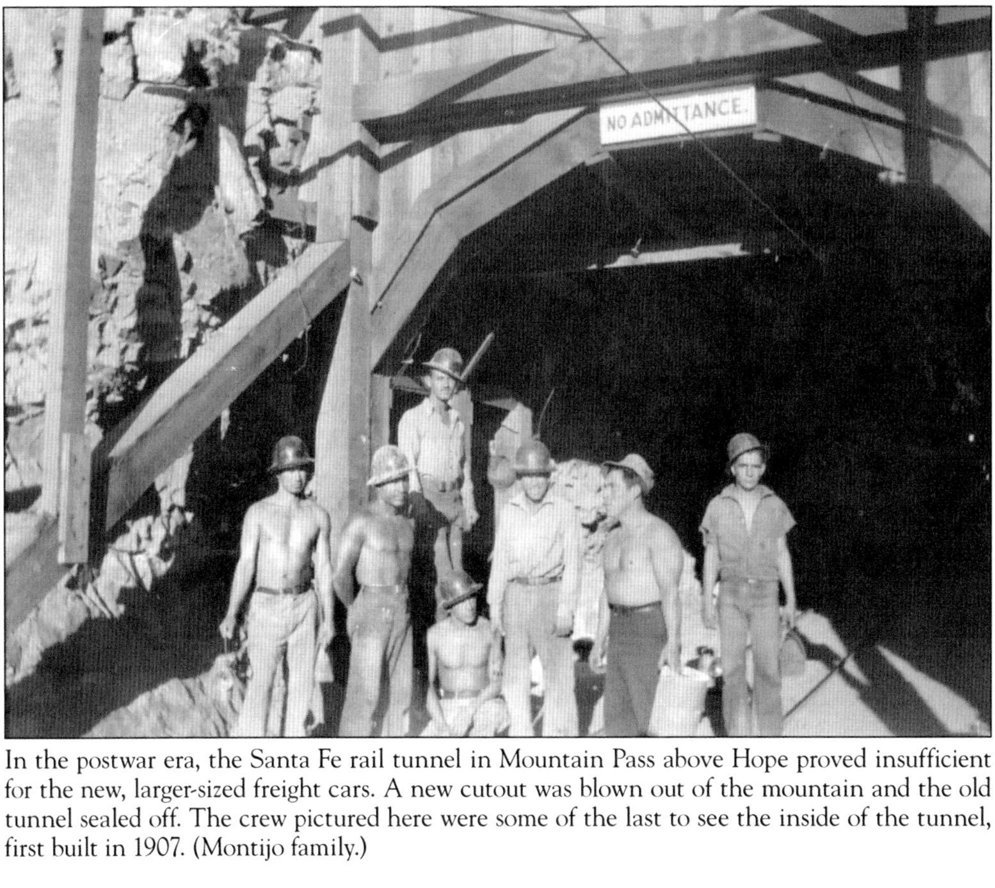

In the postwar era, the Santa Fe rail tunnel in Mountain Pass above Hope proved insufficient for the new, larger-sized freight cars. A new cutout was blown out of the mountain and the old tunnel sealed off. The crew pictured here were some of the last to see the inside of the tunnel, first built in 1907. (Montijo family.)

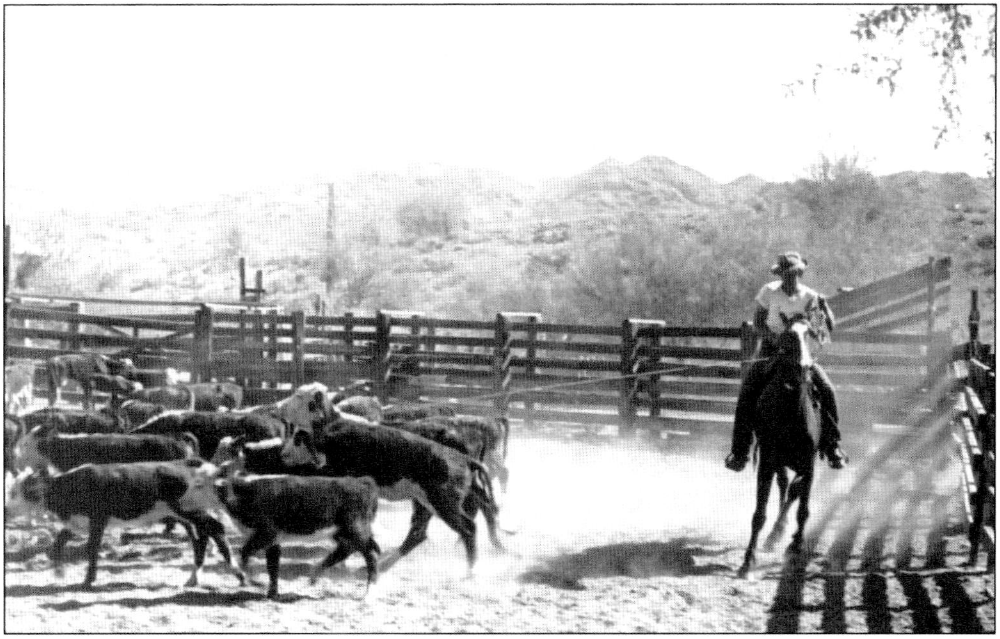

The Nord Ranch passed to August's surviving sons, Jack and Albert. The war years had taken their toll. Their brother Donald never returned and was buried in Belgium. Before going to work in the oil industry, they still found time for one last round-up. Albert Nord is pictured in 1946. (Nord family.)

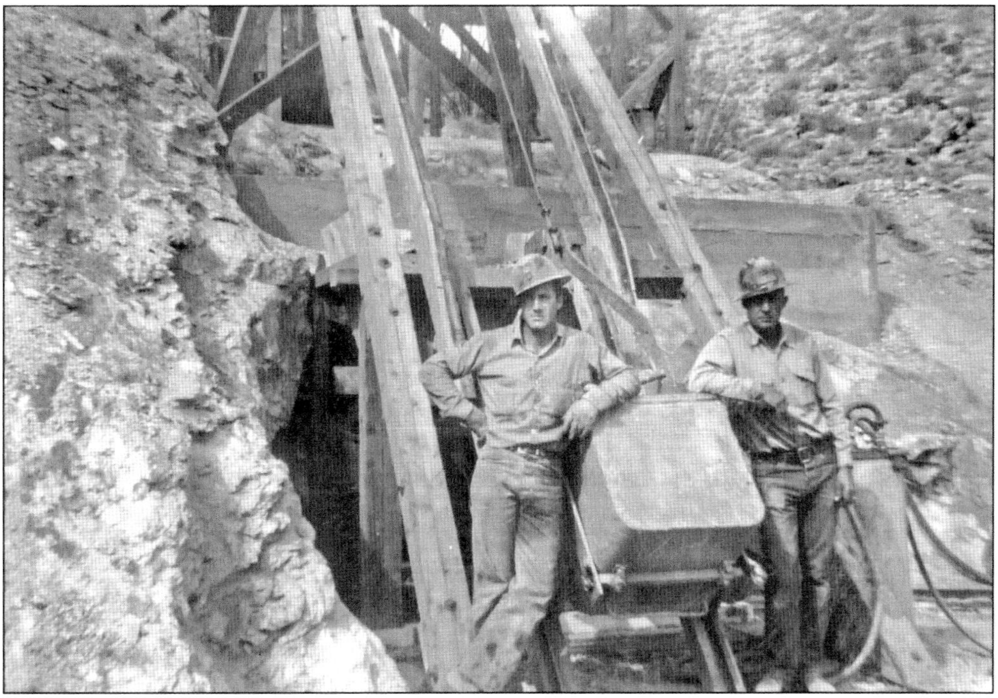

In 1951, a father-son mining team, the Darlands, worked Centroid Mine in Cunningham Pass. In 1960, father Tony (right) purchased acreage to live permanently in Mountain Pass (also called Harcuvar). Son Jack (left) and his wife, Linda, have resided there since 1990. (Darland family.)

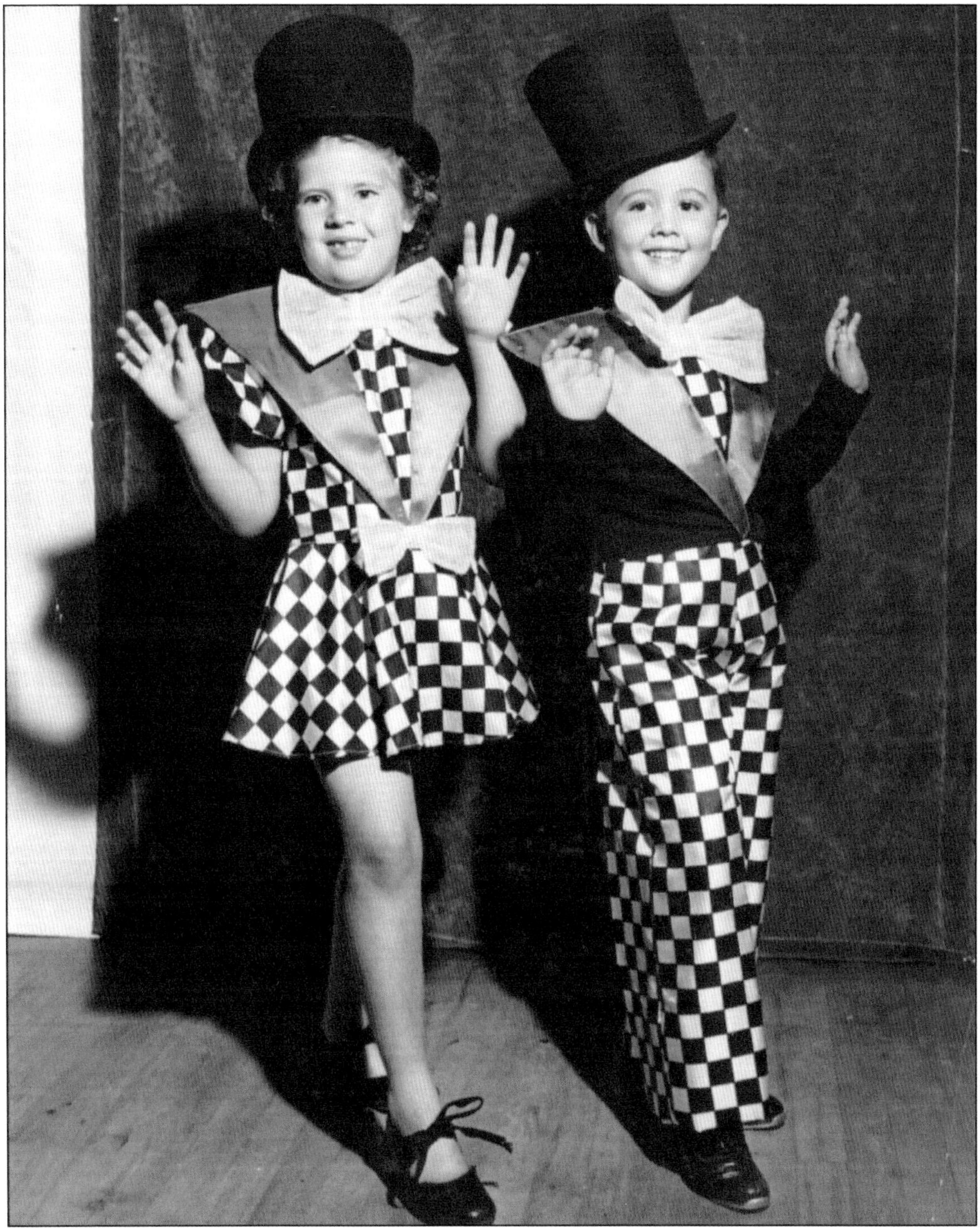

Toni Packham Brown first came dove hunting in Salome in the 1960s. After marrying Kemper Brown, she moved to town. A country girl growing up in Scottsdale, she had her own boarded horse from an early age. She grew up to become an equestrian of international competitive caliber. Toni owns and operates the T Bar B Feed store, where she shares her extensive knowledge about many different kinds of four-legged animals. Disciplined, dignified, and graceful, she still works her horses at the same time every day. By nature she is a reserved person, but at a riding competition or on stage, Toni proves herself a natural performer. Her performance at a recent local Red Hat Revue brought down the house. Toni is pictured in 1954 with her brother John Packham at the beginning of her entertainment career in a musical performance on the legendary *Wallace and Ladmo Show* on Phoenix television. (Brown family.)

Six

Cash Flows and the Community Grows

At mid-century, the McMullen Valley became everything Dick Wick Hall could have dreamed. With the armistice, truck, bus, and automobile traffic flowed through the necklace of communities as never before. Throughout the McMullen Valley, service stations, motor courts, and restaurants were built to meet the demand. A new economic paradigm with more jobs than people to fill them was created. The eclectic little enclaves in the desert became oases of economic opportunity.

Major oil companies established fuel depots and truck maintenance facilities as Route 60 became the main thoroughfare between Phoenix and Los Angeles. Young and old residents alike waited 5 to 15 minutes just to cross to the other side of the road.

Cars once only seen in magazines were stopping for gas or slowing to gawk at the "tourist-luring" diversions. Without leaving home, the people of the McMullen Valley were seeing, meeting, and experiencing people from across the nation. America was driving in, getting something to eat, and taking a look around. Some were staying overnight and doing some sightseeing. Others were coming back and taking even longer stays in the area. Good times were just beginning.

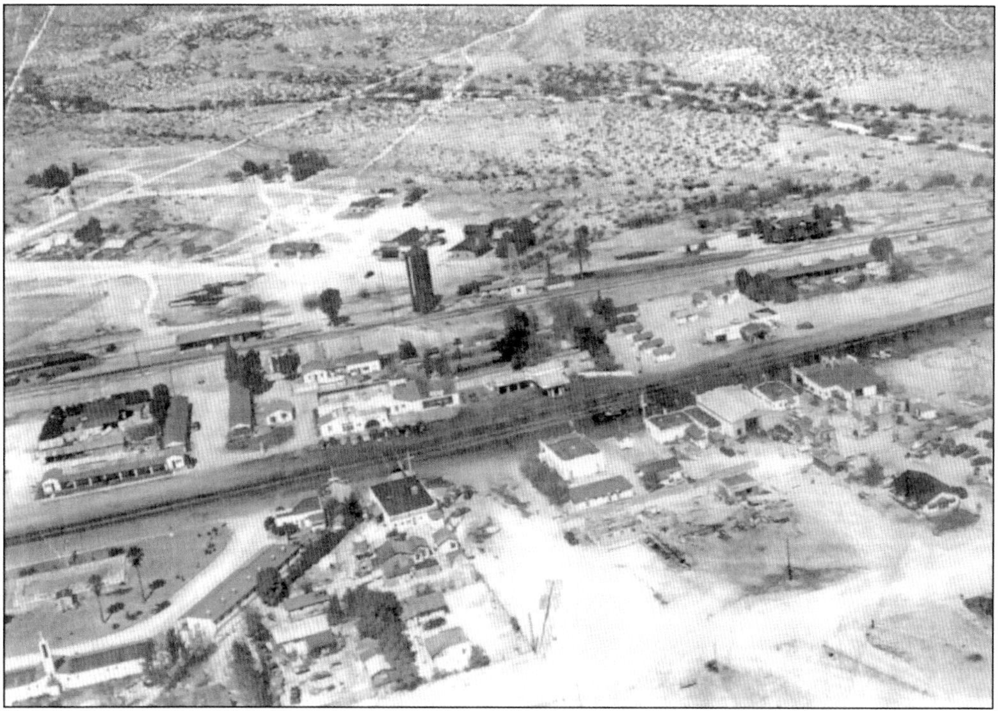

The economic growth that catapulted the middle class into prosperity in the postwar era had a profound effect on the McMullen Valley. For the first time, road trips were within reach of millions of American families. With the advent of air-conditioning, the number of overnight motel visitors increased. Local service stations sold over half a million gallons of gas annually. Roadside businesses never closed. Above, an aerial photograph of Salome was taken in the early 1950s. Pictured below, stick figures were resurrected from the 1920s and town businesses advertised on this billboard during the same period. (Above, Montijo family.)

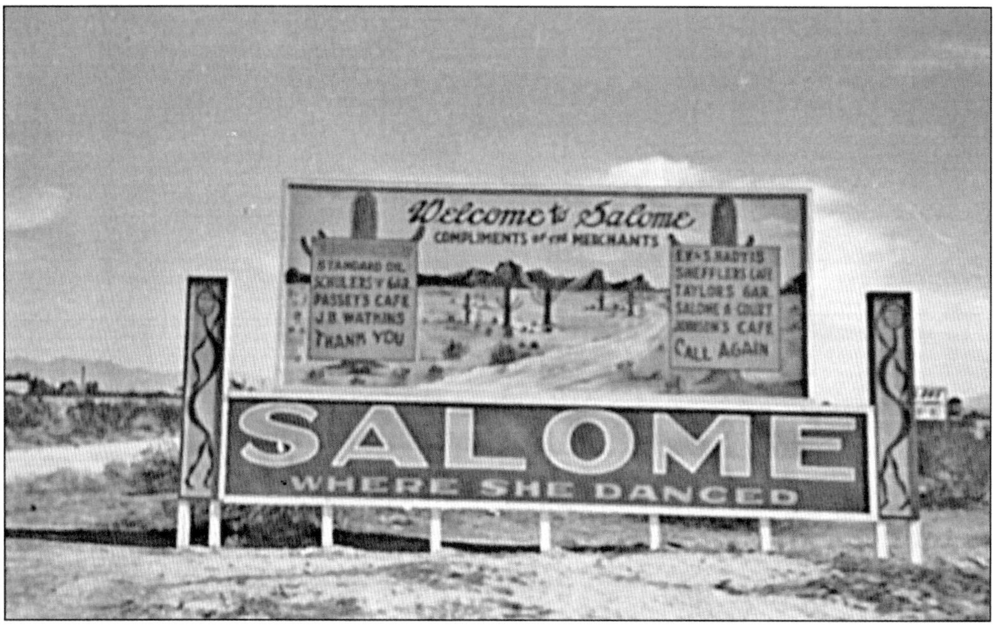

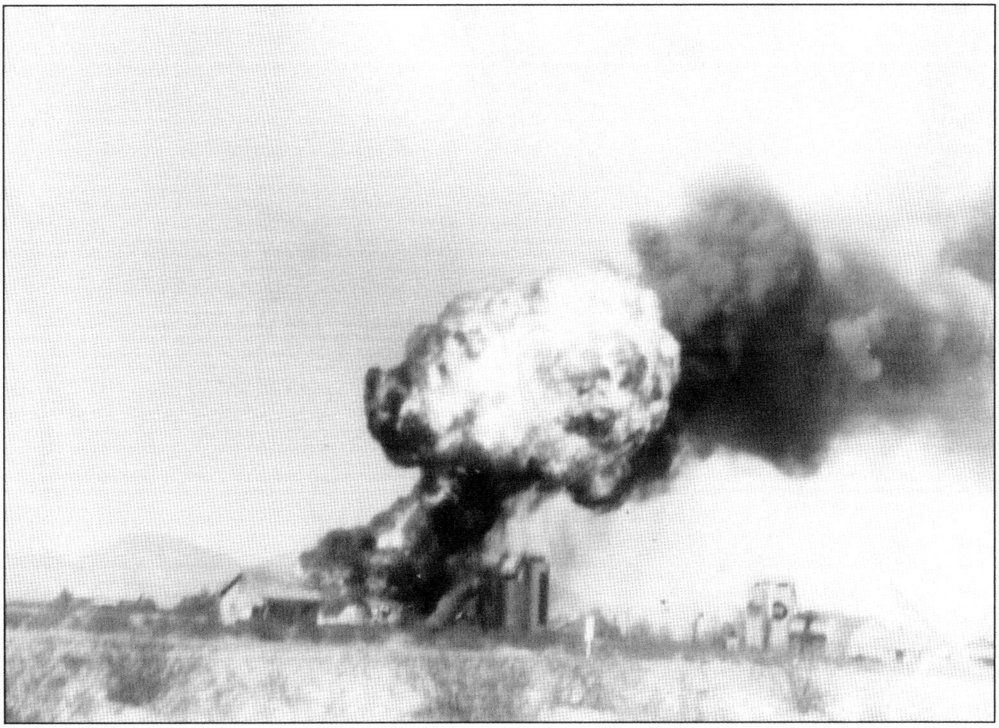

After the paving of Route 60, major oil companies Standard, Richfield, and Shell Oil chose Salome to locate bulk storage, truck maintenance, and driver turnaround facilities. In the late 1940s, an explosive fire damaged the Shell Bulk Oil facility, operated by Sam Haydis and pictured above. Flames filled the desert with a toxic cloud that extended for miles. The Mountain Pass Truck Stop is pictured below several years later, located just east of the Richfield facility. Curt Mork was among the first to offer free showers for truckers. Renovated and renamed in recent years by Dennis and Kathy Westergreen, becoming Harcuvar Plaza, the location now offers imported pottery, storage units, a bed-and-breakfast, and a barbeque restaurant. (Above, Wolfe family.)

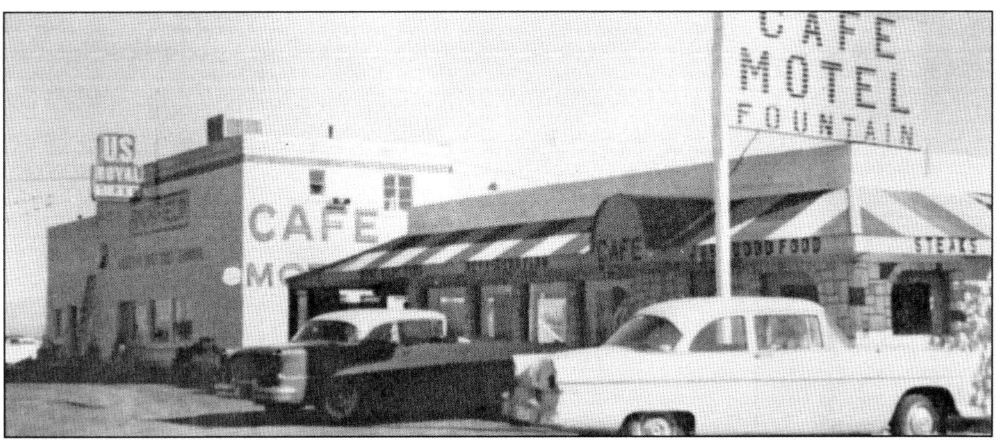

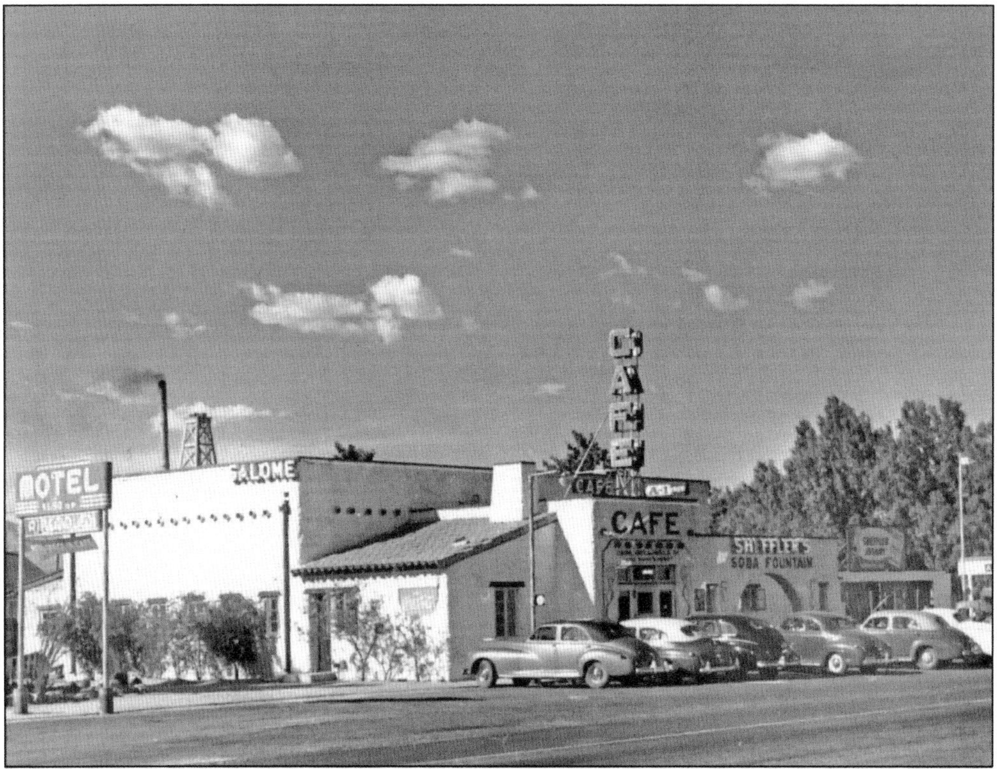

By the 1950s, Shefflers thrived under the management of Ralph and Billie Farr, formerly Wilma Freidel. A good team, they would make friends and money. Gambling at Shefflers had taken the form of Ralph Farr's legendary backroom poker game. An enduring story recalls the night the Shefflers janitor, whose name has been lost, could not lose a hand. By midnight, the equivalent of a month's pay in cash lay in front of him. Try as he might, the other card players would not excuse him, for even a breath of fresh air, until 2:00 a.m. Casually gathering up his winnings, the janitor slowly strolled to the door, ran to his car, and drove like a demon to the postmaster's home in Wenden. The janitor woke up the postmaster so he could quickly turn the cash into an untouchable postal money order. Pictured above is the Shefflers exterior. Pictured below is the interior of Shefflers restaurant. (Both Billie Farr.)

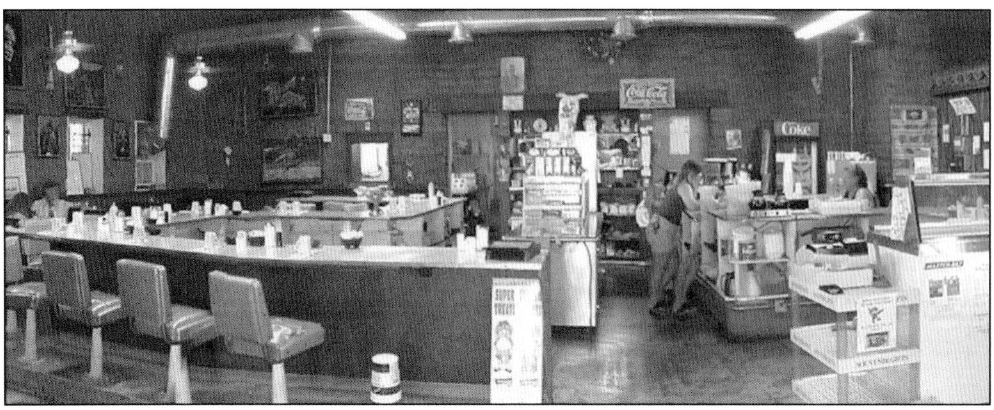

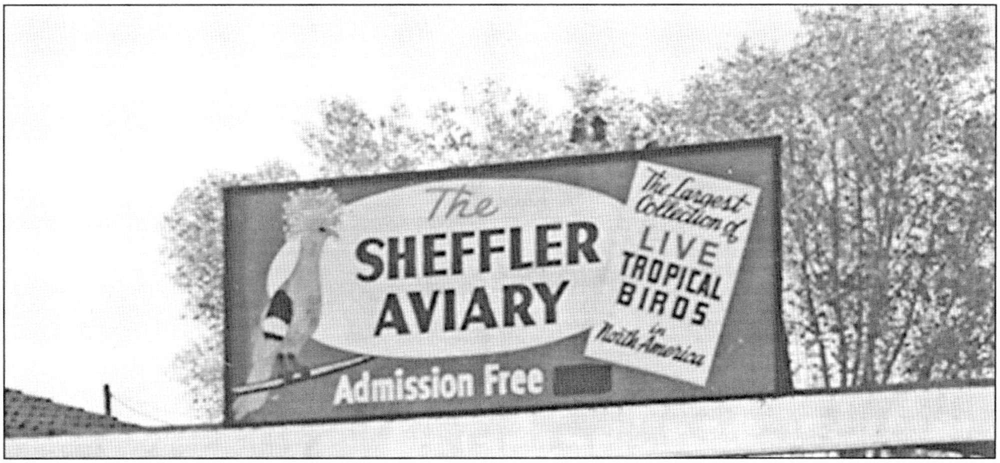

"Bus" Sheffler was the driving business force in the brothers' partnership. Bill Sheffler was an ornithologist whose collection of tropical birds had begun to overwhelm his home. The idea of a bird aviary adjoining their establishment was a roadside attraction the Shefflers could promote. They displayed the largest private collection in North America, offering tourists a riot of color and sound in feathers. Rare specimens such as Peachface and Blackmash lovebirds, yellow-rumped parakeets and Chinese silver pheasants, macaws, cockatoos, and parrots were viewed on over a quarter of an acre of cages and pens. Several residents clearly recall that Rosie, a white cockatoo, would "cuss like a sailor." A Sheffler heir vehemently denies that there was ever any blue language at their aviary. The billboard over the aviary is seen above. Below is the interior of the aviary in the early 1950s. (Both Billie Farr.)

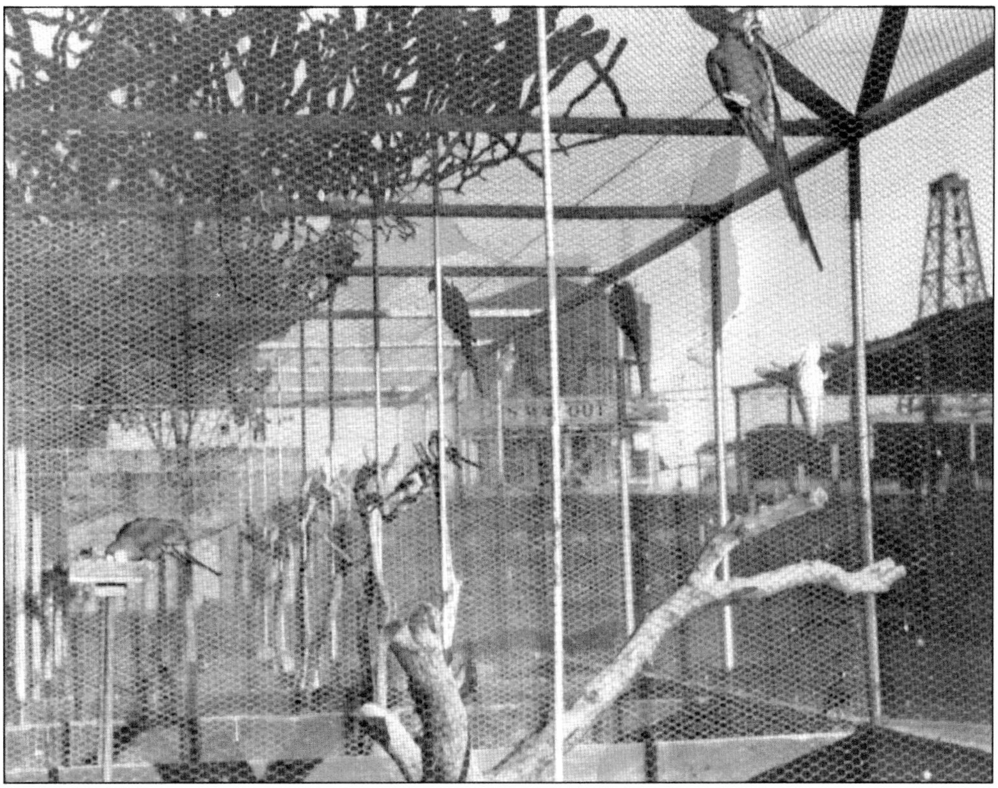

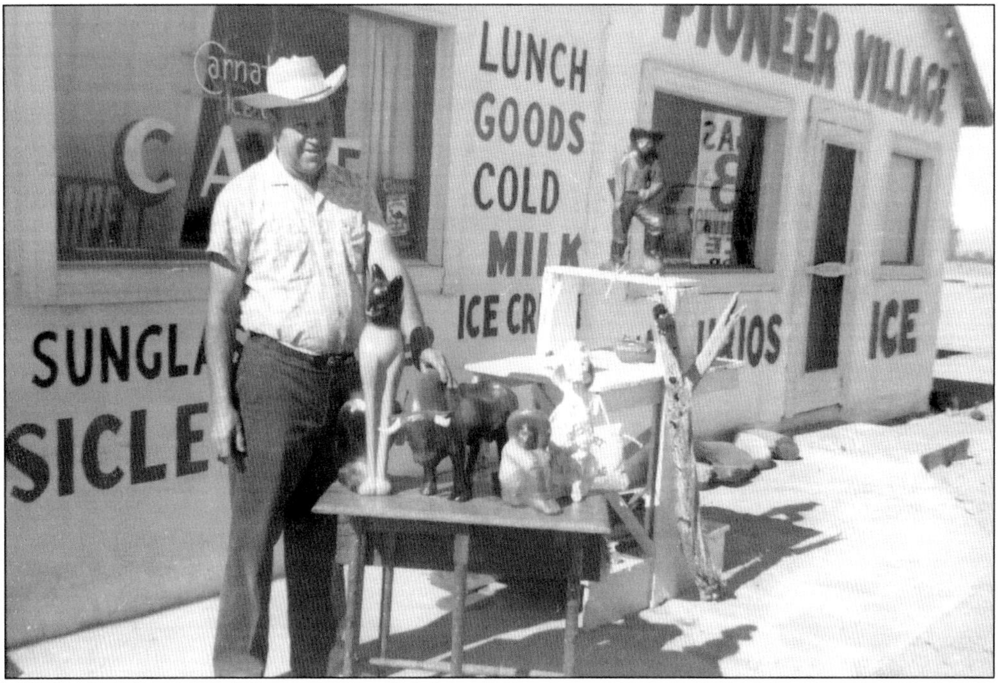

During the heyday of summer road vacations in the 1950s and 1960s, there was sufficient traffic for many entrepreneurs to open businesses along Route 60. Paul Drach, pictured above, first opened Pioneer Village near Vicksburg with his wife, Dorothy. When his landlord learned how well Paul was doing, the rent was raised. Paul moved his collection of curios to the Shady Rest location, closer to Salome. (Bev Kurth.)

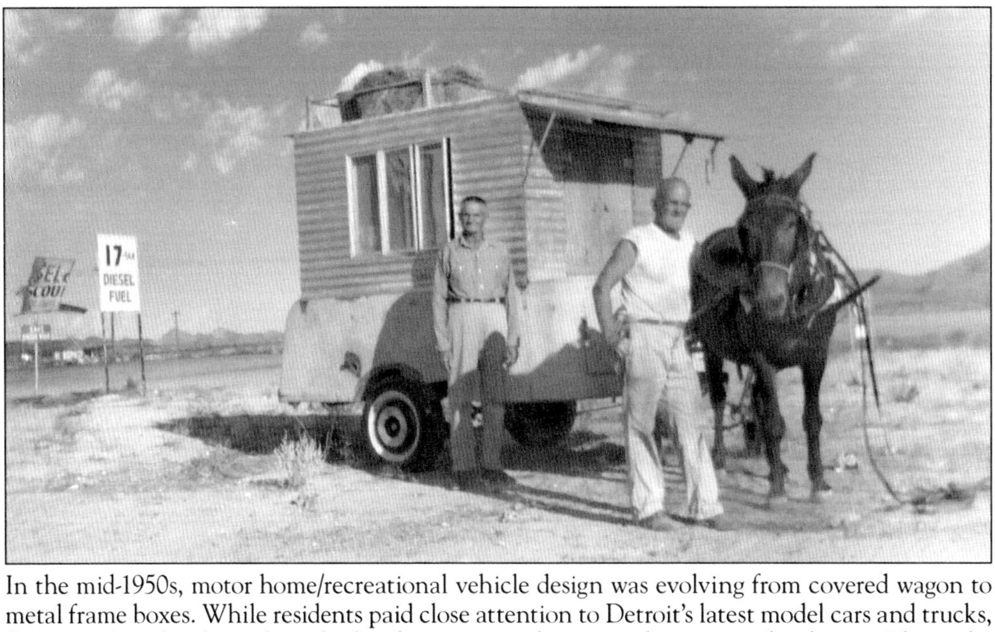

In the mid-1950s, motor home/recreational vehicle design was evolving from covered wagon to metal frame boxes. While residents paid close attention to Detroit's latest model cars and trucks, few even thought about the vehicles that came to dominate their winter landscape. The early-model hybrid mobile home pictured visited in the mid-1950s. Note the price of diesel fuel 50 years ago. (Wolfe family.)

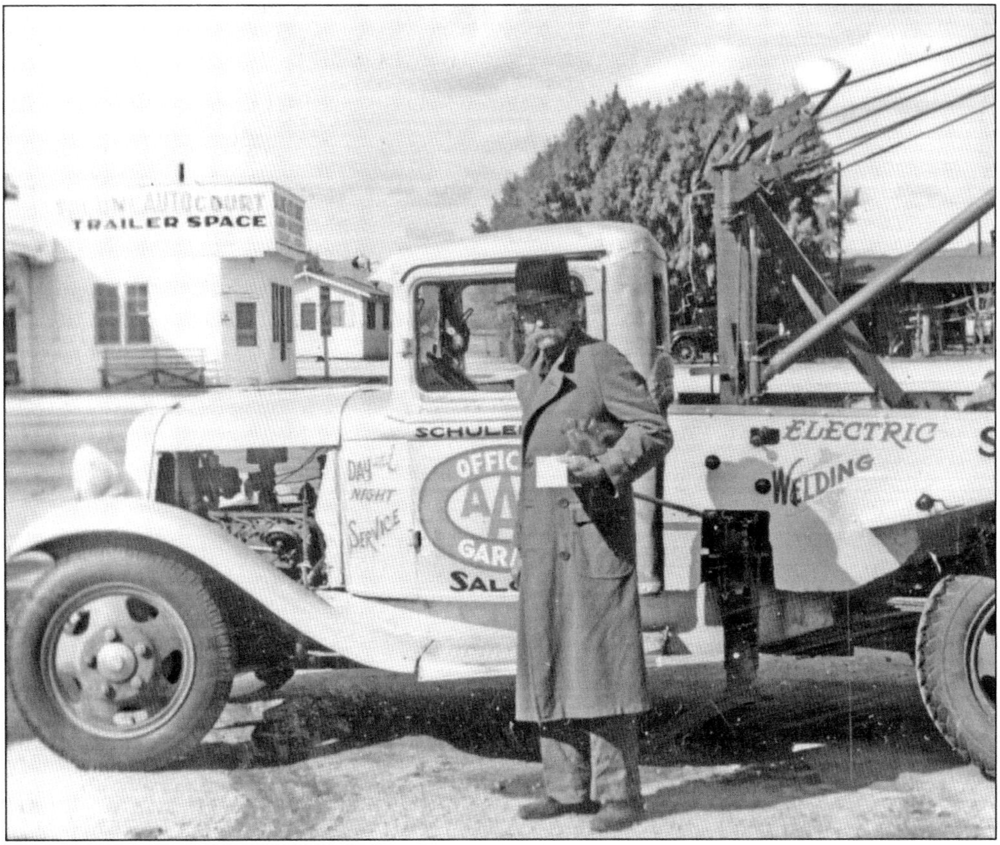

Remembered only as "Mr." Franks, this miner, pictured in the 1950s, was sometimes seen around Schuler's garage, occasionally doing an odd job or two. Fred Schuler, who operated his station for over 20 years, seems to have been an enigma. Few remember ever seeing Fred anywhere around town except at work. He and his wife, Eva, appeared to live quietly. (Wolfe family.)

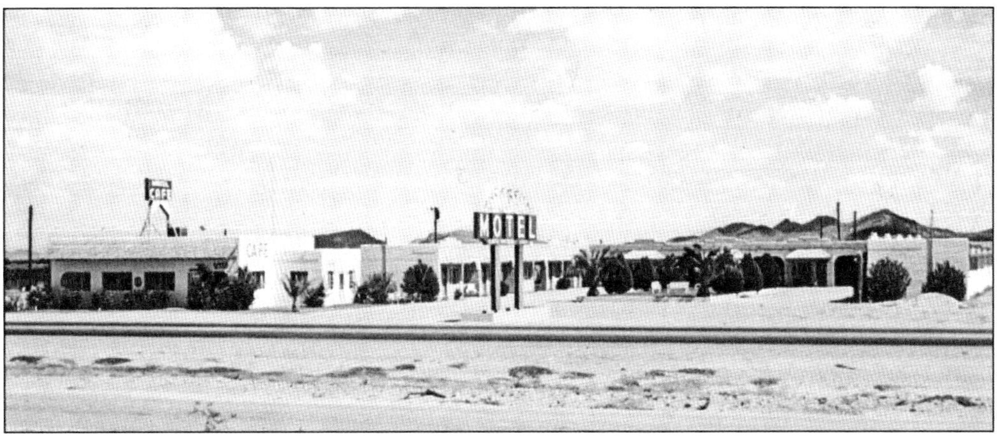

Of all the roadside inns catering to overnight guests, none surpassed the Amber Hills Motel and Café in Mountain Pass. Its architectural distinction was based on its hacienda-style courtyard and pastel-colored adobe walls. Every room offered privacy and covered parking. Long after the other motels fell into disrepair, the Amber Hills maintained its dynamic profile, as commercial and movie producers appeared regularly to repaint before using it as a film location.

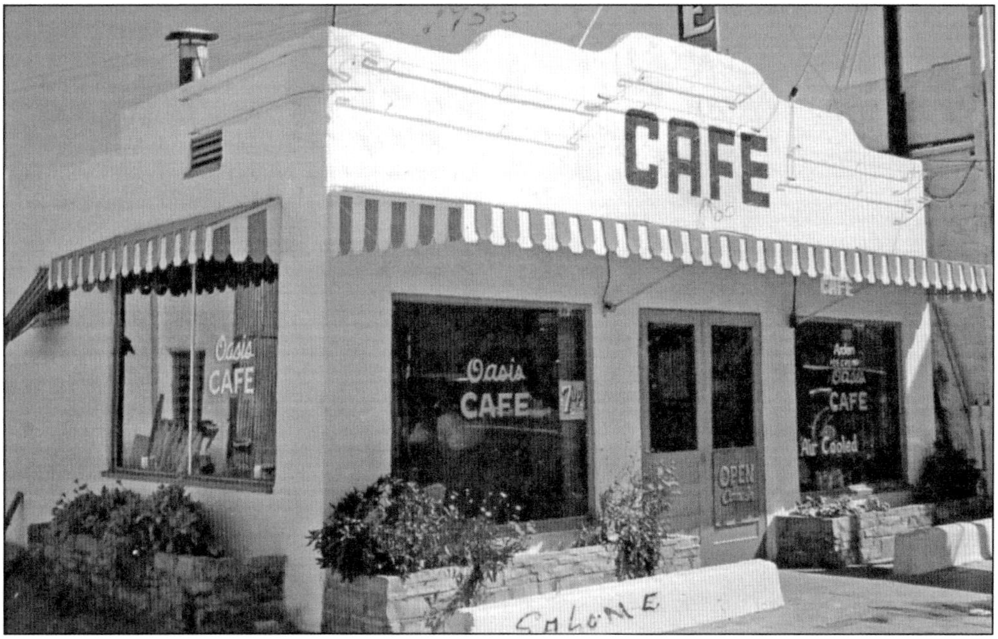

The Oasis Café and Randall Brothers Garage were located adjacent to each other on the east side of Route 60 in central Salome. For years, the Oasis was owned and operated by the Pettigrews, Harold and Eula. The Pettigrews are remembered fondly, 50 years later, especially by their waitresses. Now middle-aged women, they recall weathering the traumas of their teenage years while employed at the Oasis. (Ann Davis Rees.)

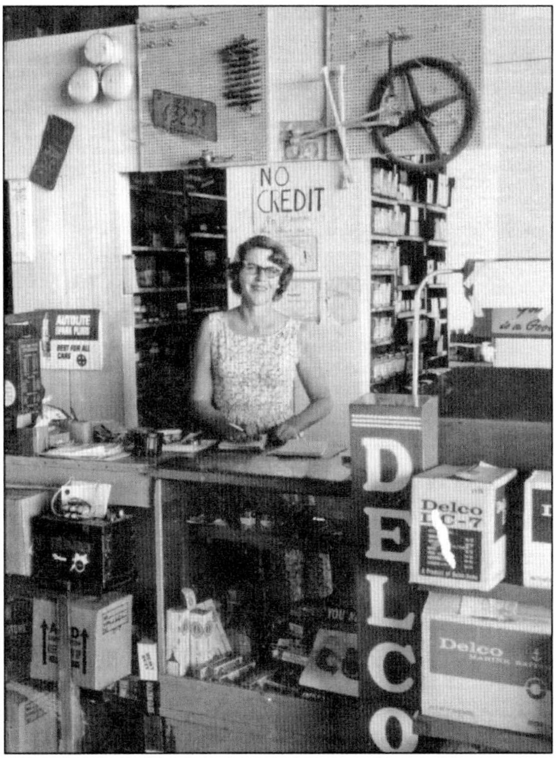

Behind the counter at the Randall Brothers Garage through the 1970s, Anita Randall was always ready to offer help with a smile and the latest in stylish eyewear. (Montijo family.)

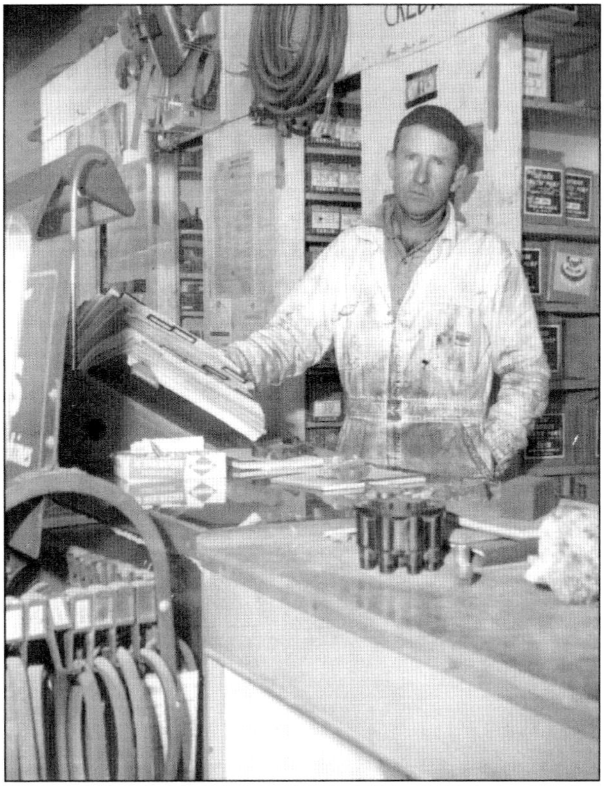

Despite the high quality of American workmanship in the 1950s, vehicles still broke down crossing the desert. Communities in the McMullen Valley offered help, sustenance, and car repairs. Conscientious service mechanic K. K. Randall, pictured at right, checks the parts catalog. (Montijo family.)

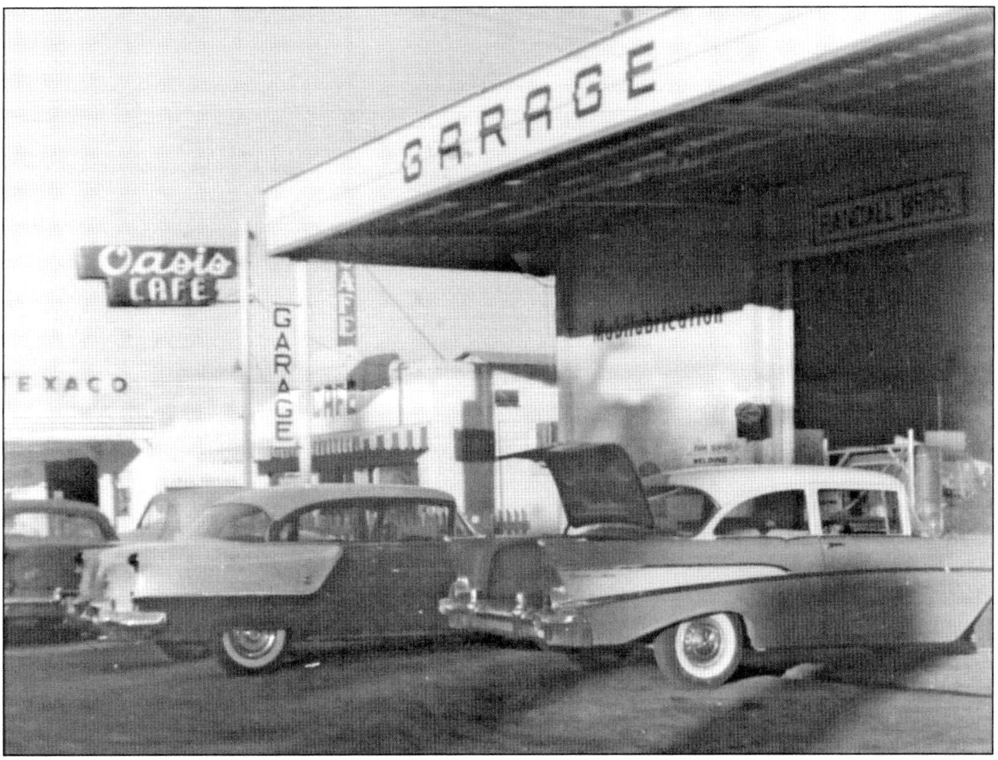

The classic whitewalls on the Oldsmobile and Chevrolet parked at the Randall Brothers Garage and the picket fence in front of the Oasis Café evoke that bygone era of 1950s America. Life was good. Families piled kids into the car for vacations in America. Route 66 was America's famous highway, but Route 60 led directly to Disneyland. (Montijo family.)

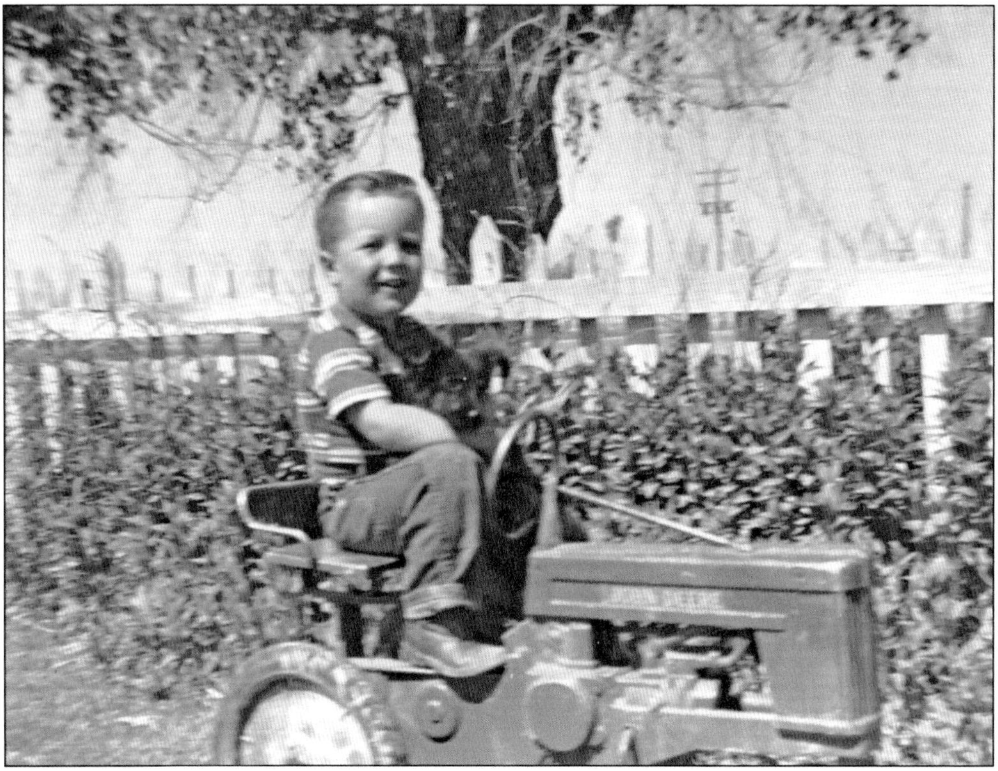

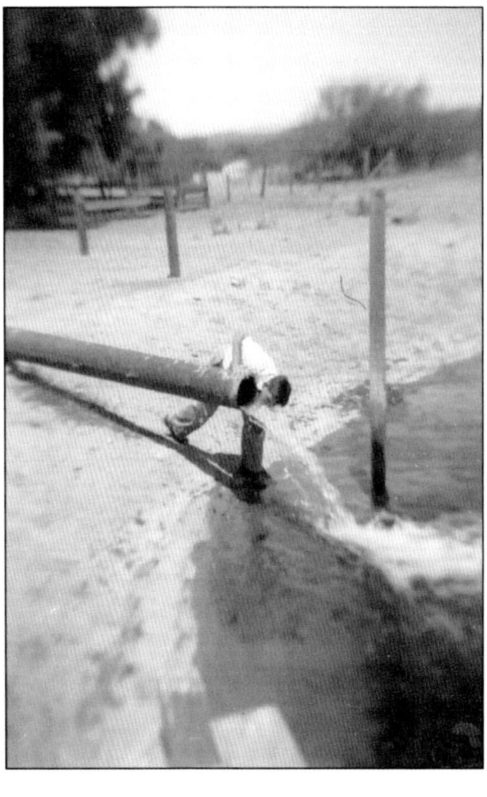

Even as roadside businesses dominated the economy in the 1950s, a new generation arrived to revive farming and ranching in the valley. Land was cleared, wells sunk, natural gas lines laid to power the water pumps, and irrigation ditches dug. From the outset, cotton was king. Melvin Hancock's grandson Larry started training early. He would be among the last to still be farming in the valley after the millennium. (Hancock family.)

In Arizona, everything ultimately depends on water. The original native inhabitants, called the Hohokum (translated as "those who left"), did so, it appears, because their water sources dried up. Drought, unrestrained growth, and climate change threaten the future. Raised near Bouse, Armando "Mo" Montijo, pictured in the early 1950s, quenches his thirst at the Planet Ranch, where his mother Marcella's family, the Esquerras, had lived for generations. (Montijo family.)

Finally a part of the American mainstream, McMullen Valley had it own postwar baby boom. After the number of youngsters in the valley increased significantly, pressures began to mount for new local schools. By the time Oral and Leona Hunter's daughter, Judy, would be ready for high school, there would be one built in Salome. (Misty Russell.)

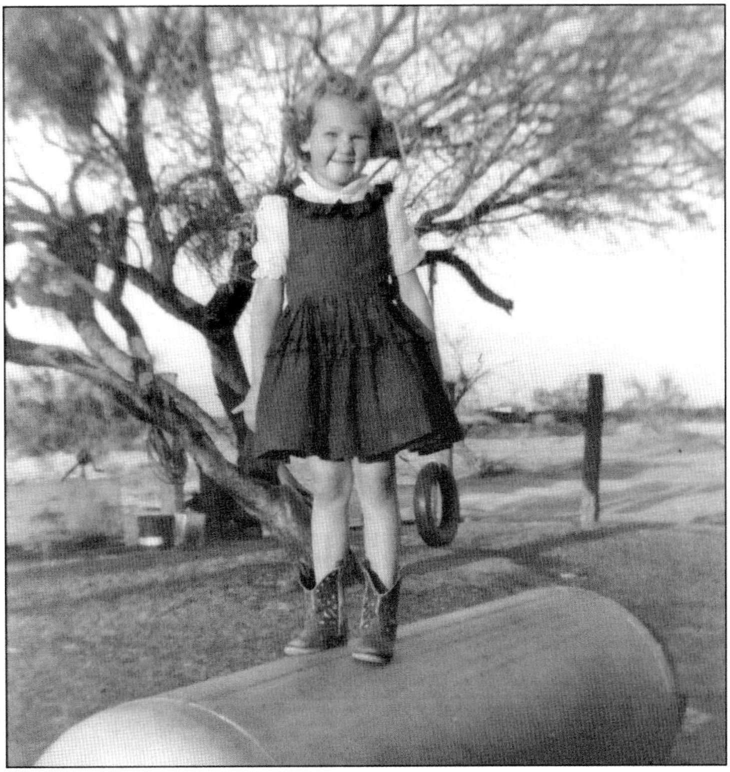

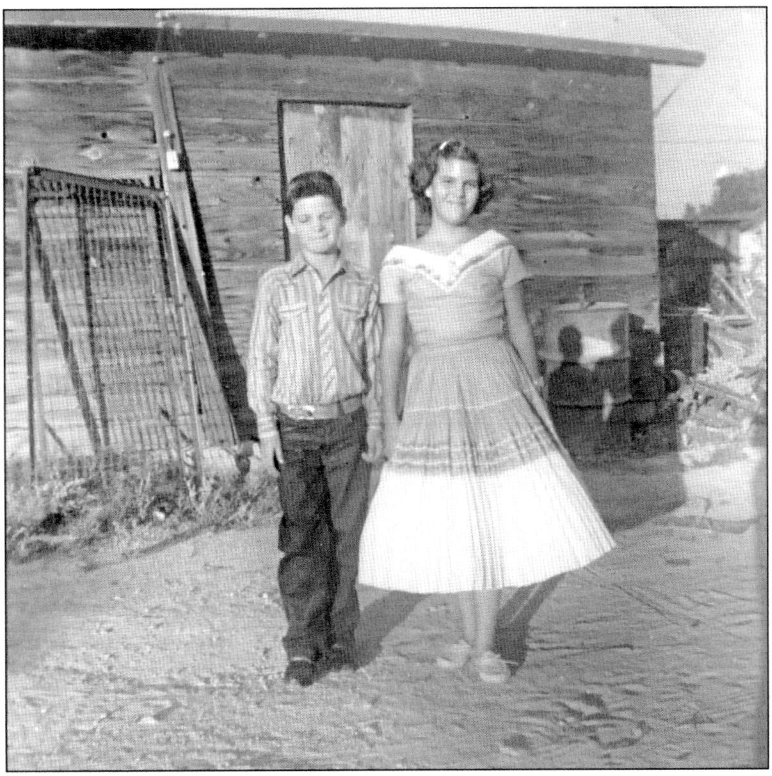

In the 1950s, Dick Wick Hall Days were a celebratory weekend of events for kids of all ages. Pig roasts, dances, games, and all sorts of entertainments encouraged former valley residents to return for a weekend of fun. Dressing up Western style, cousins Richard Randall (left) and Cheryl Randall (right) are pictured in 1957. (Montijo family.)

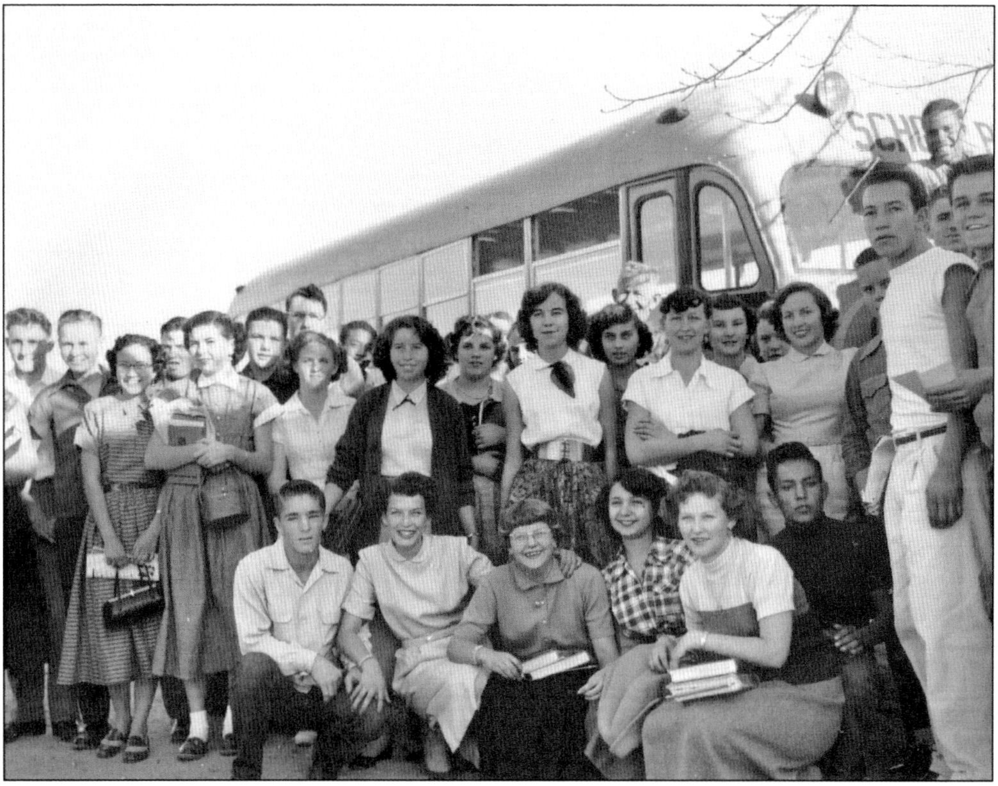

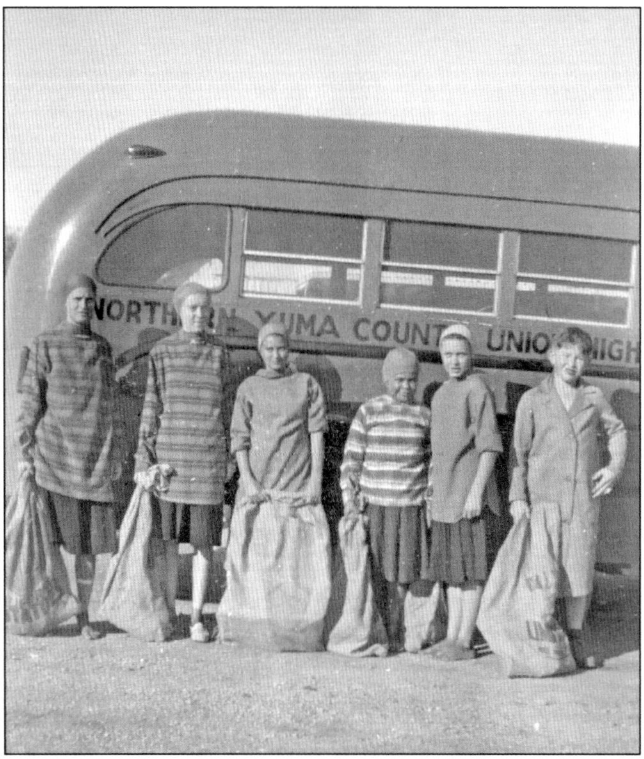

Before North Yuma County Union High School in Salome opened in 1956, students commuted daily to high school in Parker. Boarding as dawn broke over the Harquahalas, they traveled on a school bus lovingly known as "the Galloping Ghost." Its aged shock absorbers did not always cushion bumps, and its metal bench seats lacked decent padding, but "the Ghost" always delivered its students safe and sound. The friendships made as "the Ghost" crossed the desert have lasted a lifetime. Above, 1950s students are pictured with their beloved school bus. Six freshmen stand in front of "the Ghost" during initiation at left. (Both Montijo family.)

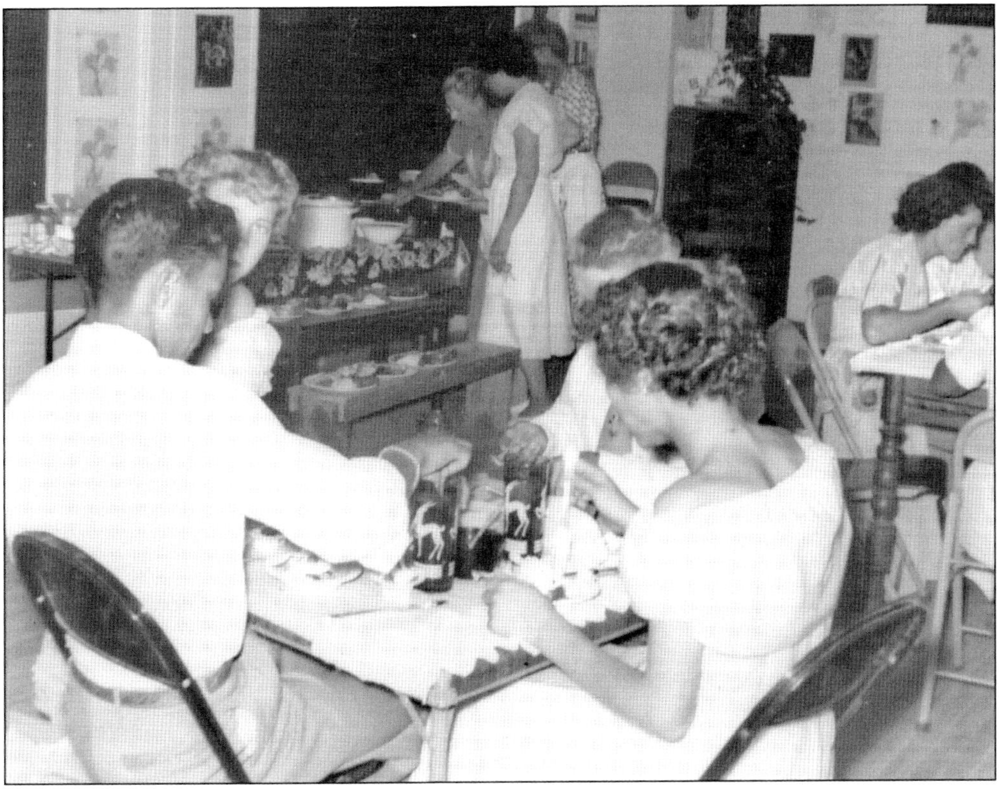

The schools in the valley sought to deliver quality educations and offer students the same extracurricular activities available to city kids, such as proms and their attendant post-prom dinners. By necessity, classrooms substituted for tony nightclubs and fashionable restaurants. Prom nights, no matter where, are about getting formally dressed, dancing close with a special date, and dining with both friends and table manners. In this Bouse School eighth-grade prom from the early 1950s, graduates enjoyed an evening of dinner and dancing. Girls dined in long dresses at folding card tables (above), then danced close with their dates (below) under the watchful eyes of chaperones, while reviewing the standard and cursive alphabets. (Both Montijo family.)

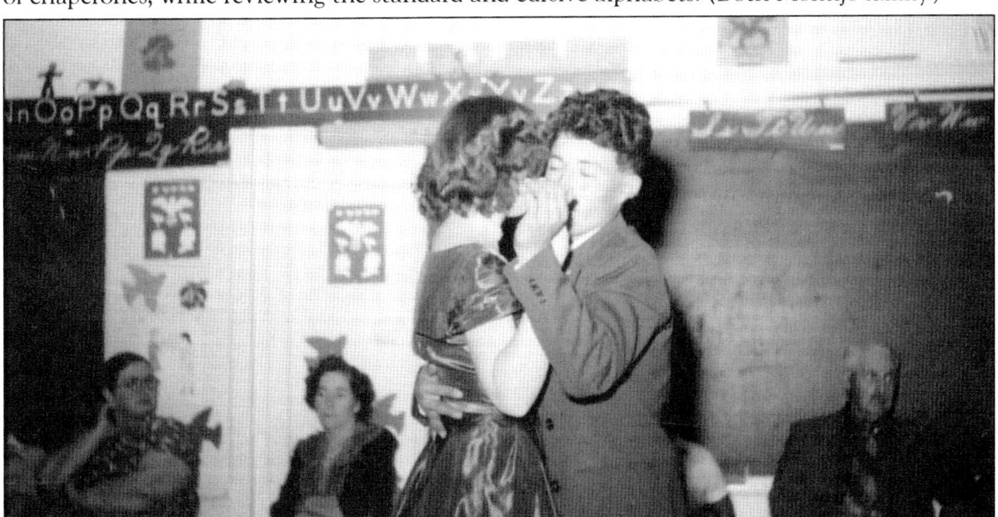

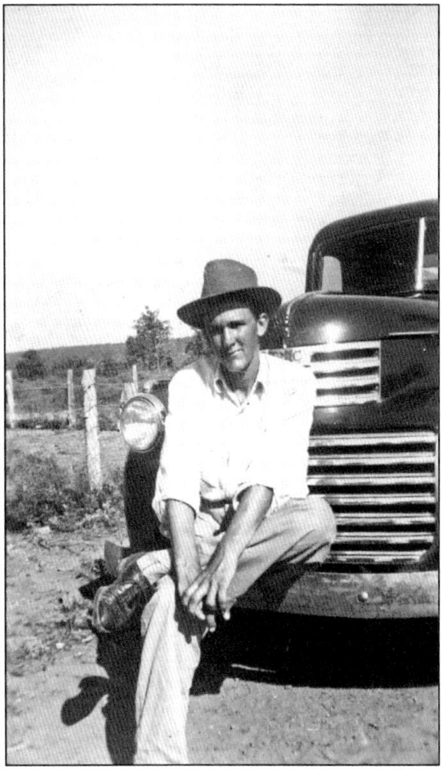

Surviving veterans came home eager to start fresh, begin life anew, and fulfill their dreams. Originally from Oklahoma, after service in the South Pacific, young Oral Hunter came to the McMullen Valley with a vision. He saw himself as a successful farmer who would work hard at it but also enjoy life, taking the time to hunt, fish, and fly airplanes. (Misty Russell.)

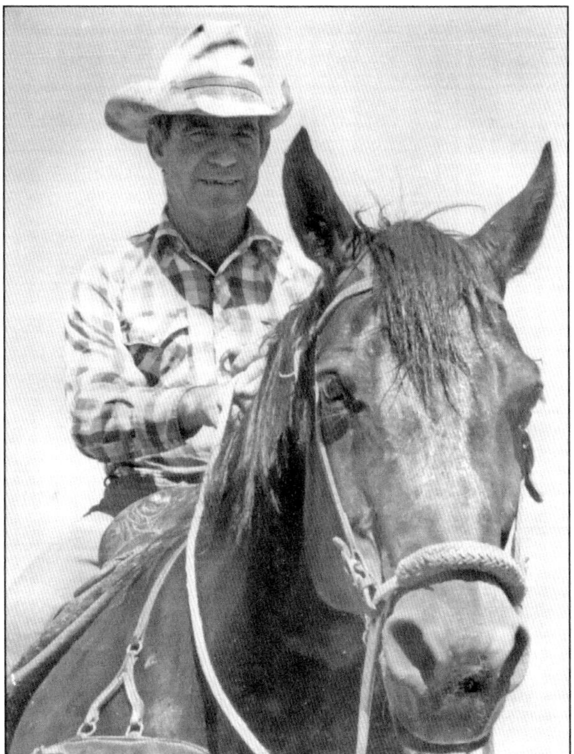

The revival of cattle ranching brought the Conleys up from Maricopa, south of Phoenix, in 1955. Initially ranching on BLM land, they were mandated not to build a house for more than $500. Eventually they moved to a ranch with a proper home, where Burt and Betty Conley raised four children—Larry, Elaine, Alberta, and Bob, all graduates from the high school in Salome. Burt Conley is pictured on his horse, Puddin. (Conley family.)

Ben and Dorothy Matthews came to farm in 1954. Arriving young and energetic, they were active members of the community. Ben served numerous terms on the school board. He was elected to the Board of Supervisors of La Paz County. Dorothy became president of the ViSaWen Women's Club. They were people who felt the responsibility to contribute all they could. Ben and Dorothy Matthews are pictured in the 1970s. (Dorothy Matthews.)

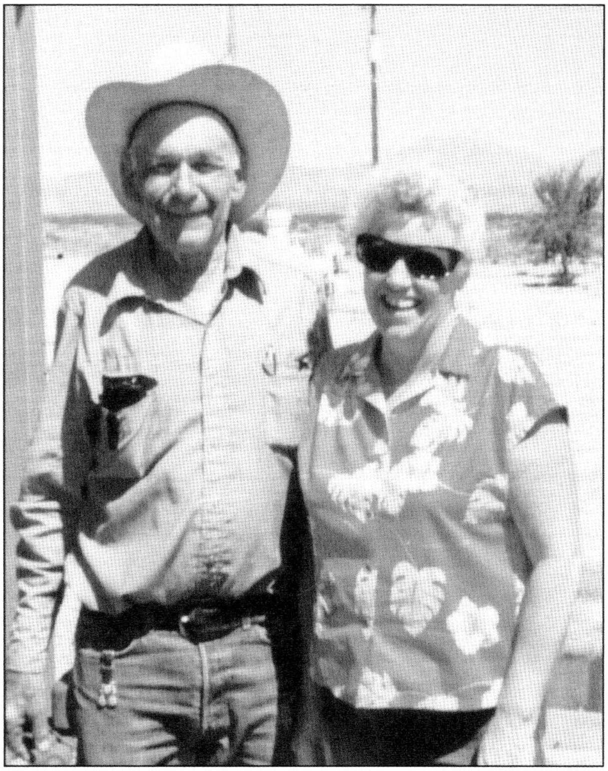

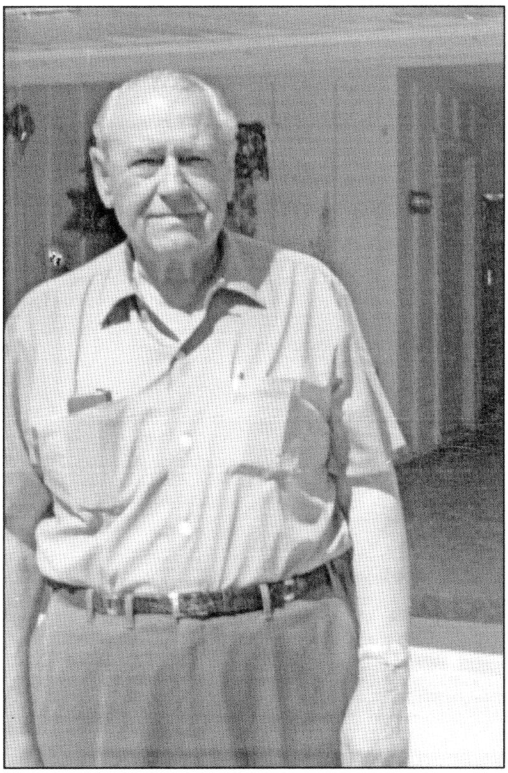

Don Brown is legendary among the farmers who came in the 1950s. The largest and most influential landowner, he found success growing high-quality cotton before introducing melons, founding the local industry. Former Boy Scouts, who received free melons to sell to tourists, remember Don Brown fondly. His melons provided them with the means to earn the money they needed to spend their summers at Scout camp. Don Brown is pictured late in life. (Brown family.)

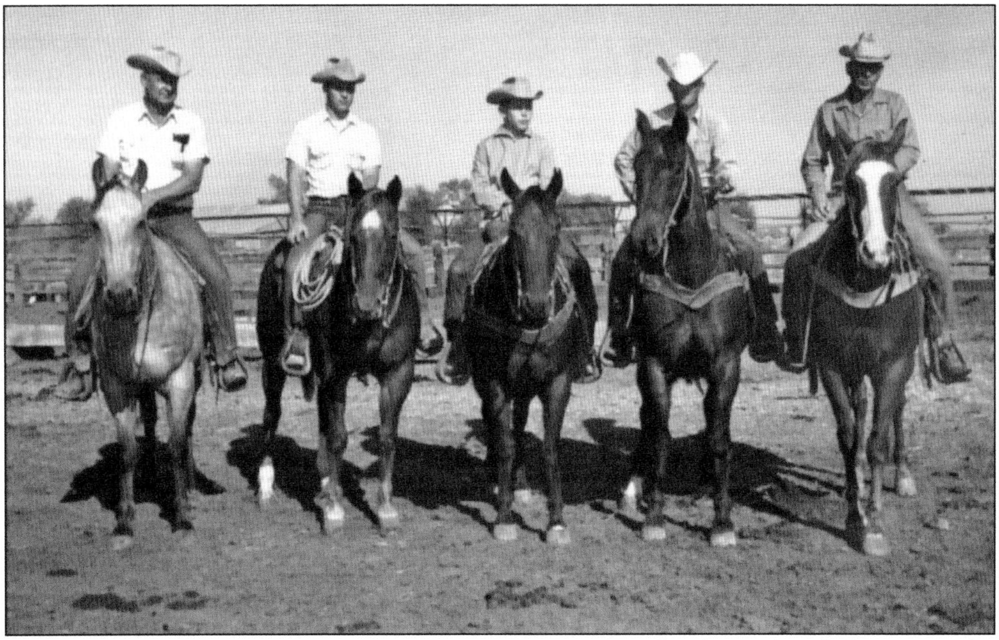

In 1936, Bob Crowder first met original Kofa rancher Jack Wilbanks. A decade later, Crowder purchased Wilbanks's cattle spread and was joined by his brother-in-law, Karl Weisser, to form the Crowder-Weisser Cattle Company. Between their ranches in Kofa and Vicksburg and their feedlots in Phoenix, they ran a substantial operation. Karl's sons, Steve and John, would become full-time residents of Vicksburg. Steve, a collector, would own and operate an antique shop in Hope until his death in 2008. John would drive race cars, become a master of water pumps, and continue the family tradition of raising cattle into the 21st century. Pictured above in 1964, from left to right, are Karl Weisser on Buckwood Thomas, R. E. Crowder III on Mr. Crowder's Filly, John Weisser (age 12) on Dooley McCue, John Mahan on Scooter, and Bob Crowder on Hecks Bells. Pictured below is a corral near Kofa. (Above, Weisser Cattle Company; below, Brian De Ganahl.)

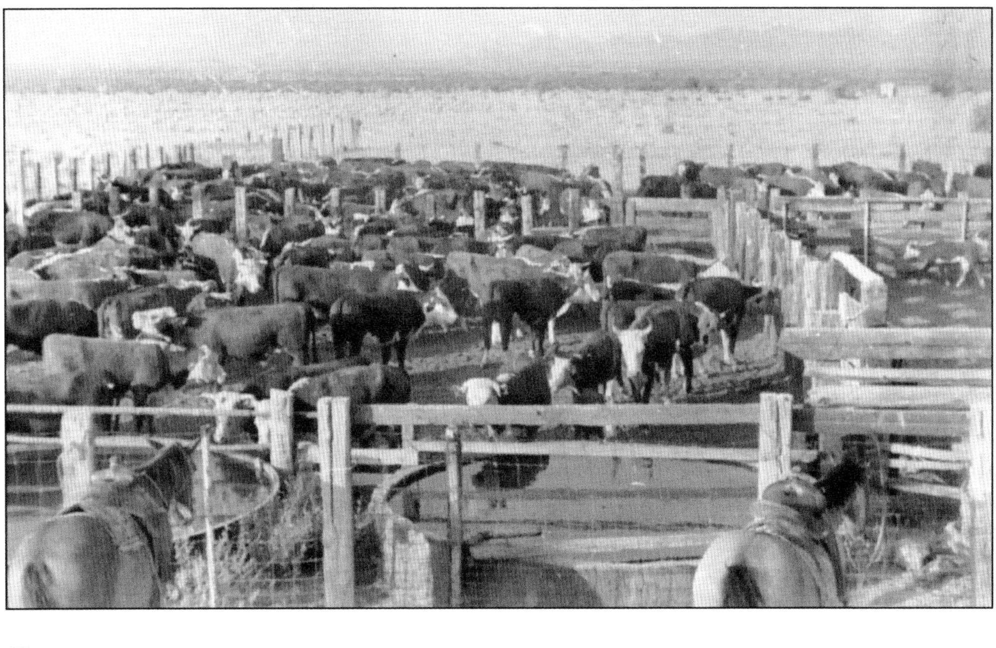

Seven

Let the Good Times Roll

Economic activity created the substantial tax base needed to get the Yuma County officials to pay attention to the needs of local residents. For decades, high school students had been forced to room and board in distant Parker in order to complete their education. When a school bus was finally provided, high school students were commuting for over three hours each day. Finally in the 1950s, E. V. Haydis, a no-nonsense high explosives dealer and school board member, spearheaded the effort to get a high school built in Salome.

Neon signs illuminated the bustling businesses on the highway. The motels and motor courts began luring overnight stays with refrigeration, then air-conditioning. The advent of cable television technology brought residents their first view of black-and-white images on 7-inch television screens.

New buildings were built and old ones refurbished. With a few recipes, a stove, and refrigerator, an old adobe building could be fixed up and reopened as a café.

Hard-working people, who had long found pleasure in their leisure hours playing in the desert before they had an extra dollar to spare, began to enjoy the benefits of their newfound prosperity. The face of consumerism, like so much else in the McMullen Valley, took an eclectic turn. While most urban dwellers were purchasing hi-fi stereos, sectional sofas, and other trappings that would lead them in the direction of the couch potato culture, McMullen Valley residents were buying, restoring, and customizing a wide variety of off-road vehicles, including army surplus Jeeps, motorbikes, and a surprising number of single-engine airplanes.

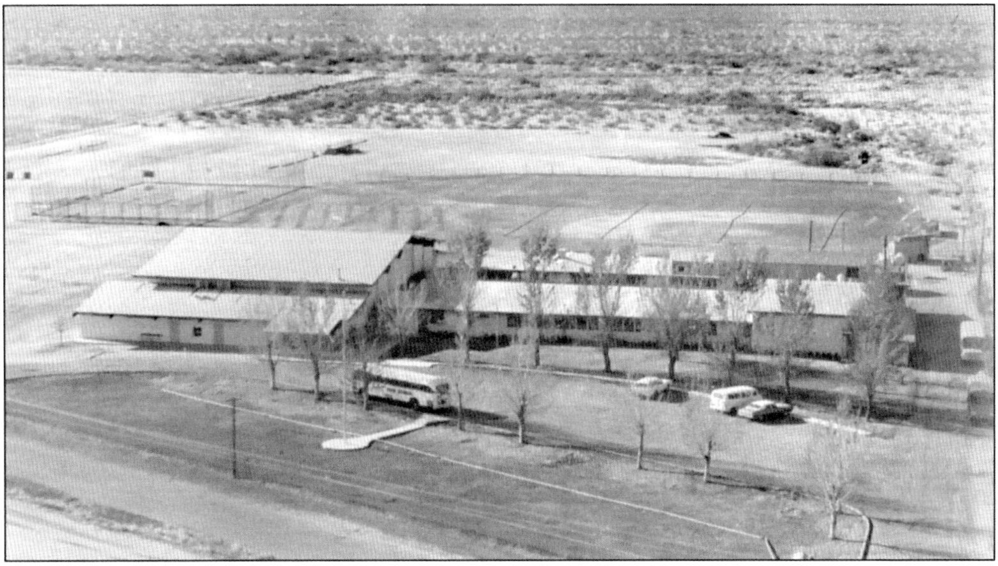

With the baby boom bulge pushing its way through the schools, it was clear the region would have a substantially larger high school–age population by the 1960s. Simultaneously, a high school education attained greater recognition as a necessity for young people. E. V. Haydis, a woman who regularly drove truckloads of high explosives and who was a district school board member, knew of the dangers on the highways and spearheaded the effort to get a local high school built. Haydis believed students would have more study time and be safer without the 100-mile commute. Pictured above, North Yuma County Union High School opened in 1956. Four years later, E. V. Haydis, pictured below, stumped the panel, who never guessed her profession, on the nationally broadcast television show *What's My Line?* (Both Montijo family.)

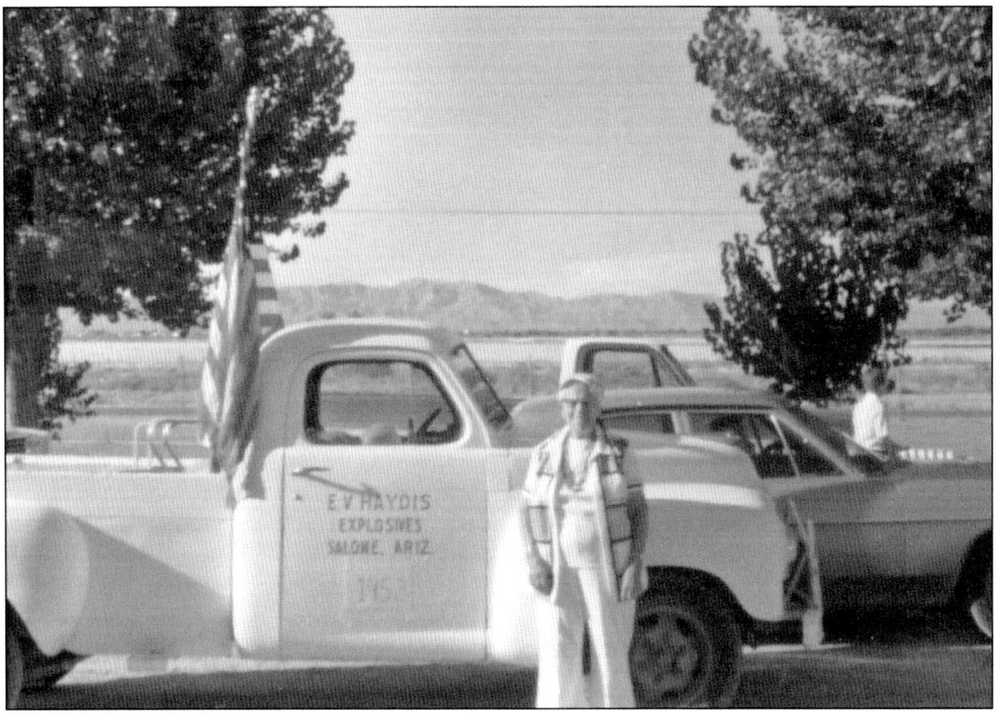

Seven boys and two girls graduated from North Yuma County (also known as NYC Union) High School in 1959. The total school enrollment was barely 40. The five teachers on staff and Principal Robert Charman each taught no less than three subjects. It was small, it was cozy, and most importantly for the entire community, it was local. The availability of teenagers after school for part-time employment eased the job crunch in the towns. Even with after-school jobs, students still had the time to engage in extracurricular activities. Pictured at right are Robert Charman and his wife, Anita. Below, the 12-member school band is seen in the 1960s. (Both Montijo family.)

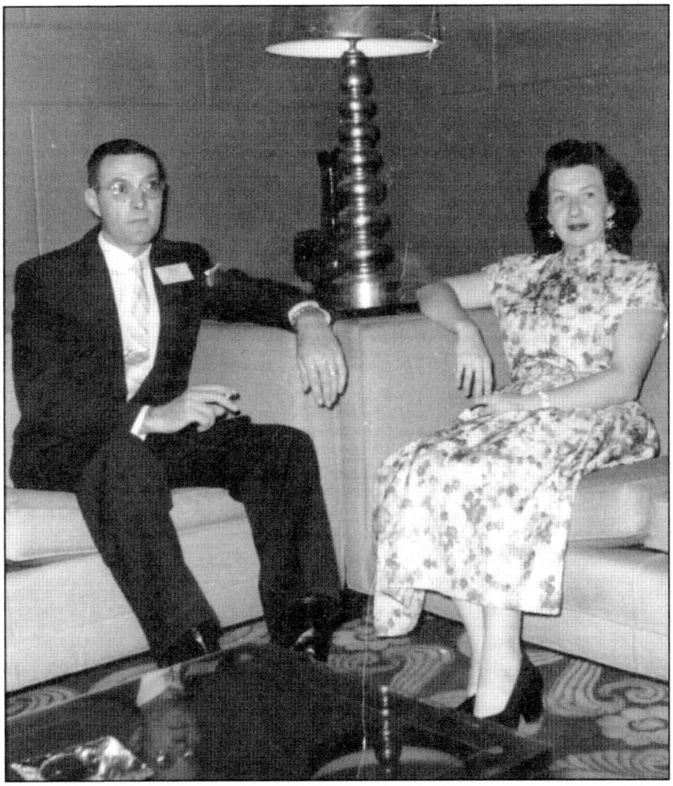

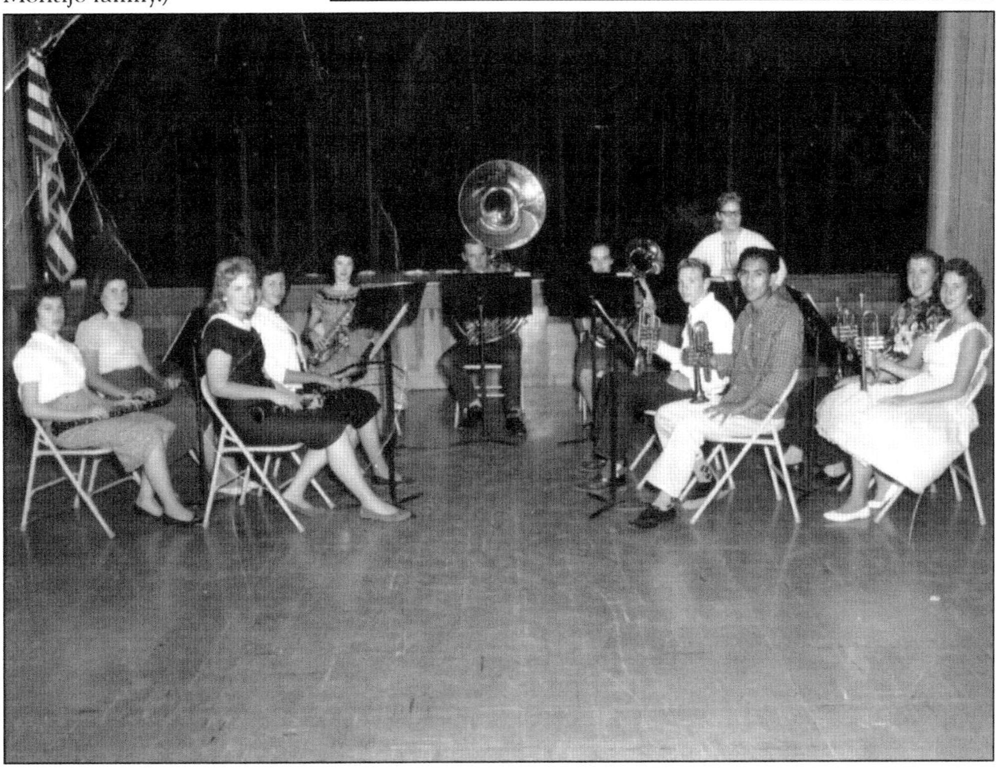

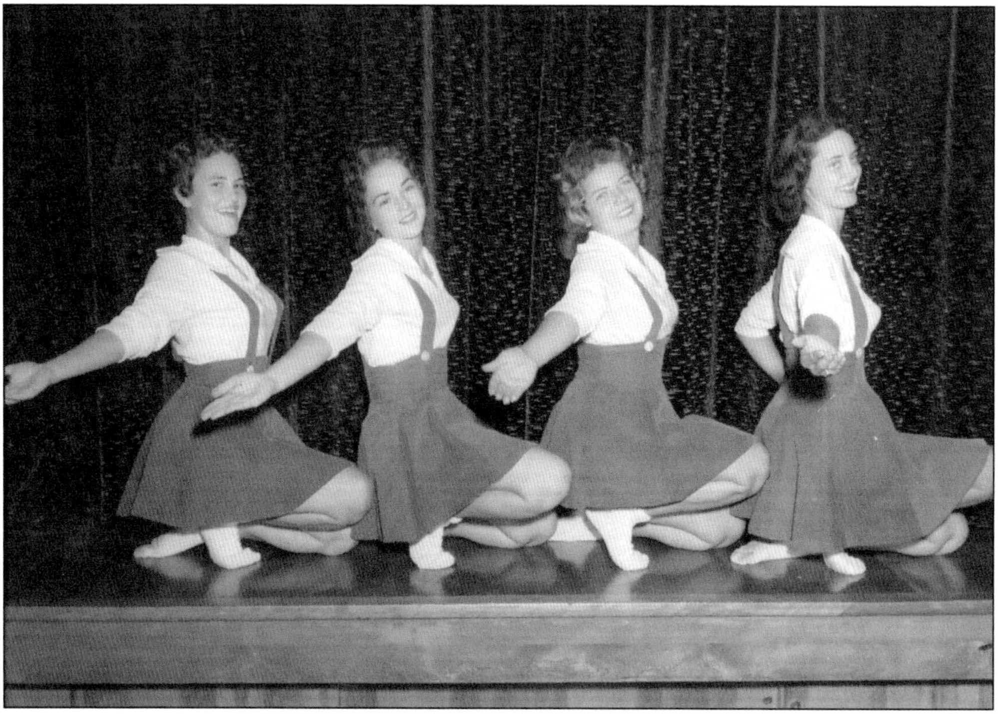

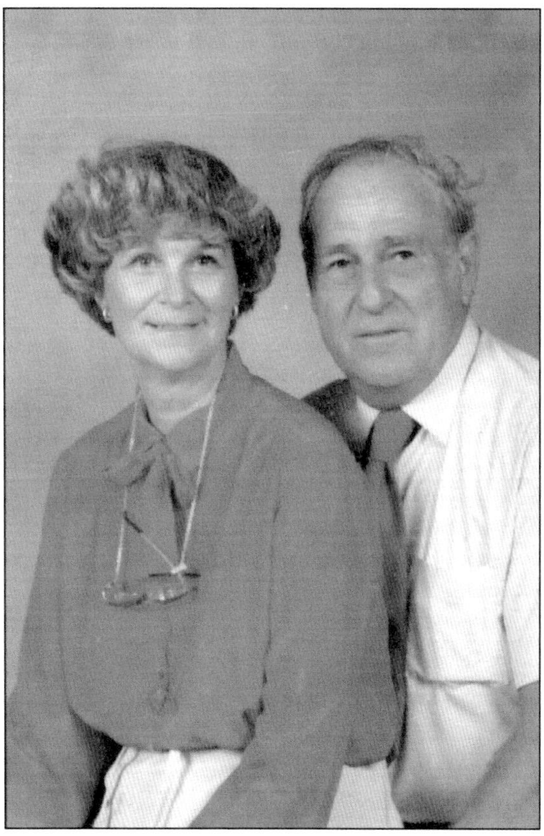

North Yuma County High adopted Dick Wick Hall's renowned frog as the school mascot. Overnight, the Frogs were competing in various sports. The low school enrollment made the athletic teams dependent on enthusiastic supporters. The peppy school cheerleaders led the charge. From left to right are Dianna Randall, Barbara Webb, Betty Anne Randall, and Dorie Balliett in 1958. (Montijo family.)

Arriving in 1947 to run the 60/70 Truck Stop, Lee and Wayne Sweetland led lives in a whirlwind. They ran businesses, such as Wayne's Merchandising and Lumber Supply, raised four children, and served as U.S. postmasters. The high school stadium was named in Wayne's honor for his years on the school board, and the governor appointed Wayne to serve on La Paz County's first board of supervisors. (Montijo family.)

Understaffing by Yuma County Sheriff's Department was common, and deputies in the valley were routinely overworked. Deputy Floyd Balliett, pictured, moved his family into the jail building during his tenure, 1960–1975. His wife, Laura, prepared home-cooked meals for prisoners. One rancher, believing Floyd's workload could not satisfactorily explain his failure to arrest cattle rustlers, told him he was too much of a gentleman to be in law enforcement. (Dorie Appelhans.)

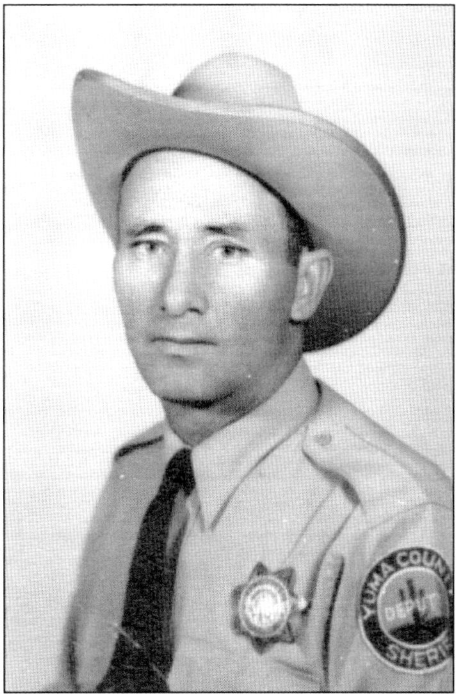

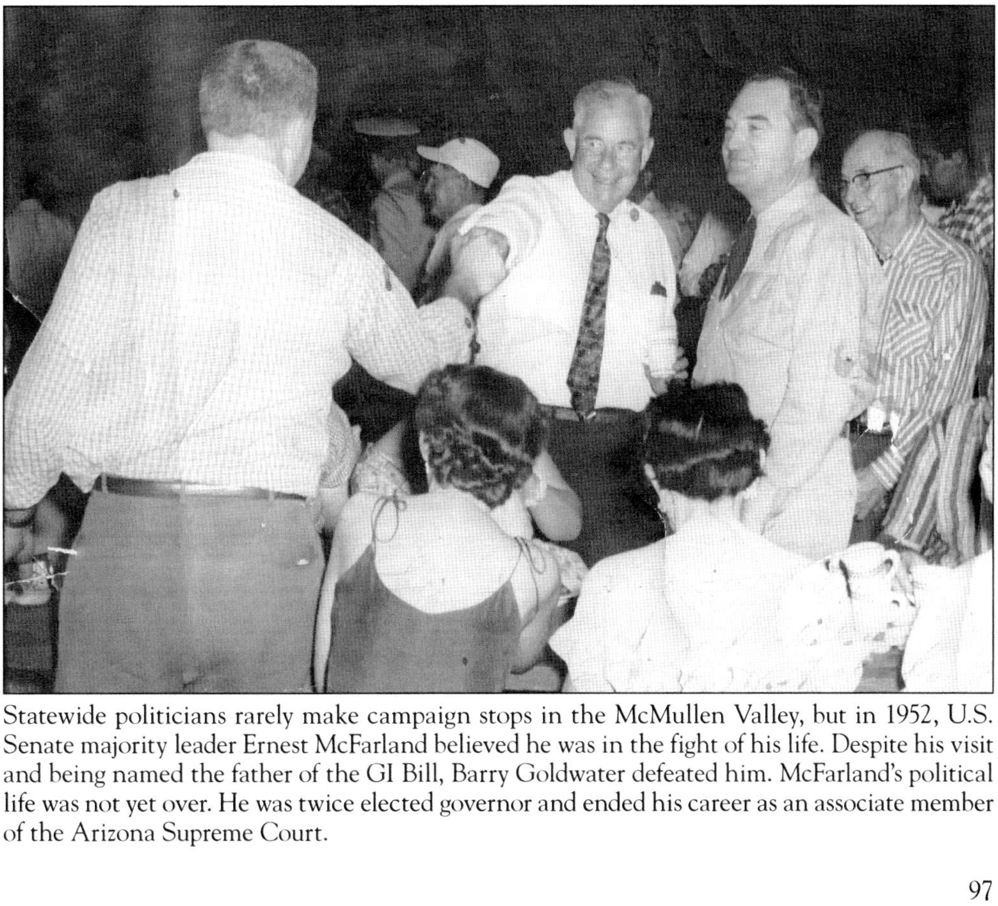

Statewide politicians rarely make campaign stops in the McMullen Valley, but in 1952, U.S. Senate majority leader Ernest McFarland believed he was in the fight of his life. Despite his visit and being named the father of the GI Bill, Barry Goldwater defeated him. McFarland's political life was not yet over. He was twice elected governor and ended his career as an associate member of the Arizona Supreme Court.

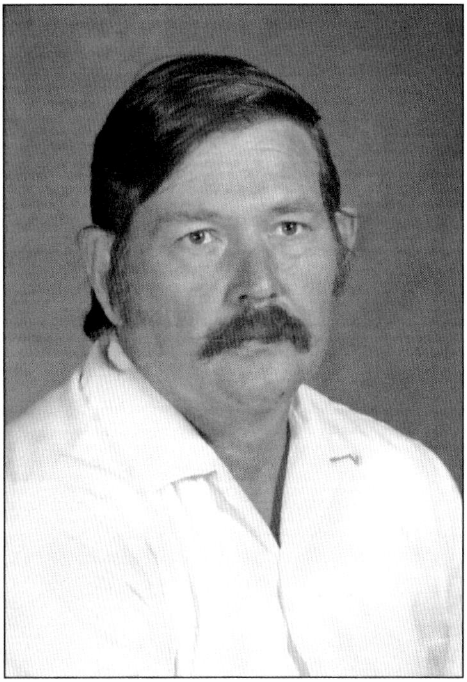

Charles Antoni, pictured at left, was a beloved elementary school teacher/principal for over 20 years. His guidance helped many kids through rough spots growing up. (Charles Antoni.)

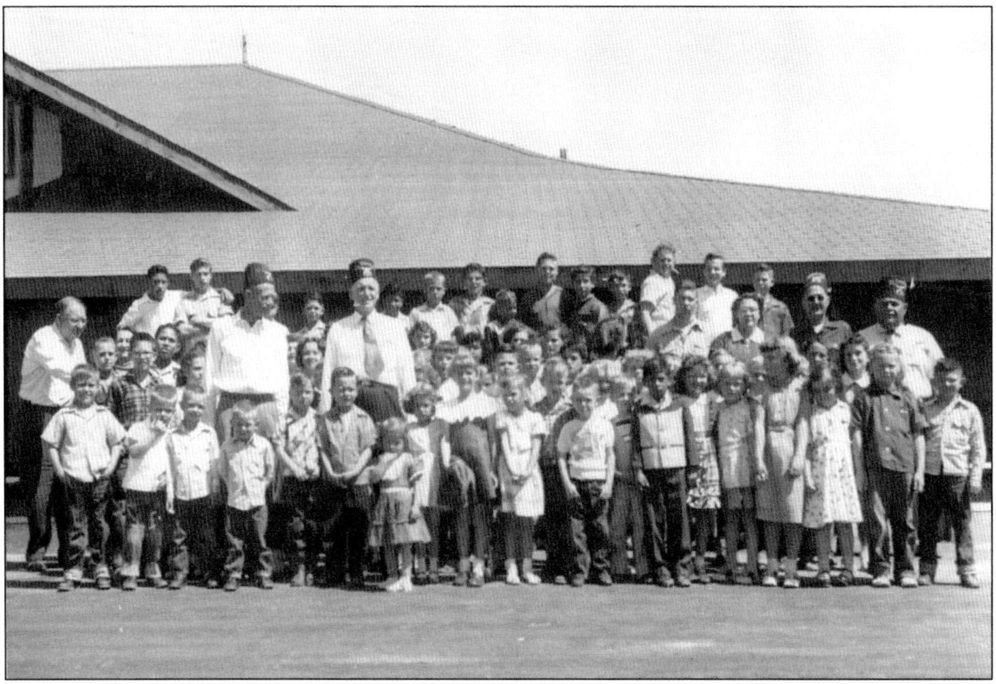

Every year, the local Shriners took the Salome Elementary School students to the Shriner's Circus at the state fairgrounds in Phoenix. Among those pictured above, at the extreme right in a Shriner's fez, is Justice of the Peace Bill Davis. He served as a dutiful surrogate parent to many young people. Several successful businessmen credit him for setting them on the straight path during their teenage years. Simultaneously serving as a Yuma County sheriff, Judge Davis is remembered for the marriages he performed with a weapon on his hip. (Wolfe family.)

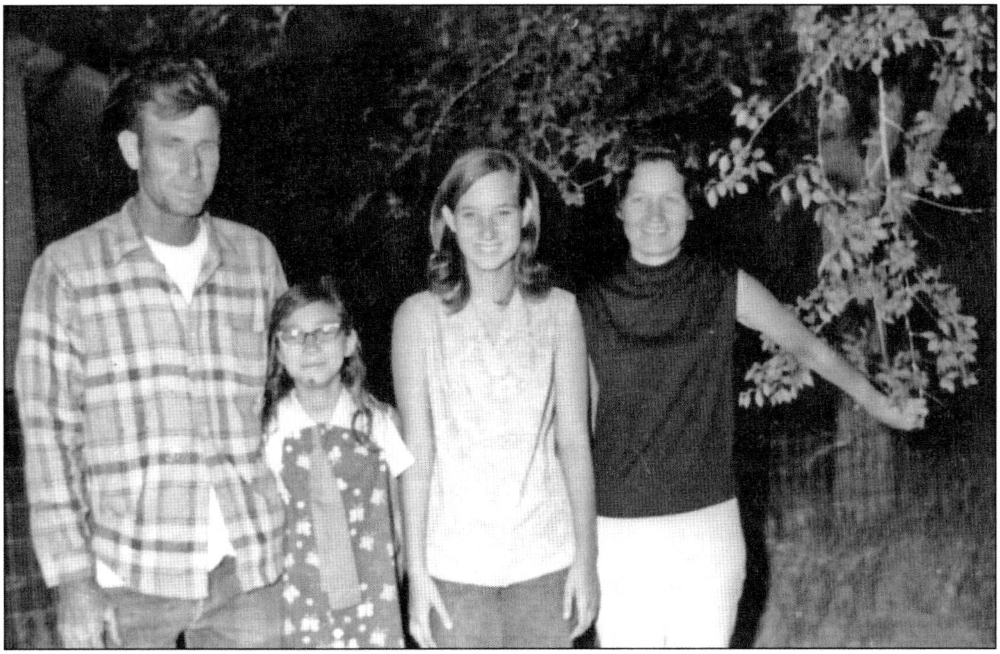

As Oral Hunter's farming operations grew, he called on his brother-in-law James Dalton to take over as his farm operations manager. With his wife, Pauline, James came to Salome and found a home. Pauline would be a much-beloved kindergarten teacher at Salome Elementary. Pictured in the 1970s are James, Tonya, Kim, and Pauline Dalton. (Dalton family.)

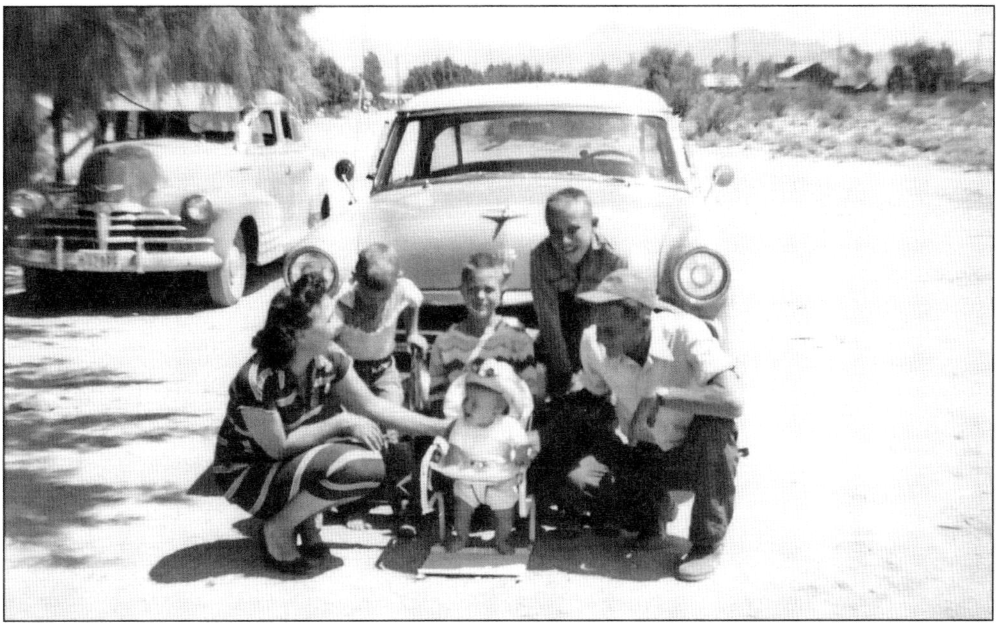

In 1950, the Wolfes left Nebraska, initially residing in a house owned by Dollie Wiley. They moved to Mountain Pass after their fifth son, Doug, was born. Doug would become a partner in Growers Oil, the local NAPA outlet, and an active member of the McMullen Valley Volunteer Fire Department. Pictured from left to right are Lucy (the 1948 Chevy at left), Ruby, Angie, Chuck, Steve, infant Doug, and Jim Wolfe. (Wolfe family.)

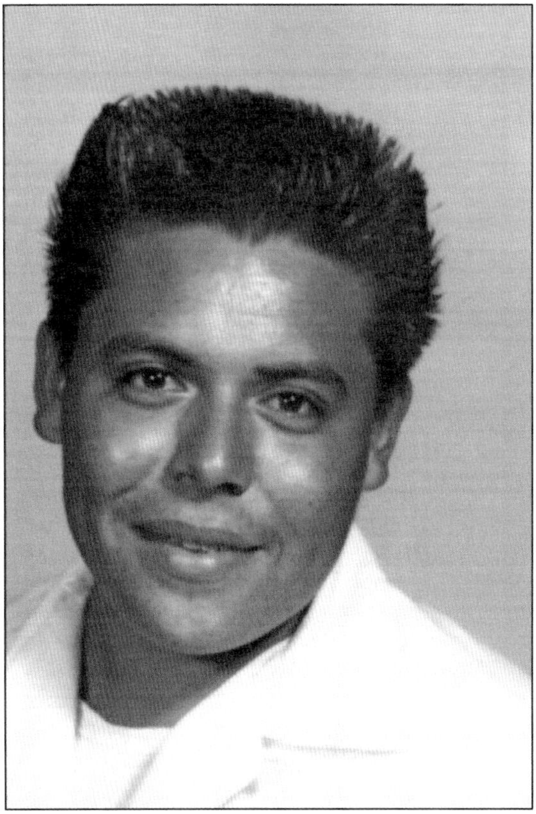

"Mo" Montijo came from Bouse to attend high school in Salome. For over 50 years, he has done anything that needed to be done in town: driving the school bus, operating a hardware store, organizing the Chamber of Commerce Chili Cook-Off, and cooking some of the best in-ground barbeque beef and pork of his generation. (Montijo family.)

The Palma clan produced an interesting and diverse group of contributors to community life. Gabriel would become a chef extraordinaire/volunteer fireman; Pam Wolfe, the owner the Nu Vu beauty salon; and Gloria Dean serves as principal and superintendent of Wenden schools. Gloria's husband, George, holds the same positions at the Salome Elementary School. Pictured from left to right are (first row) Martha Palma and Robert Lopez; (second row) Rachel Palma, Gloria Dean, Gabriel Palma, Pam Wolfe, Robert Palma, Rudy Palma, and Ramona Palma. (Palma family.)

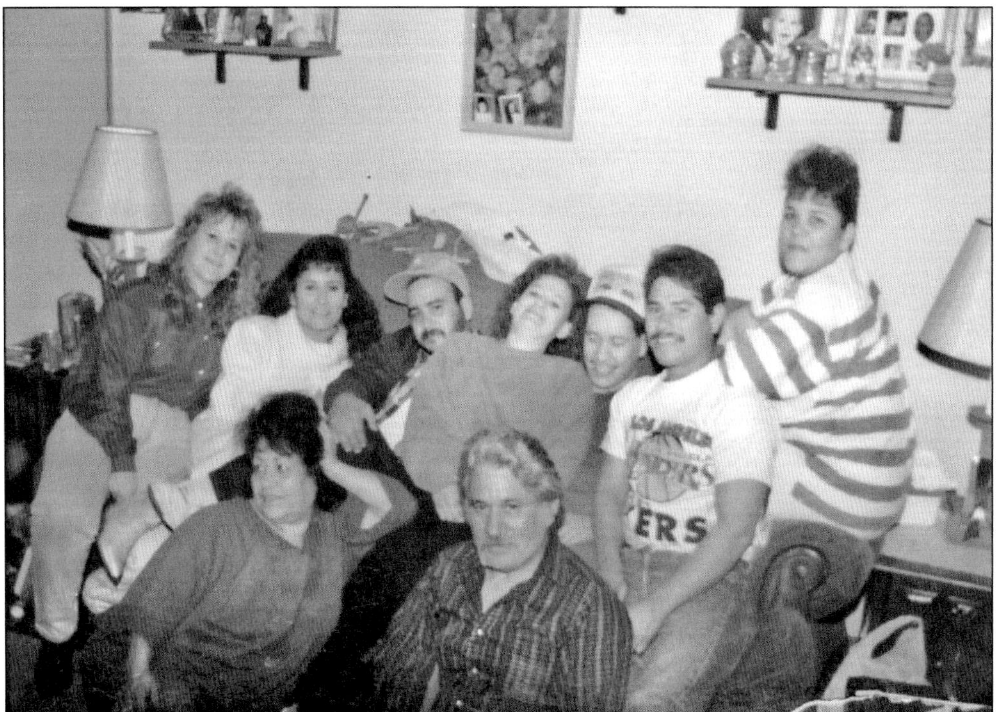

After graduating from high school, Cheryl Randall (pictured in 1968) became a community leader and a pillar of Salome and La Paz County. Active in numerous service organizations, including 4-H, she was executive director of the McMullen Valley Chamber of Commerce and sits on the boards of both the Salome District Schools and La Paz Regional Hospital. Cheryl married "Mo" Montijo in 1970. (Montijo family.)

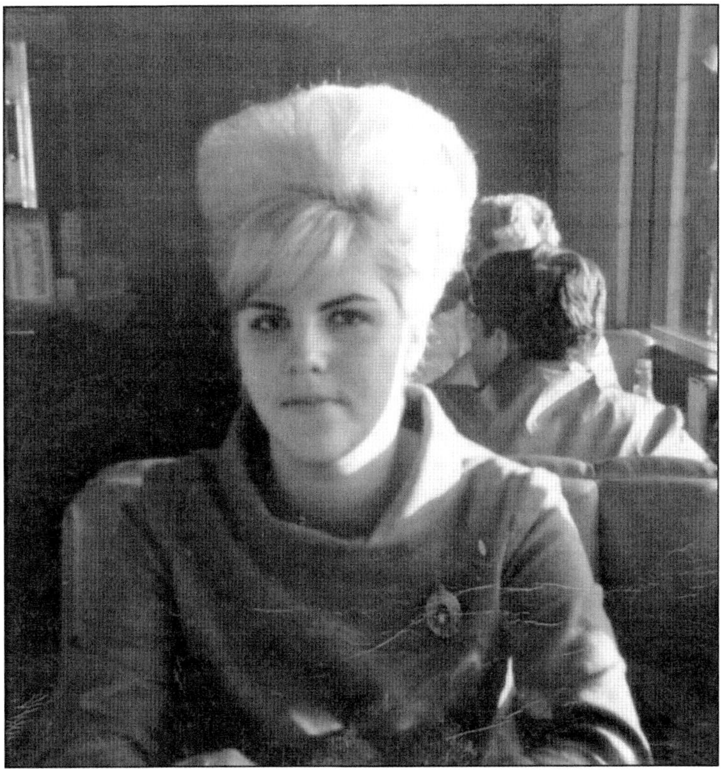

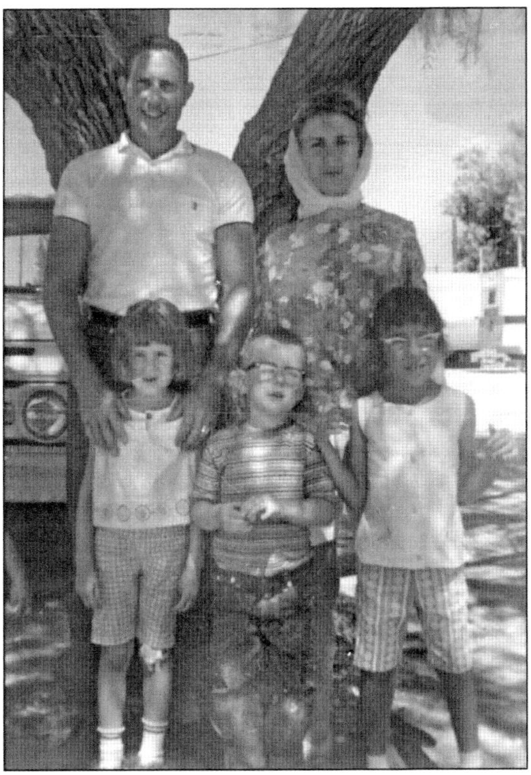

For 15 years, Cecil Buchta was the justice of the peace in Wenden. He operated a service station and rented cabins in the 1960s. Cecil also served as the fire chief of the Wenden Volunteer Fire Department. Cecil Buchta is shown with his wife, Dorla, and (from left to right) children, Leslie, Lonnie, and DeLana. (Buchta family.)

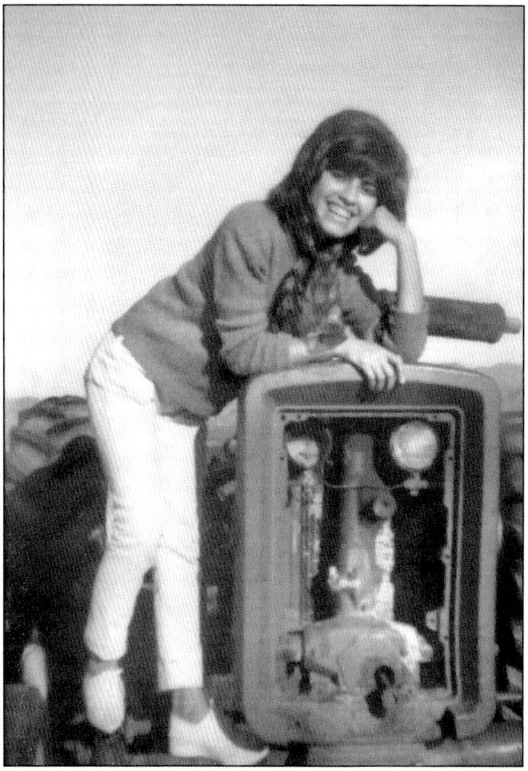

Gloria Ramirez arrived in Wenden in the mid-1960s. Marriage and children took her away, but she always longed to return home. Her dream to open an art gallery and café came true when she and daughter Devona Saiter opened Ingredients in 2003. When Jeanne Brownd joined them, they became known as "Wenden's three incredible women." Gloria married longtime Wenden resident Curt Parrett in 1993. (Parrett family.)

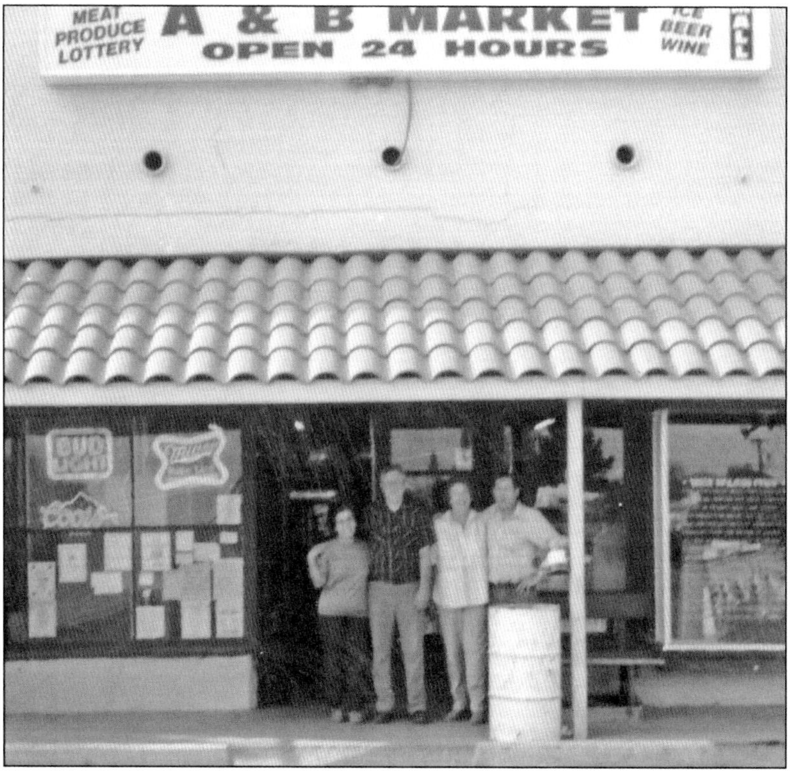

Tom Davis and sister Ann Davis Rees took over the A&B Market in 1980. For 14 years, the children of Davis, Salome's first fire chief, stocked their shelves with the provisions local residents needed. Ann's son, Sam Rees, would buy the historic Outback saloon and restaurant in Wenden. From left to right are Gigi and Tom Davis, Ann Davis Rees, and John Hepfer. (Ann Davis Rees.)

Tot Tothero was an artist who built the loveliest adobe home in Salome. She is known to have worked at Shefflers. Those are the verifiable facts, but fanciful rumors still swirl about her, decades after her passing. Allegedly, Tot was a French starlet discovered in the 1930s by an American film director. Brought to Hollywood, she hated it. Driving deep into the desert, she found a home she loved.

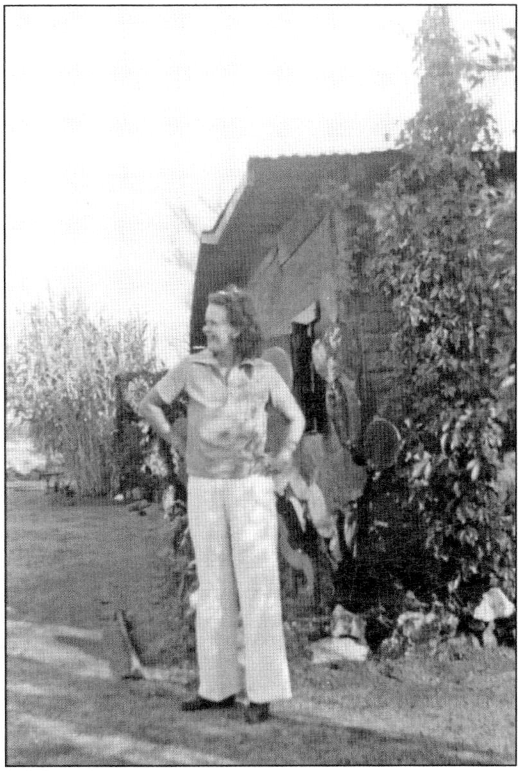

Work on the railroad first brought Jose Jordan and his family to Wenden. All the children attended Wenden schools. Daughter Mary married Jeff Campbell. They live in the original stone house once owned by F. J. Brown, Jeff's great-grandfather. Pictured from left to right are (first row) Gina, Marsha, Frances, and Jose Jordan; (second row) Jerry, Toby, and Fred Jordan; Mary Campbell; and Patsy and David Jordan. (Mary Campbell.)

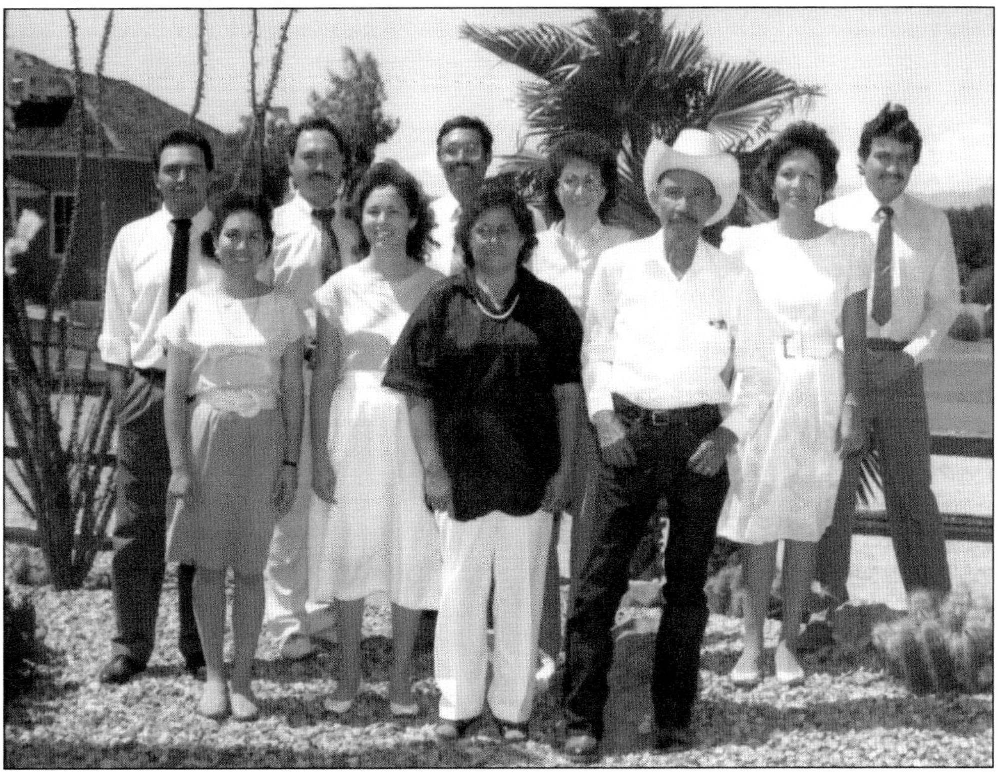

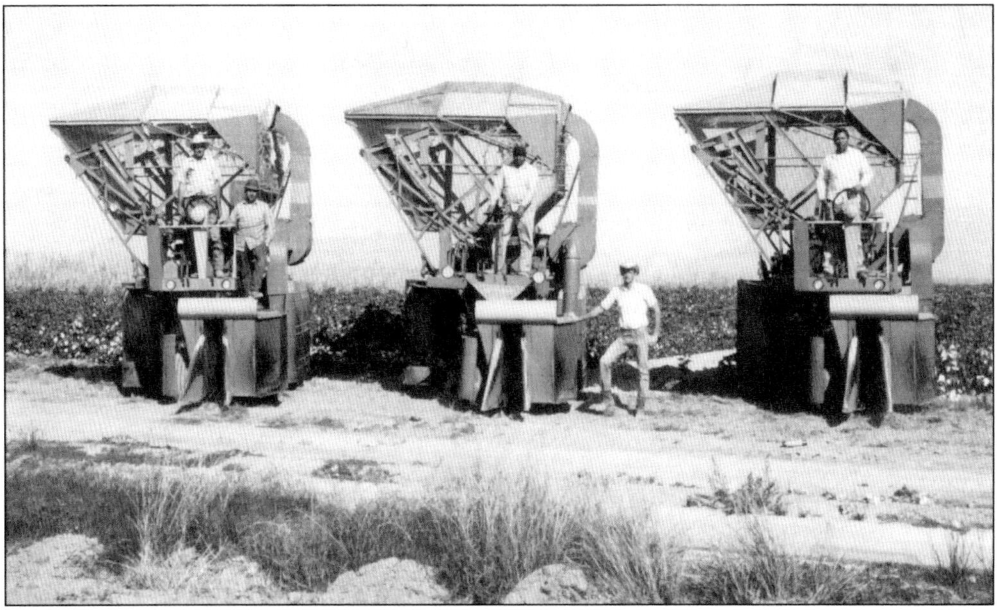

By 1966, cotton was king in the McMullen Valley. A dozen farming operations grew extra-long-staple cotton and upland cotton on 20,000 acres of arable land. The Egyptian or pima cotton is high-grade cotton that was initially smuggled into the country and first grown by the Pima Indians. As long as available groundwater could be pumped, the economics of cotton worked for farmers. But in the coming years, deeper wells had to be sunk, and utility prices to pump the water would increase dramatically. Farmers like Don Brown began growing melons; others tried planting pecans and pistachio groves in search of ways to keep their operations profitable. Pictured above is Ben Matthews (center, on the ground) with day laborers operating single-row cotton pickers in 1966. Below is a view of an extra-long-staple cotton field. (Above, Dorothy Matthews; below, McMullen Valley Water and Irrigation District.)

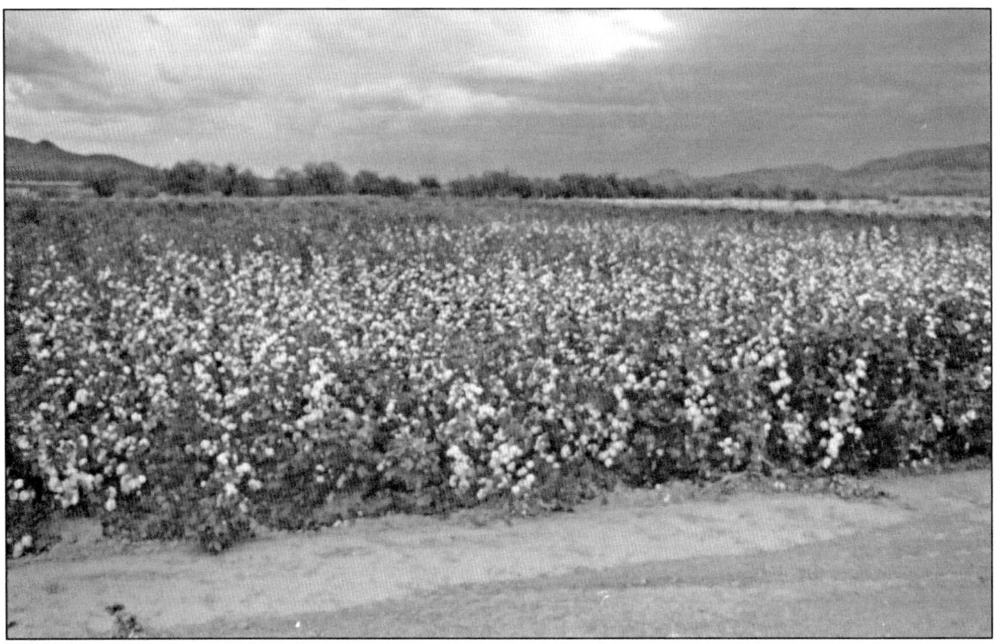

Eight

Times of Transition

Beginning with the Reid and Nord Ranches in the early days, through Jack Wilbanks in the 1930s, there had always been cattle business in the valley. However, between the expansion of the Crowder-Weisser Cattle Company, Kemper Brown's cattle operation, and the others who came after 1960, the cattle business had gone large-scale and commercial.

In the decades after mid-century, the McMullen Valley farmers exploited the unique weather and climate that enabled them to grow high-grade extra-long-staple Egyptian cotton. This strain of cotton, which originated in Egypt, thrived in the valley, as the abundant waters of the McMullen Valley aquifer nearly replicated the annual flooding of the legendary Nile River.

The extensive cotton yield from nearly 20 farms growing in the valley motivated the Francis brothers, Gesford and Jack, to build a cotton ginning facility in Wenden. Known under the name Valley Industries, the Francis brothers serviced the needs of farmers like Don and Kemper Brown, Ben Matthews, Oral Hunter, Jeff Alder, and Don Anderson. The cotton gin, farms, and ranches all provided employment in the days after the road business on Route 60 had ebbed.

By the late 1970s, a confluence of political and economic forces created times of transition for all the businesses and residents of the McMullen Valley. A troubled national economy, rising energy costs, falling commodity prices, and the opening of the interstate between Phoenix and Los Angeles demanded reevaluation of priorities.

The breakup of Yuma County, the creation of La Paz County, and the sale of 12 major farms and ranches to the City of Phoenix all occurred in quick succession. With most of the City of Phoenix–owned land initially leased back for farming, there was no immediate impact to the residents of the valley.

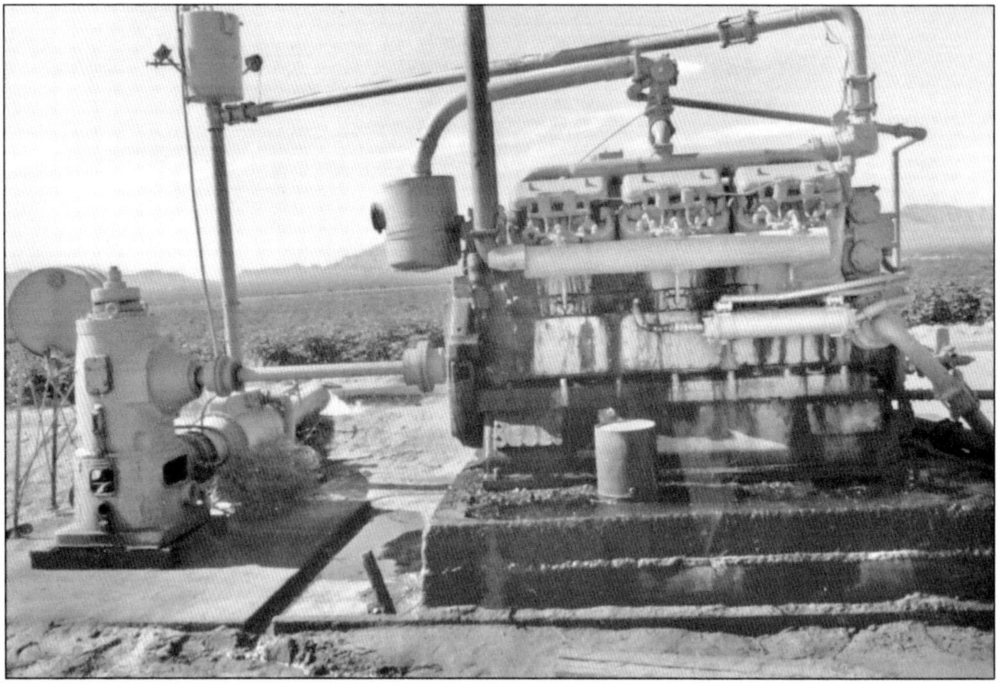

The commercial cotton-growing operations of the postwar years required power, pumps, and water. In the 1950s, Arizona Public Service (APS) finally brought gas and electricity service to the McMullen Valley, nearly two decades after rural electrification legislation was passed. As natural gas was less expensive at that time, the farmers installed large Caterpillar engines, above, to pump water from the deep wells. The large aquifer beneath the valley supplied the required water. Concrete ditches were laid to deliver the irrigation water. As electric pumps became more economical, 250-horsepower electric-powered pumps were installed (below). (Both McMullen Valley Water and Irrigation District.)

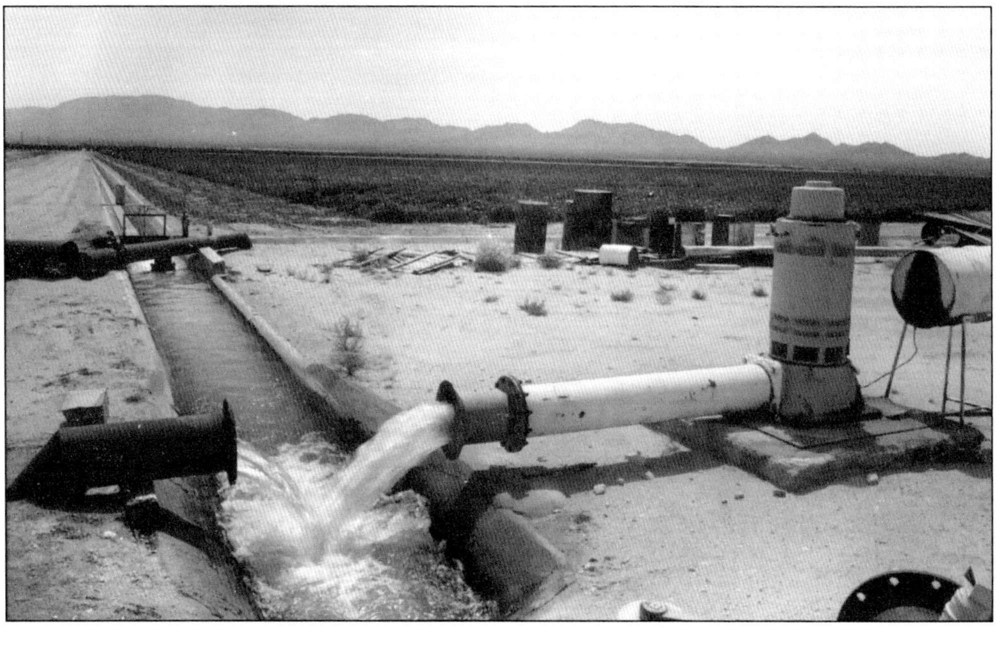

In 1961, after military service, Kemper Brown came to run his father Don's cattle ranching operation. Within a decade, it would fall on him to run the farming component of the business as well. Discovering his own intrinsic capabilities, Kemper became both a successful farmer and rancher. He took to the lifestyle of riding, branding, and flying his airplane to get the morning report from his cowhands. (Brown family.)

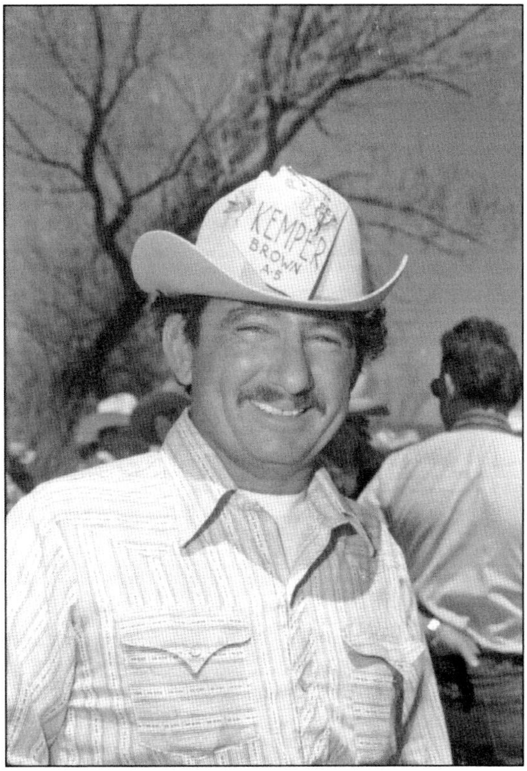

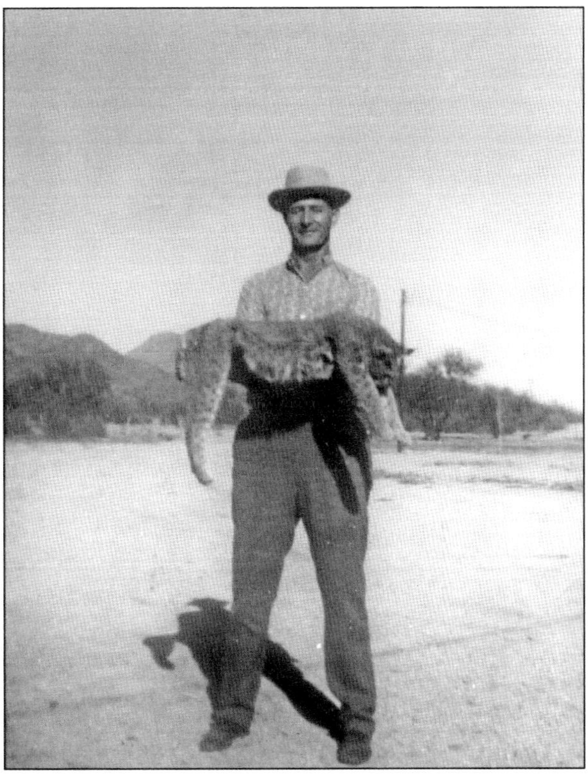

Born in Oklahoma, Woodrow West first came to the valley in 1954 to manage Don Brown's farming operations and protect his interests. Standing 6 feet, 9 inches tall, he is remembered for his immense hands, gentle manner, and loyalty to the Browns. His experience in a German POW camp helped him to find religion. His great size distorts perspective on the very large bobcat he shot before it destroyed livestock. (Karen Thomas.)

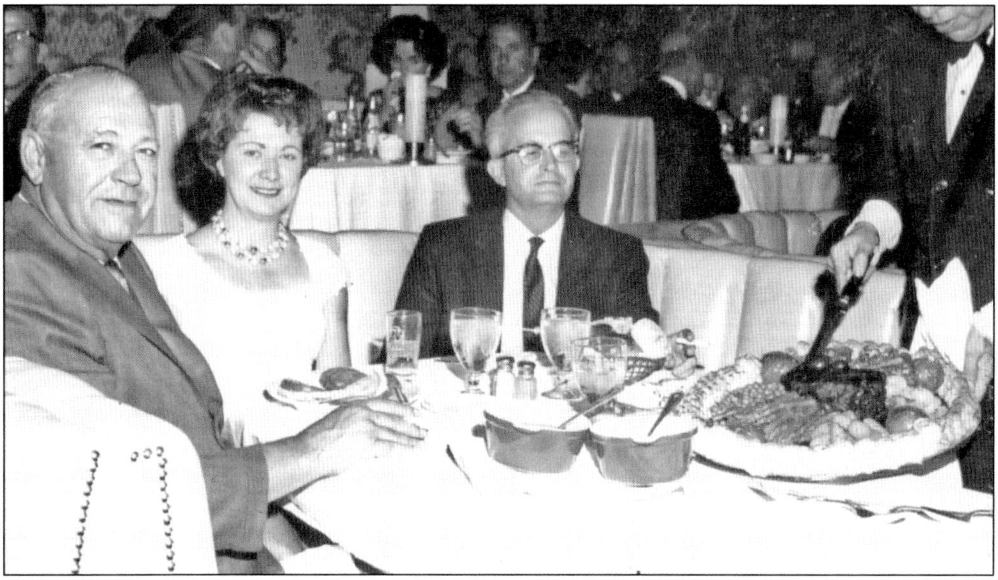

Socializing with friends in the McMullen Valley has always manifested itself in many different ways. In the early 1960s, landowner Don Brown and his wife, LaVerne, (left) dined with Ralph Farr of Shefflers (right) at Wilbur Clark's Desert Inn in Las Vegas. Ralph was in the process of purchasing the entire Shefflers operation after managing it for over 15 years. (Billie Farr.)

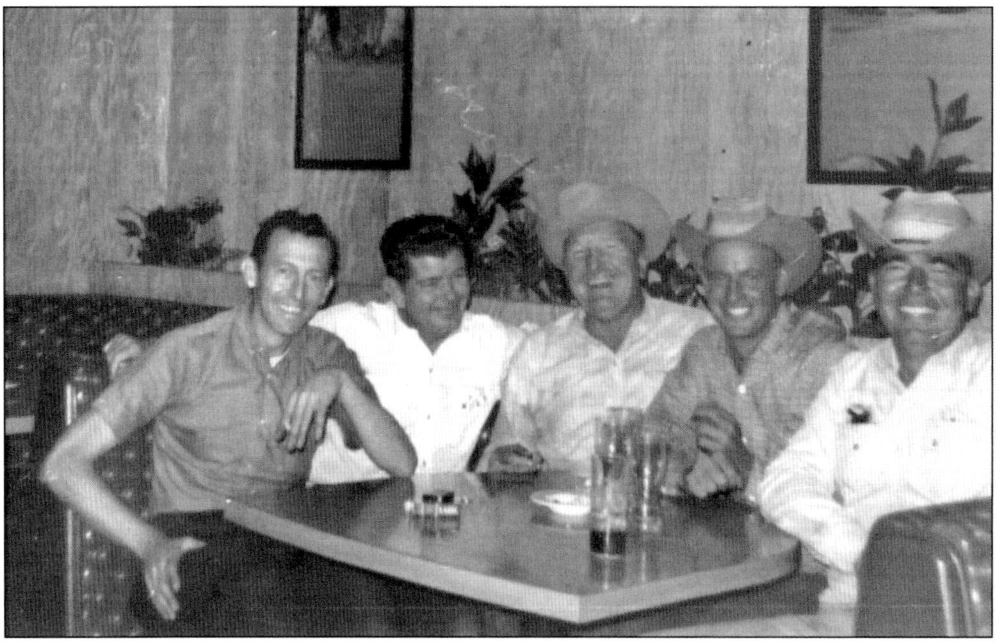

Valley farmers often met over cold beers. Pictured from left to right, Bozo Darnell, Elton Britt, Jerry Hancock, Ronald Norton, and Jeff Alder socialize in the early 1970s. Years later, Jerry's son Larry married Jeff's daughter Lori. Jeff perished tragically in a plane crash, along with Don Anderson and Forest Cooper. (Hancock family.)

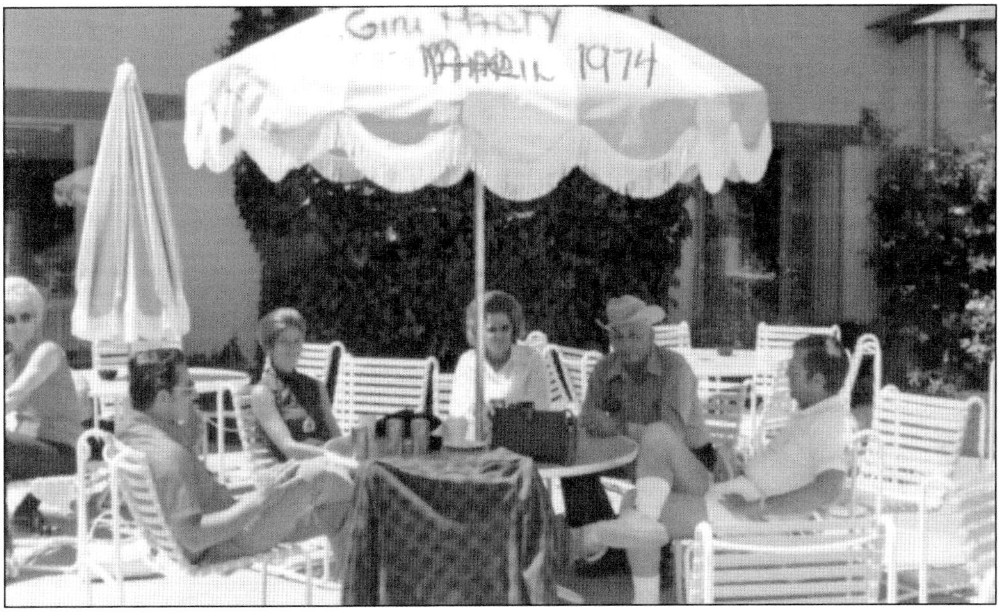

The Gin Party was a traditional gathering held after the cotton harvest and ginning at the Francis brothers' facility in Wenden. Following their intense seasonal harvest, a serious celebration was deemed mandatory. In 1974, from left to right, farmers Kemper Brown and his wife, Toni, were joined by Dorothy Matthews, Ben Matthews, and gin owner Gesford Francis at Rancho de Los Caballeros near Wickenburg. (Brown family.)

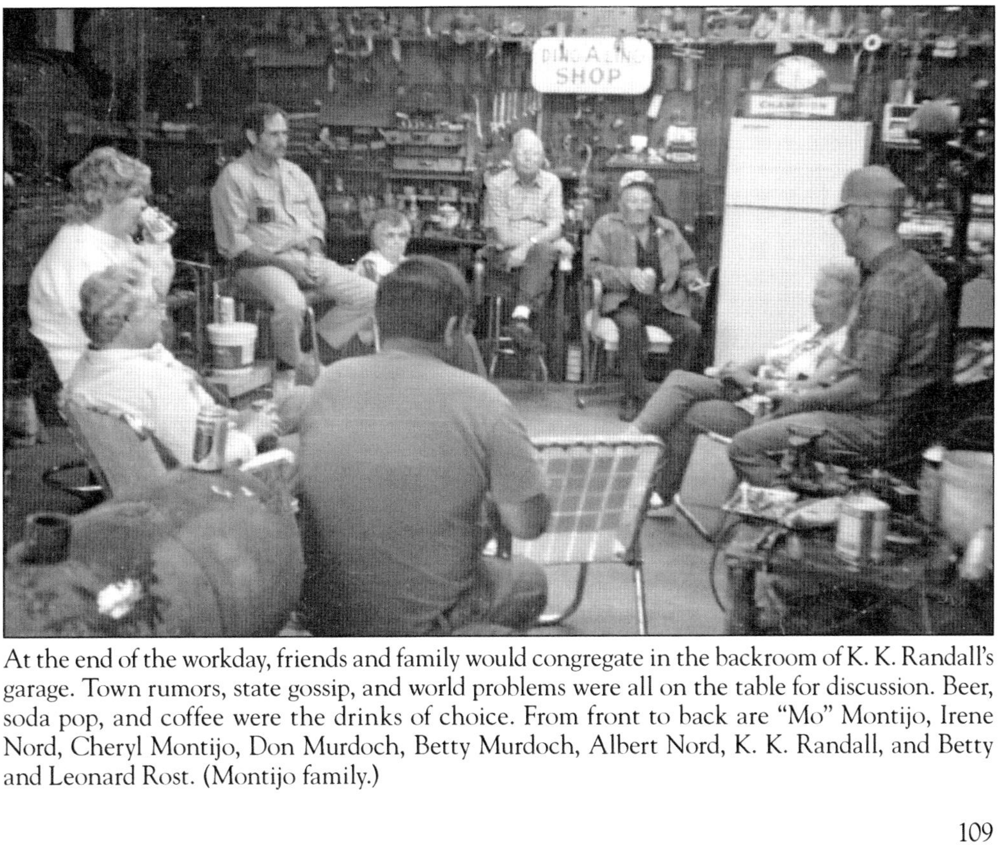

At the end of the workday, friends and family would congregate in the backroom of K. K. Randall's garage. Town rumors, state gossip, and world problems were all on the table for discussion. Beer, soda pop, and coffee were the drinks of choice. From front to back are "Mo" Montijo, Irene Nord, Cheryl Montijo, Don Murdoch, Betty Murdoch, Albert Nord, K. K. Randall, and Betty and Leonard Rost. (Montijo family.)

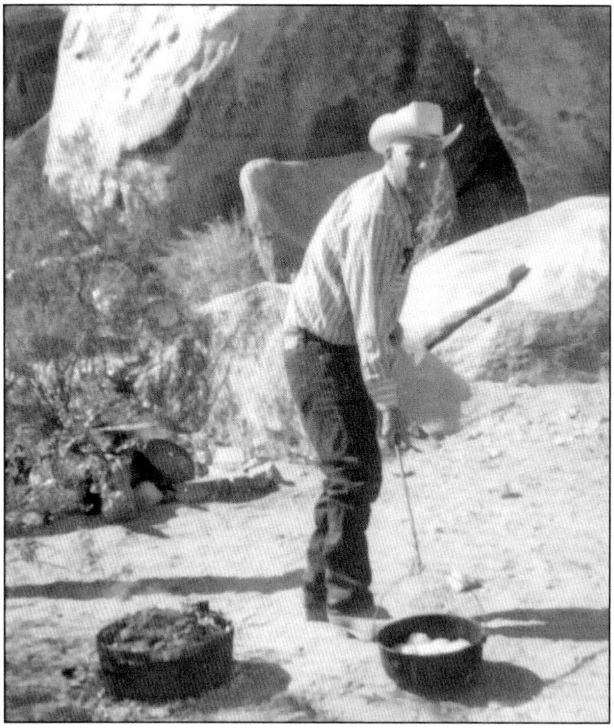

Indian Springs, long a prime destination for picnics, hikes, and Jeep rides, was the place to be on Easter morning as long as Ben Matthews was baking his beer biscuits in a Dutch oven. Over 30 years after the last time invitees feasted on Ben's biscuits, people still rave about them. Ben's widow, Dorothy, has shared Ben's recipe with those who have requested it. However, residents who received it and vividly recall the taste of Ben's biscuits question whether some key ingredient may have been lost. Repeated attempts to replicate Ben's biscuits always fall short. Ben Matthews is shown here baking in Dutch ovens in the 1970s for an Easter morning breakfast served at Indian Springs. (Left, Dorothy Matthews; below, Susan Douglas.)

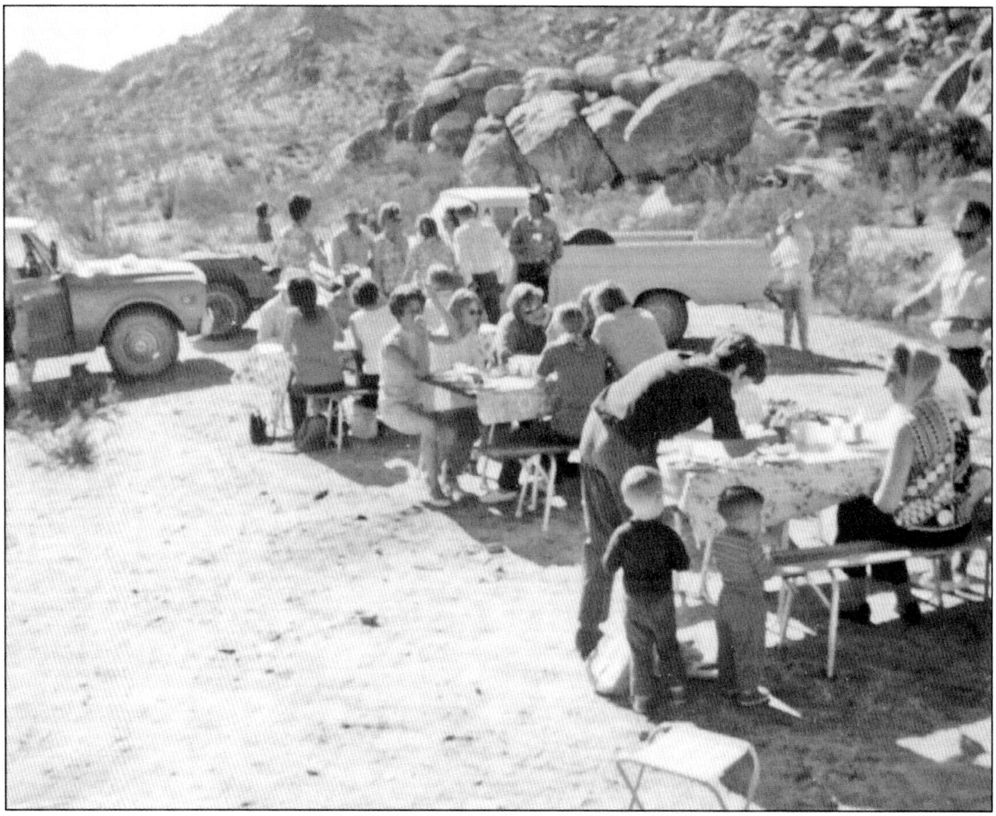

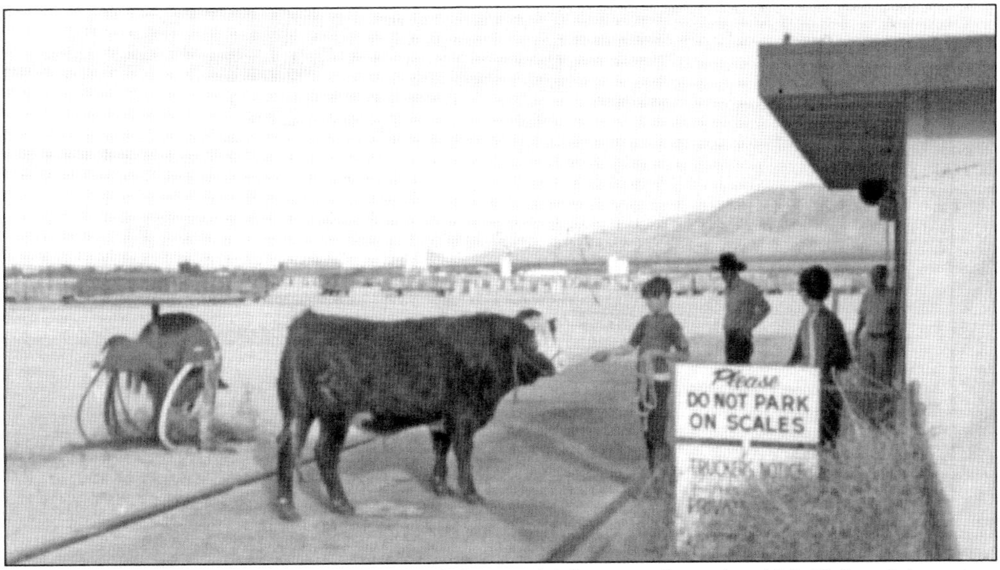

No youth activity epitomizes the ethos of the rural life more than the 4-H Clubs of America. Above is Jim Downing, former 4-H member from Mississippi, with son Will Downing. Pictured as well is Will's grand champion market steer, Red. Will would attend West Point and go on to become a battle major in Iraq and win the Bronze Star. Below, Kenneth Montijo is pictured with his sheep, Shitsuji ("sheep" in Japanese), at the La Paz County Fair. A master mechanic, Kenneth has worked on championship-winning off-road vehicles. Both were members of the Tri-Valley 4-H Club. (Above, Downing family; below, Montijo family.)

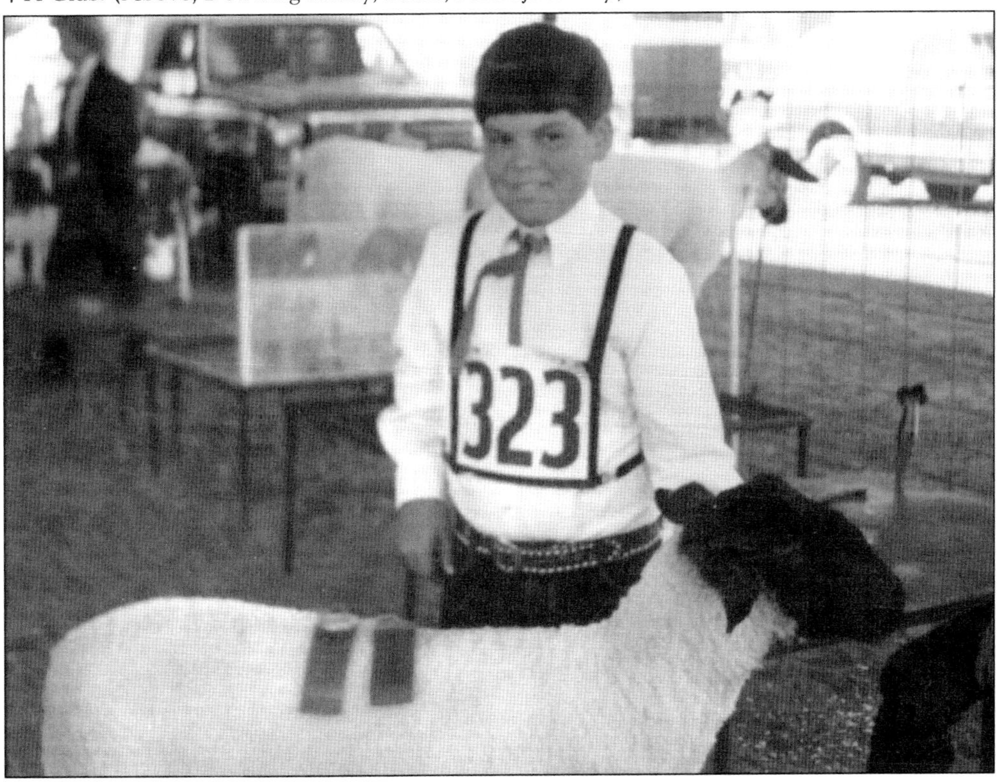

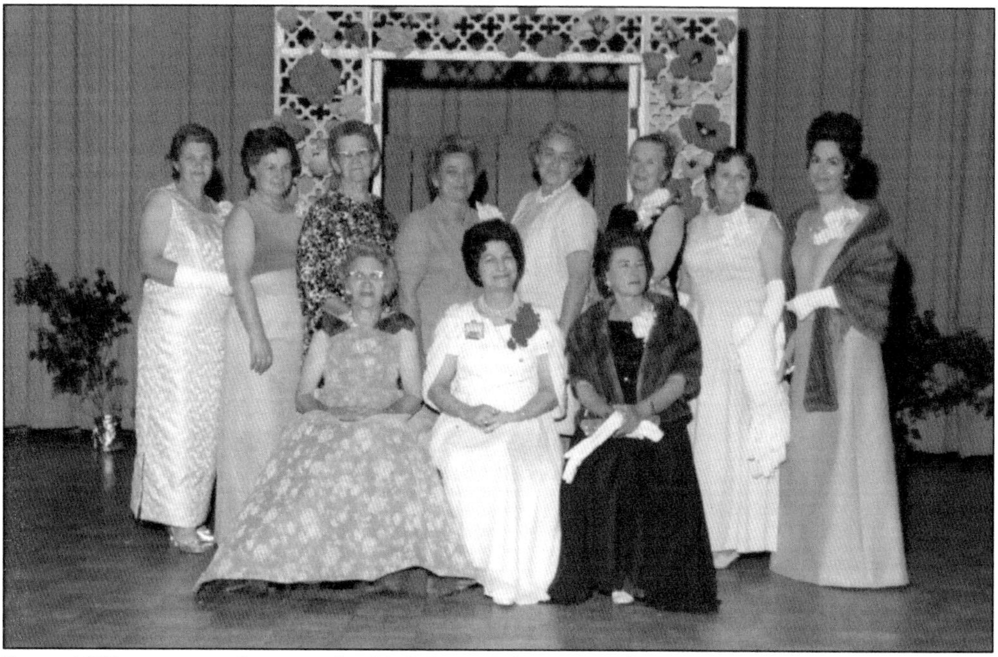

Since 1935, in war and peace, the Vicksburg-Salome-Wenden (ViSaWen) Women's Club has worked for children, veterans, and the needy. They are renowned for their quilts. Their diverse membership has included a concert pianist, high explosives hauler, saloon keeper, real estate brokers, and numerous grandmothers. At the 1966 State Convention, ViSaWen representatives pictured included Florence Matthews, Barbara Brown, Elizabeth Solper, Hattie Cox, and Ella Stein. (ViSaWen Women's Club Archives.)

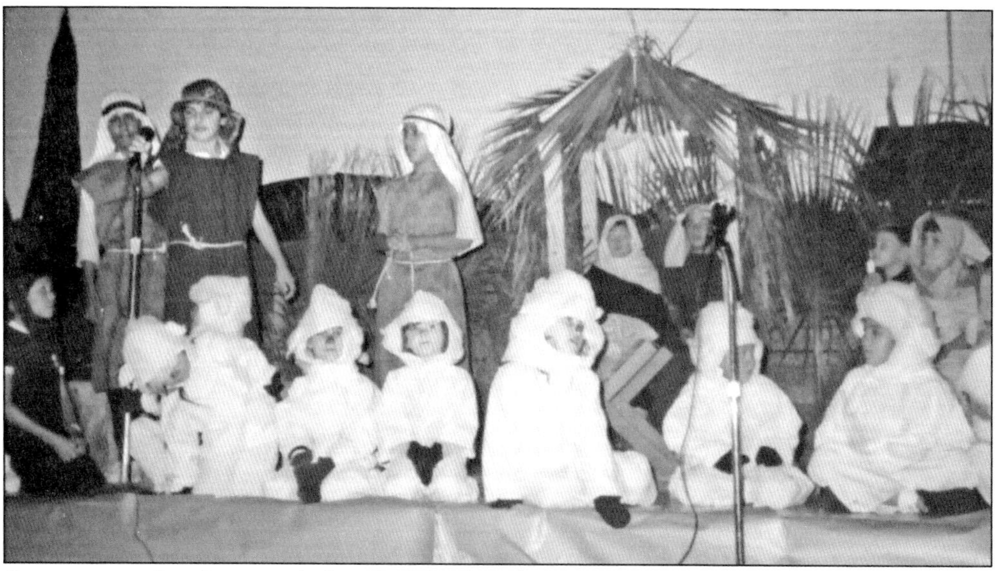

Generations of kindergarten kids at the Wenden Elementary School were cured of stage fright by being dressed up as sheep in the school's annual Christmas pageant. For many years, Herb and Betty Tillapaugh were synonymous with Wenden Elementary. Herb was the principal, while his wife, Betty, taught kindergarten through third grade as well as eighth-grade English. Pictured are unidentified students and (third sheep from the left) Jamie Downing. (Downing family.)

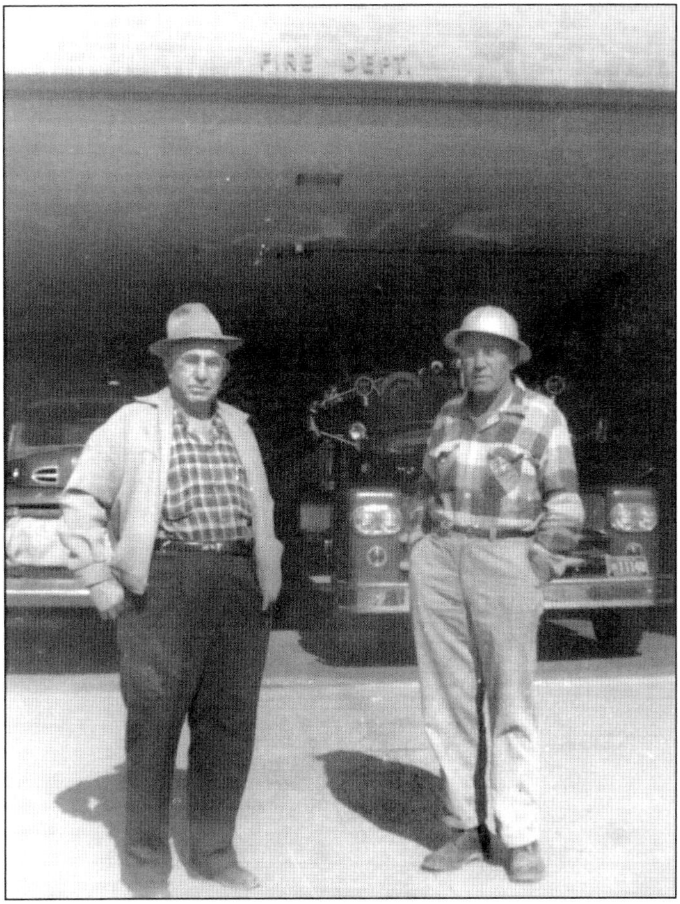

In the 1960s, Salome's first volunteer fire chief, Tom Davis, persuaded a Phoenix dealership to sell a fire truck on an installment plan. It was a precedent-setting event. Mr. Franks helped in the negotiations. At right, Tom Davis (left) is pictured with Mr. Franks (right). Wenden's first fire truck, pictured below, was purchased in 1973. Ironically, many current members of the volunteer fire departments had been victims of house fires in their youth. (Right, Ann Davis Rees; below, Buchta family.)

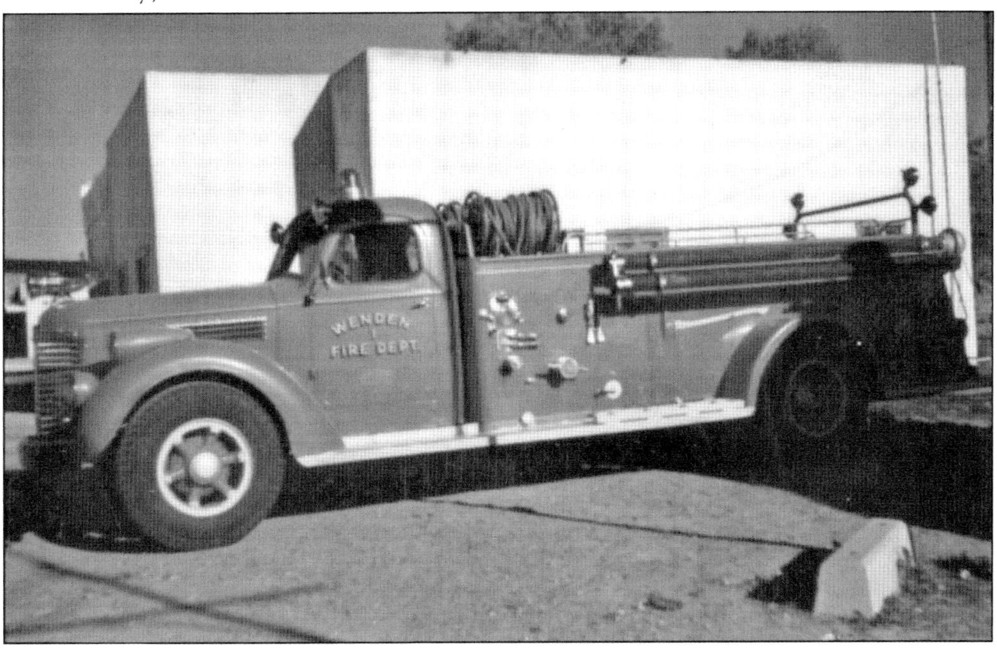

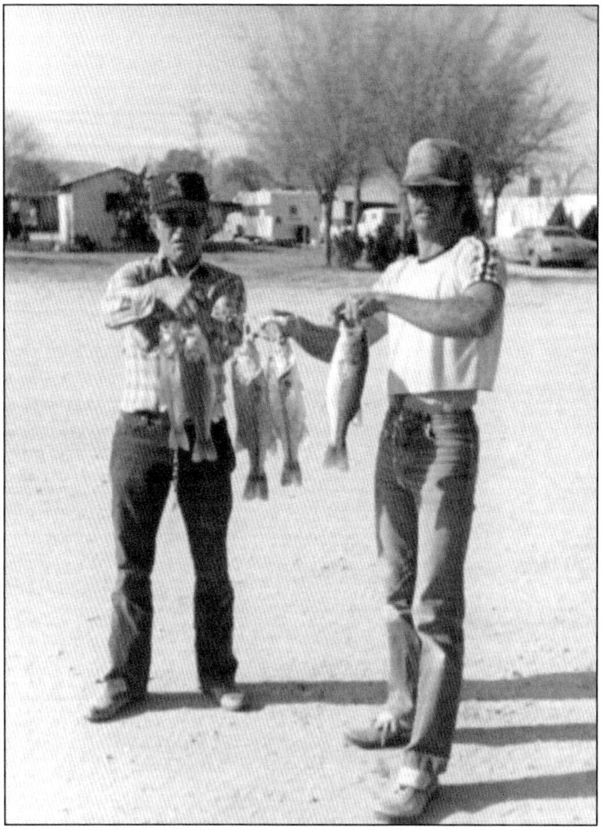

In 1968, the U.S. Army Corps of Engineers built an earthen dam where the Big Sandy, Santa Maria, and Bill Williams Rivers converge, 38 miles north of Wenden. Upon completion, Alamo Lake State Park was created. Offering stark desert beauty reflected in over 500 acres of sparkling blue water, the lake is stocked with largemouth bass, channel catfish, black crappie, and bluegill. In spring, abundant wildflowers bloom; year-round, the lake attracts waterfowl, eagles, foxes, coyotes, mule deer, and wild burros. The park is considered one of Arizona's best-kept secrets. Stargazers find a light-free, unobstructed view of the Milky Way. Pictured with a day's catch from Alamo Lake are Wally Fulks and son Terry. Below is an aerial photograph of Alamo Dam. (Left, Wally Fulks; below, Sharon Rubin.)

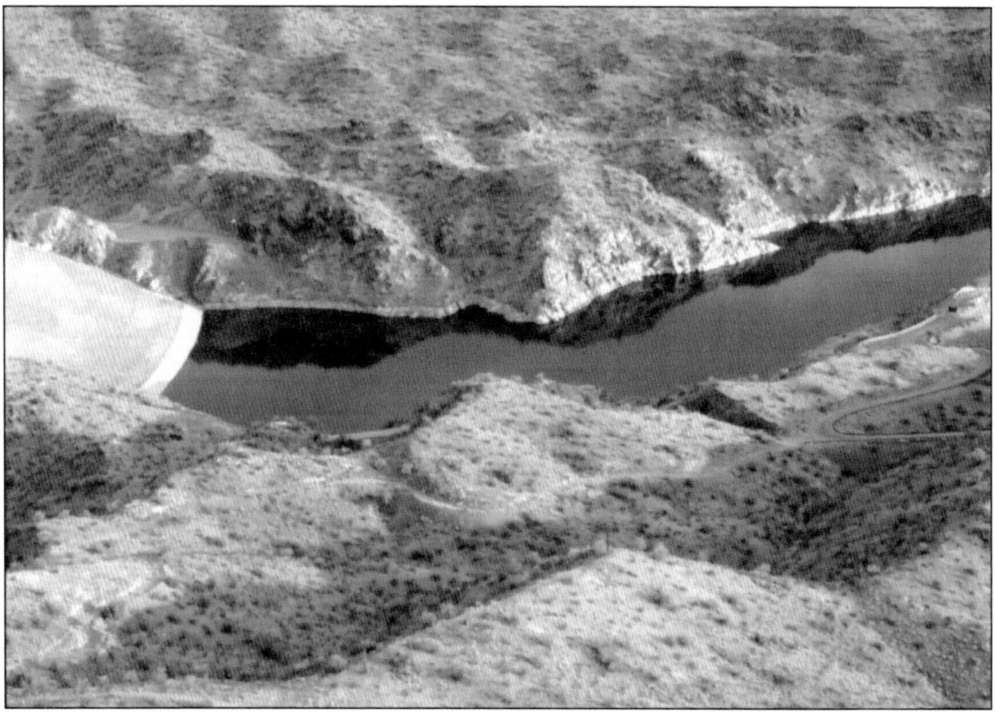

Thousands of acres surrounding the McMullen Valley communities are administered federal lands. While a battle rages to keep access to these lands open, residents have enjoyed and respected these vanishing areas for years. These days, they urge the flocks of winter visitors to do the same. In days past, the land was leased for hunting. Leland Stacy is pictured in the 1970s, hunting for relaxation. (Mona Stacy.)

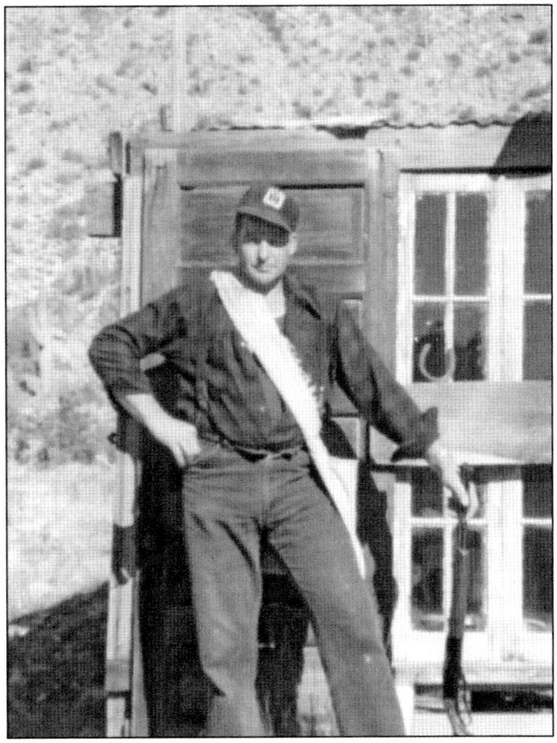

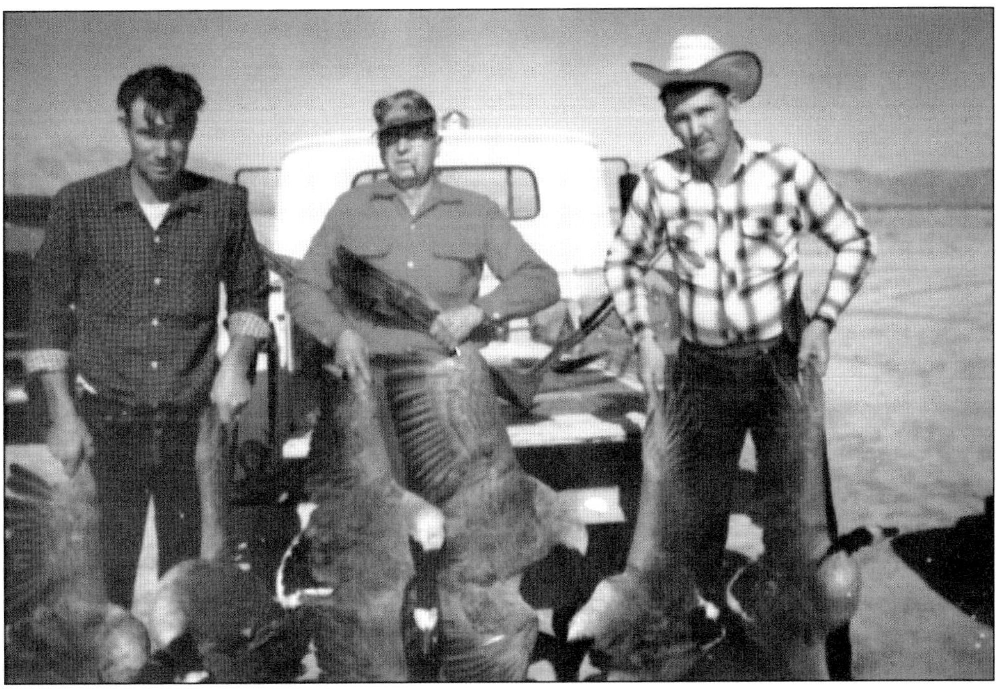

In the 1960s, Oral Hunter (center) ran a hunting preserve off Route 60. Tex Shanks (left) and James Dalton (right) are seen with pheasants shot in the Butler Valley in 1965. The birds were prepared for Christmas dinner by Leona Hunter and, after 40 years, are still remembered as tasting delicious. (Dalton family.)

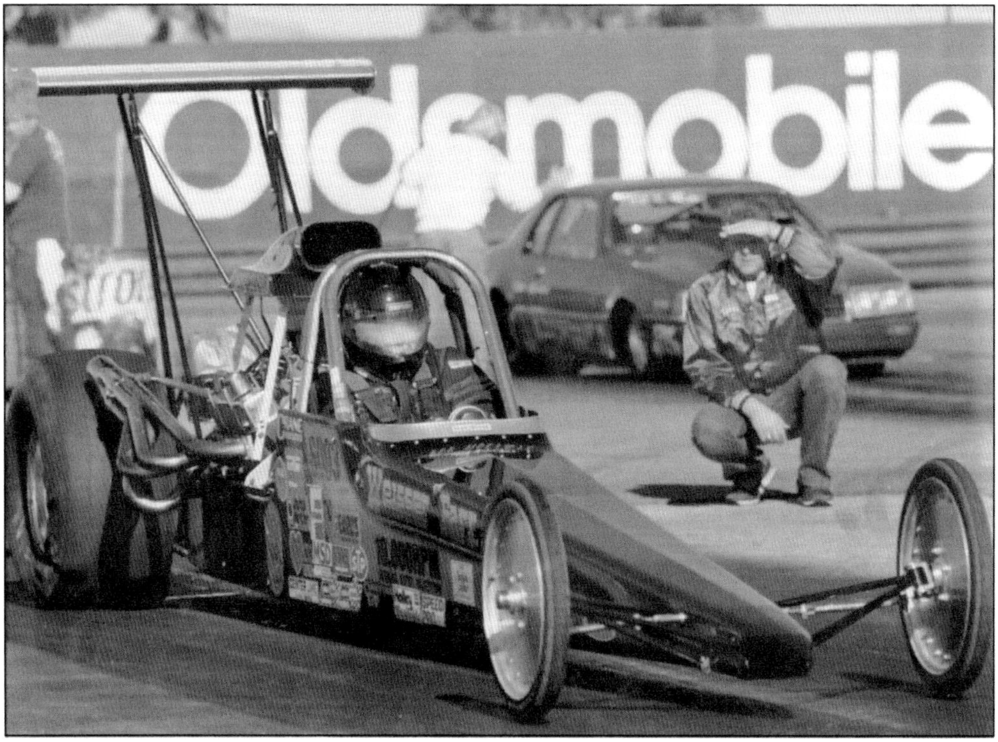

John Weisser, seen earlier on horseback at age 12 as a member of the Crowder-Weisser ranching family, grew up wanting to pursue speeds greater than a horse's gallop. Periodically he took breaks from cattle driving to pursue his passion for driving race cars. Above, John sits expectantly behind the wheel of the race car he cosponsored with Bill Farr (right). (Weisser Cattle Company.)

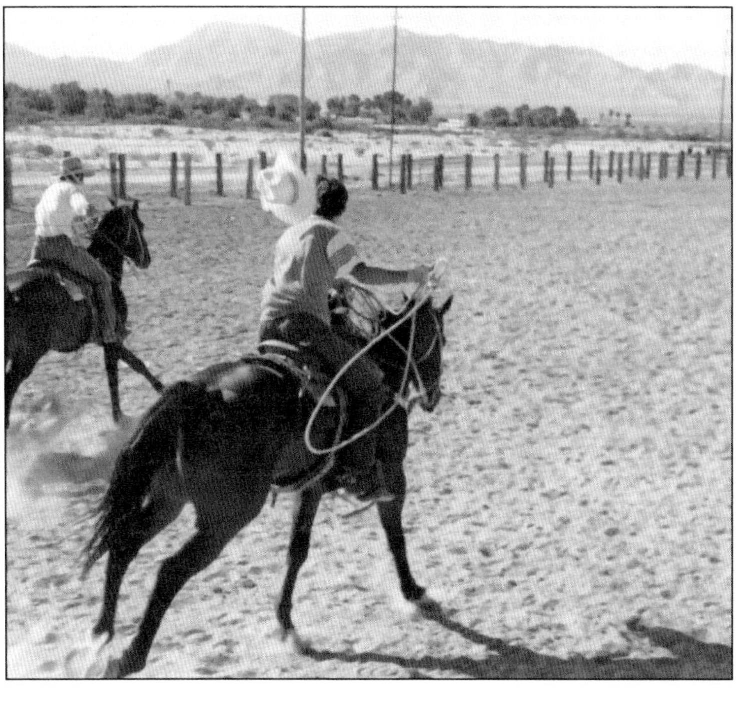

Originally from Mississippi, Jim Downing (left) and Clare Downing (right) moved to Salome in 1980. Jim was raised on a farm and Clare in the town of Greenwood. They are pictured roping at the wild burro corral in Wenden. Abandoned by miners over the years, wild burros have survived wandering for generations. (Downing family.)

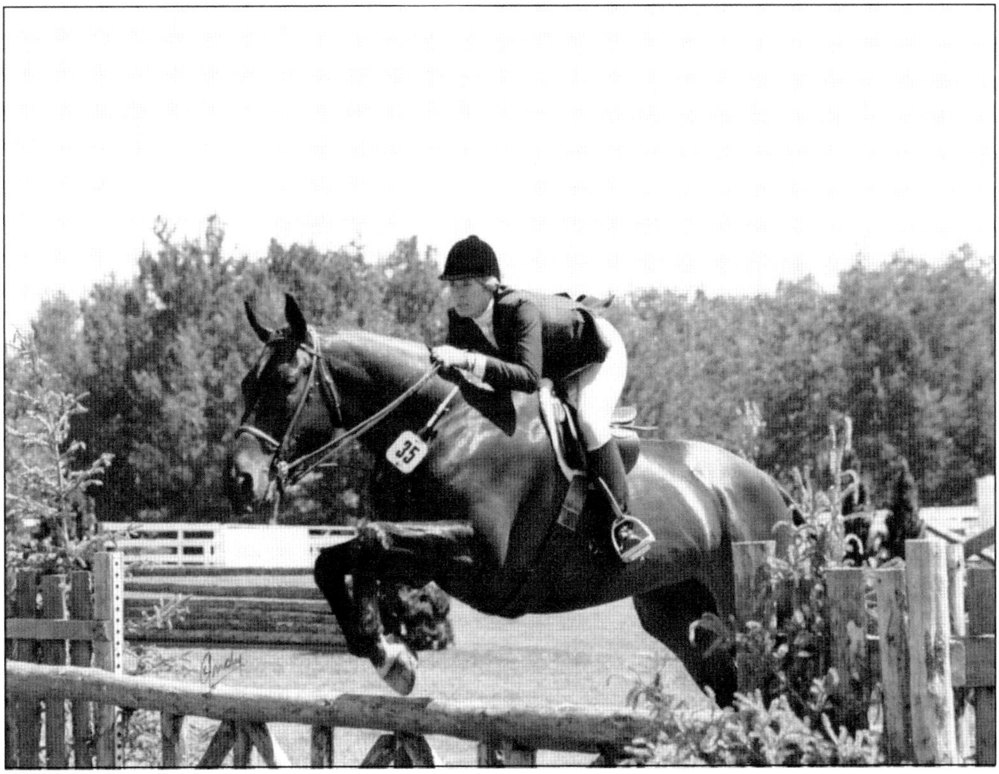

The T Bar B Feed in Salome sponsors a professional rodeo every year, but owner Toni Brown has yet to compete in any events. She may still compete in rodeo based on her success at English equestrian events. Toni Brown is seen here at an international competition in Calgary, Alberta. (Brown family.)

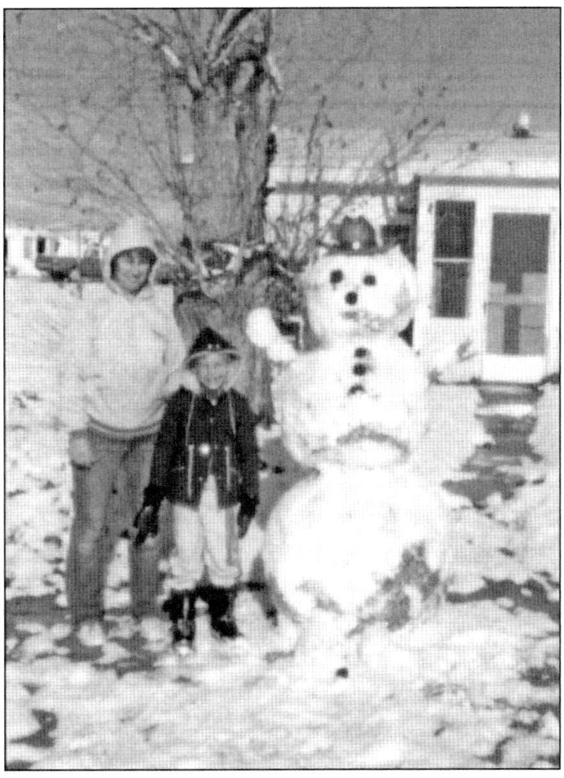

For kids coming of age in the desert at a 2,000-foot elevation, a winter storm that drops enough snow to build a snowman may be a once-in-a-lifetime event. The blizzard of 1985 was the memorable storm for C. J Stacy, pictured with his mother, Mona Stacy. C. J., now in his 30s, vividly remembers that he rolled this snowman up and down two blocks in order to amass enough snow to build one this tall. (Mona Stacy.)

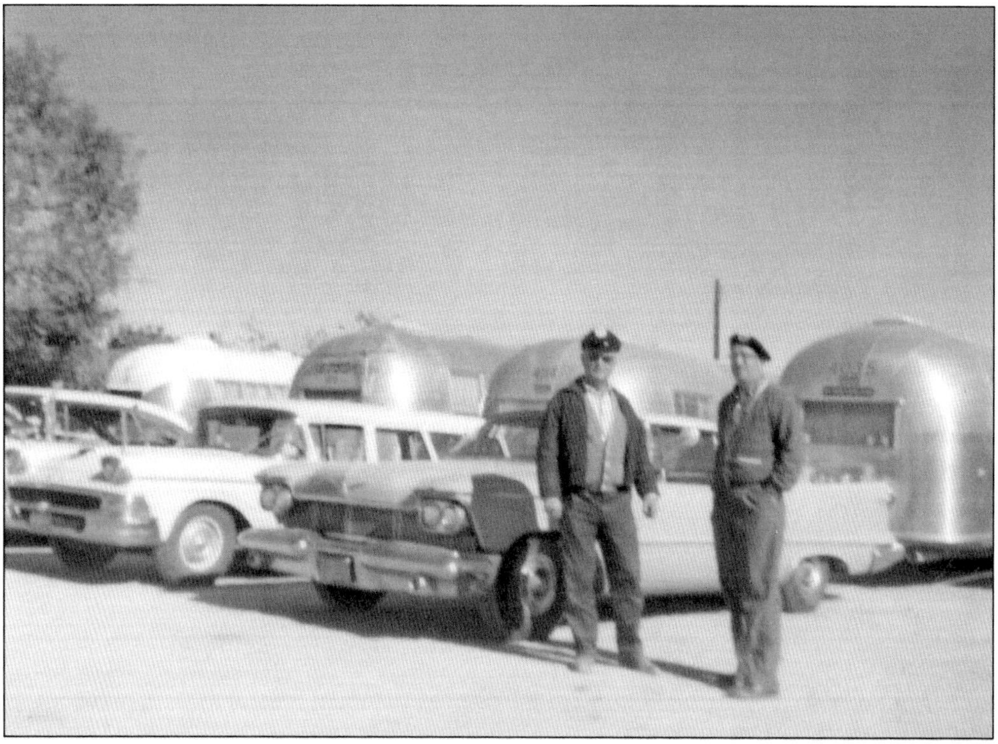

In 1962, Airstream founder Wally Byrum (left) and Airstream club members stayed overnight in Salome, beginning a perennial trend. Since 1978, Route 60 has brought visitors flocking to the recreational vehicle and motor home parks found between Morengo Palms, east of Wenden, and Ramblin' Roads in Hope. In winter, they come to pursue a myriad of activities in the clean, healthy air under the warm winter sun; year-round, they explore the exquisite desert and bountiful wildlife and enjoy the clear view of the Milky Way. Nearly 150 years after James McMullen first drove stagecoach passengers into the sunset, the unspoiled, natural beauty of the McMullen Valley endures. Perhaps that is the reason adventurous travelers seeking an authentic American experience can still be seen pulling a classic trailer down the highway and into the sunset. (Above, Montijo family; below, Sharon Rubin.)

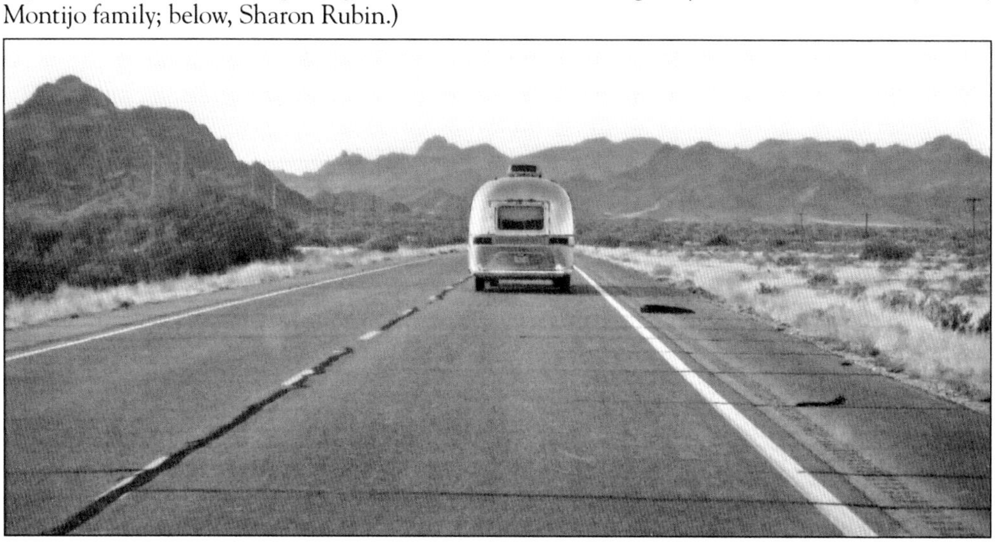

Nine

The Great Arizona Outback Rumor and Innuendo Historical Society Rescues the Past

The Great Arizona Outback (GAO) Rumor and Innuendo Historical Society was named in celebration of Dick Wick Hall. Our organization is focused on efforts throughout the McMullen Valley, including the communities of Salome, Wenden, Hope, Vicksburg, and Alamo Lake.

Founded in 2007, the society sought to uncover the area's rich history. This led to recognizing the urgent need to collect and preserve it. As we promoted conserving the stories, images, and documentation of the area's history, the idea took root, and within the first year, over 150 residents have joined us in support of these efforts.

Soon after we began, we learned of an unpublished manuscript about the early miners and the beginnings of settlement in the Harquahala Mountains. We knew we had to share it with the community. We published *Pioneer Women, Miners and Thieves: Golden Nuggets of History in the Great Arizona Outback* by Cactus Kelli in 2008. It is a collection of portraits of the enterprising men and women who first came here in the days of the Harrisburg and Harqua Hala mining camps. Kelli first came to Salome in 1919 and over her long and remarkable life has observed and chronicled its transformations.

The Great Arizona Outback Rumor and Innuendo Historical Society's first community-wide project was the restoration of the final resting place of the area's pioneers, Wenden Cemetery. We were joined by volunteers from many of the major service organizations, including the McMullen Valley Chamber of Commerce, McMullen Valley Volunteer Fire Department, Wenden Business Association, Veterans of Foreign Wars, the Master Gardeners, Salome Lions Club, the 9/11 Committee, and the Wenden Chapter of the Salvation Army. In acknowledgment of her inspiration to initiate the restoration, an area on the cemetery property has been designated the Cactus Kelli Park.

Every day, we learn more about the intriguing people and interesting times that made this eccentric valley what it is today. Every month, new sites in need of restoration are suggested as future projects. Every year, we hope to resurrect more history, hoping that with living memories of the past, we will be better informed for the choices of the present and the decisions that will guide our future.

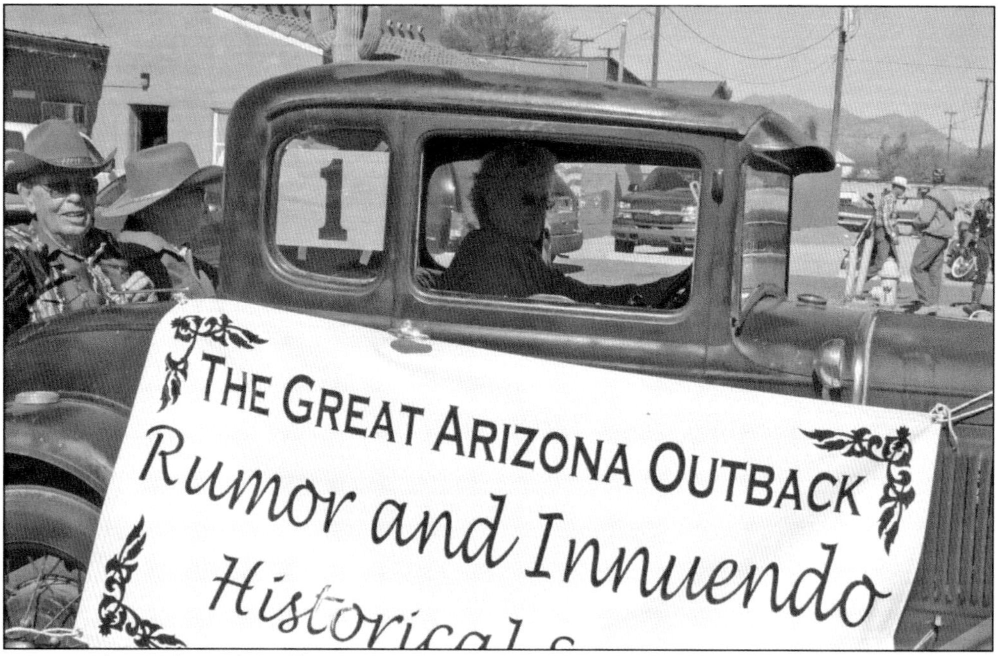

In 2007, the Dick Wick Hall Days Parade served as our first public event. Above, Albert Nord (left) and Hayden Brown (right) ride in a classic Ford. Neither had climbed into a rumble seat in 75 years, but both did it with ease.

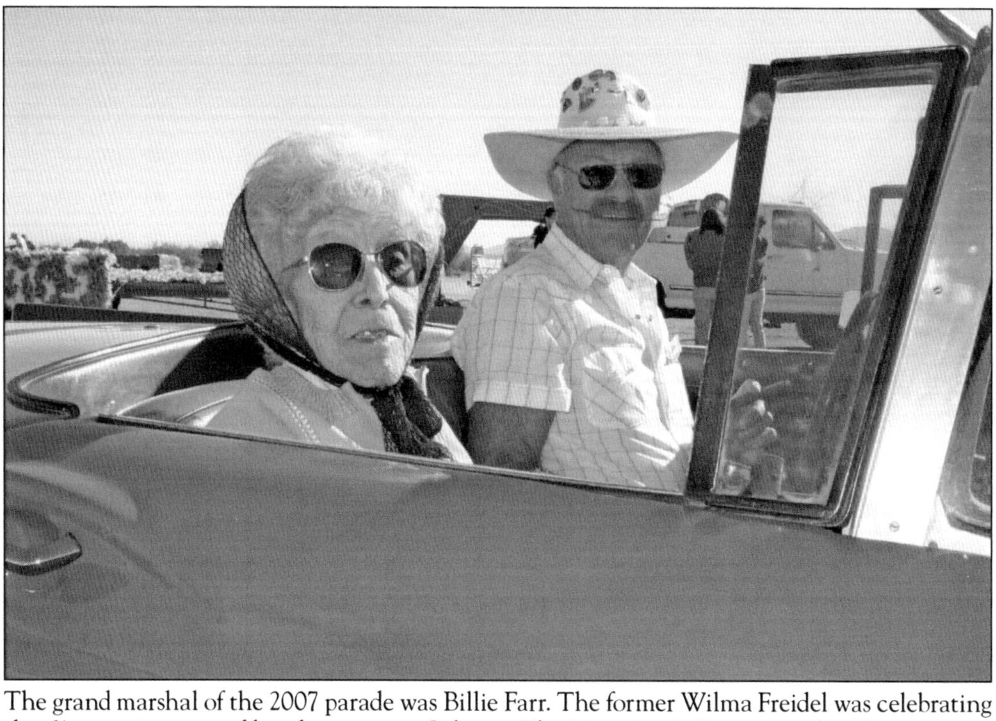
The grand marshal of the 2007 parade was Billie Farr. The former Wilma Freidel was celebrating the 61st anniversary of her first visit to Salome. The New Year's Eve attire the "first lady" of Shefflers wore while at the cash register—diamonds, jewels, and a fur coat—will not soon be forgotten. Pictured with Jerry Roach, Billie passed soon after this photograph was taken.

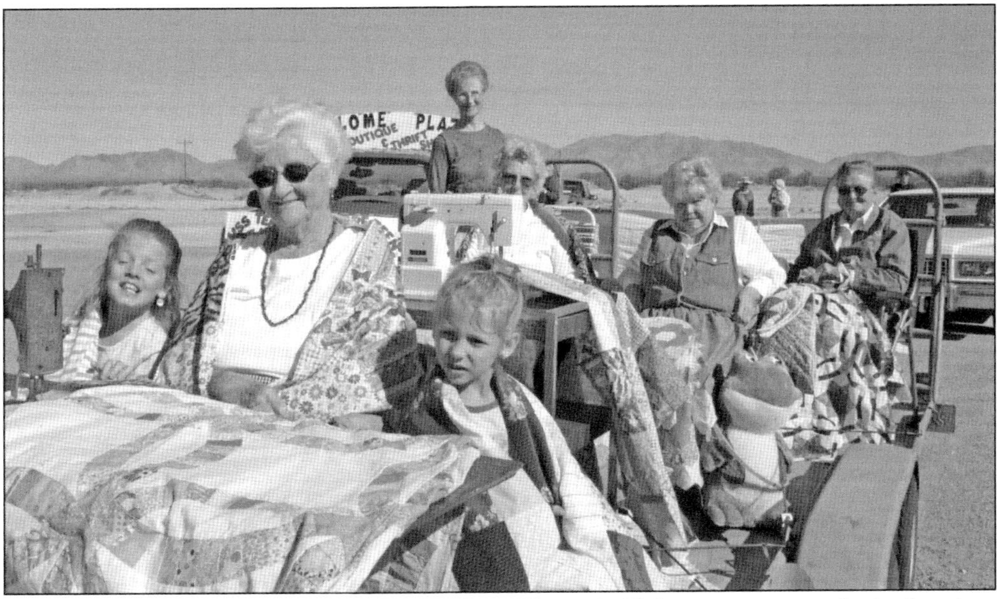

The exquisite handmade quilts by the ViSaWen Women's Club were prominently displayed on their float in the 2007 parade. Throughout their 60-year history, the members have contributed time, energy, and resources to worthwhile causes. The historical society has been a beneficiary of their support. Pictured is Irene Nord (front) with granddaughters Michaela (left) and Destiny (right), Elizabeth Bryan (standing), Pinky Andersen (partially obscured by the sewing machine), Bev Sullivan, and Louise Lindsay (far right).

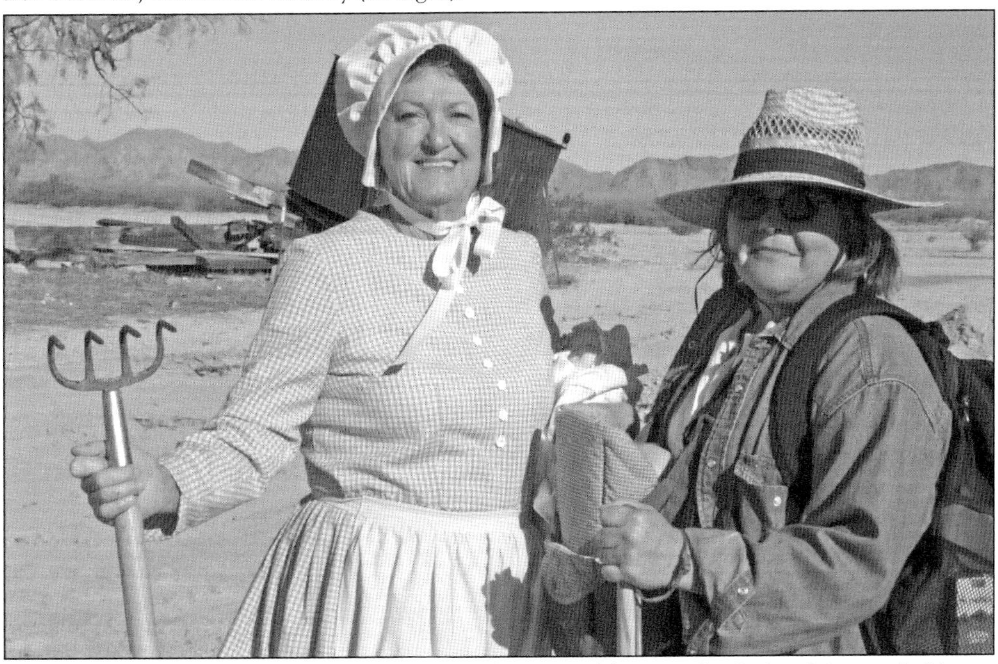

At the 2007 Dick Wick Hall Days Parade, the ensemble worn by Robin Martin (left) was designed and created by Barbara Van Diest (right). These elegant women received first-place awards for the theme "The Past Meets the Present" costumes, dressed as "old time and modern pioneer women."

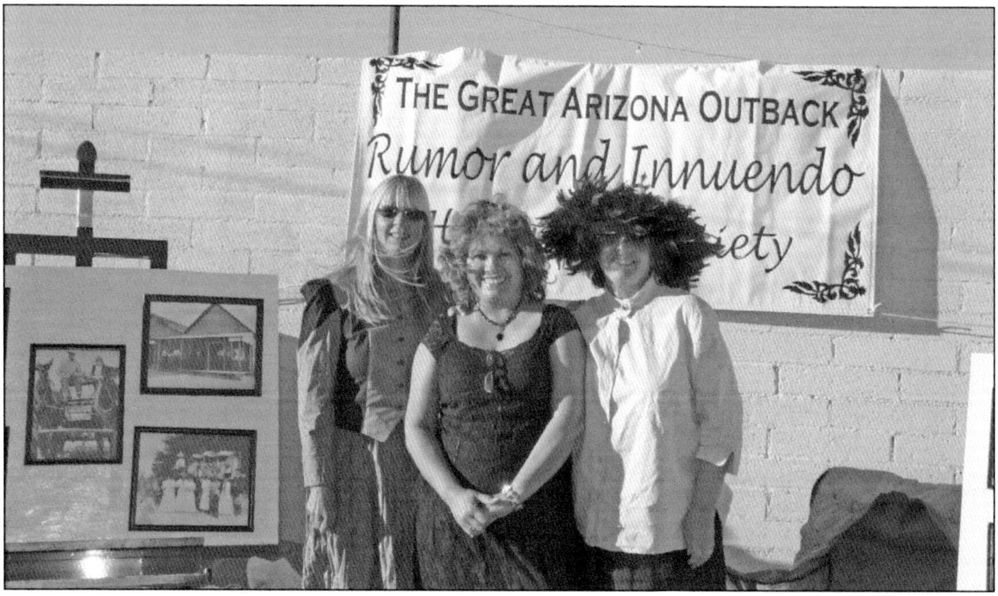

An information booth and photograph display at the Dick Wick Hall Days festivities provided the first opportunity to invite local residents to join and participate in the historical society's mission. The display of vintage photographs, seen earlier, spurred memories and stirred emotions. Membership recruitment went very well. Costumed for the event were Dawn Patterson (left), Gloria Parrett (center), and unidentified.

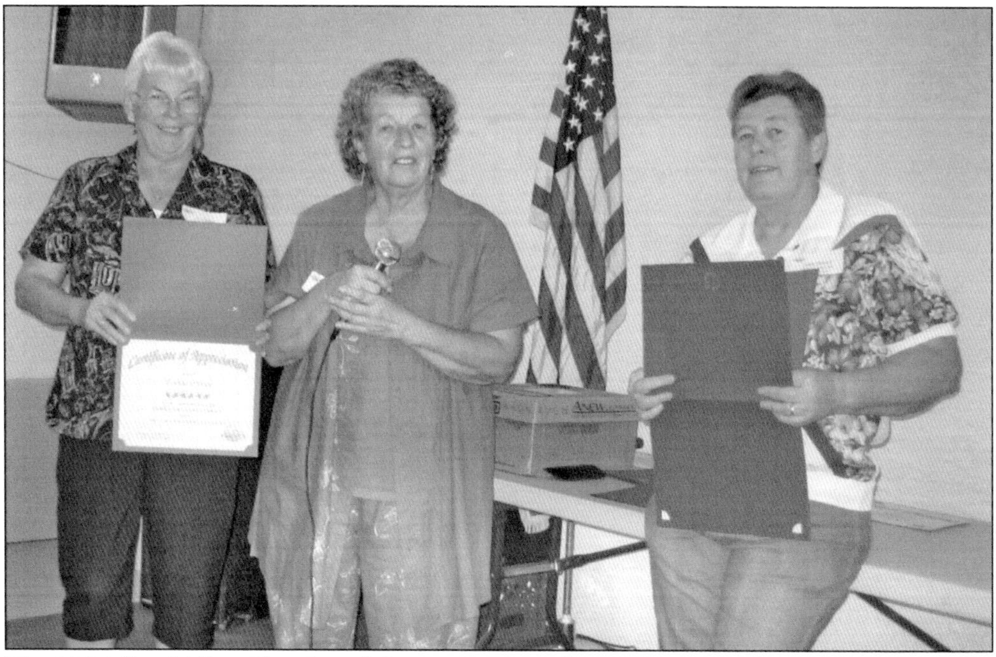

The McMullen Valley Chamber of Commerce Awards Dinner is a yearly event that draws an overflow crowd. From the outset, the chamber has actively supported the Great Arizona Outback Rumor and Innuendo Historical Society and its activities. The chamber has shared resources, publicly endorsed projects, and provided volunteers. Pictured are board of directors members Evonne O'Brien (left), Lee Vernon (center), and Linda Darland (right).

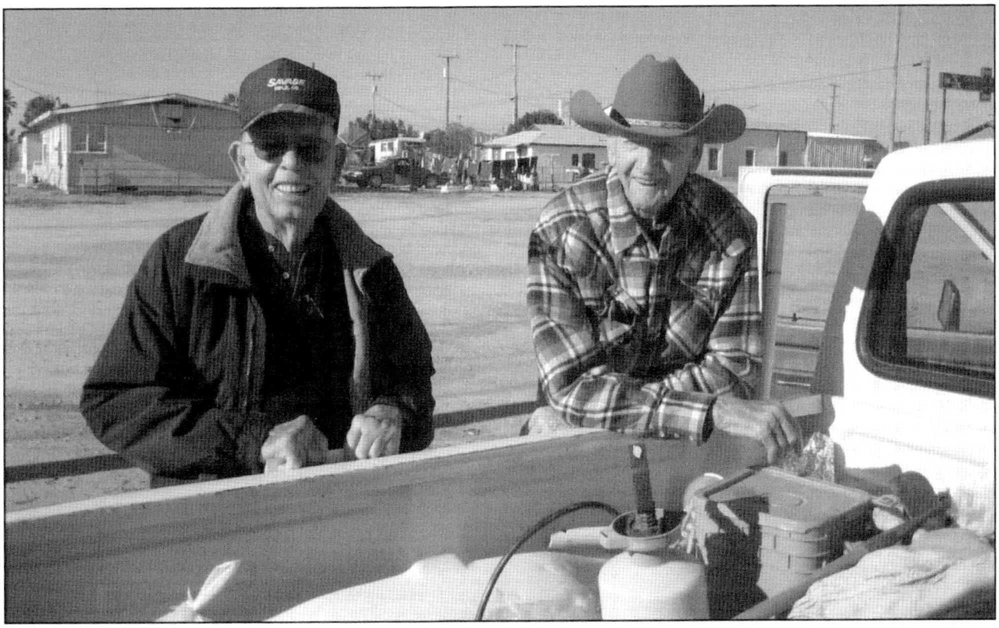

The GAO Rumor and Innuendo Historical Society gathers information from numerous sources. When confirmations of reputed facts are required, old-timers are rounded up to lean over the bed of a pickup so that they can help parse it out. Their recall of events 70 years ago is surprising. They conveniently remember only people whom they can recall positively. From left to right are Albert Nord, 82, and Hayden Brown, 95.

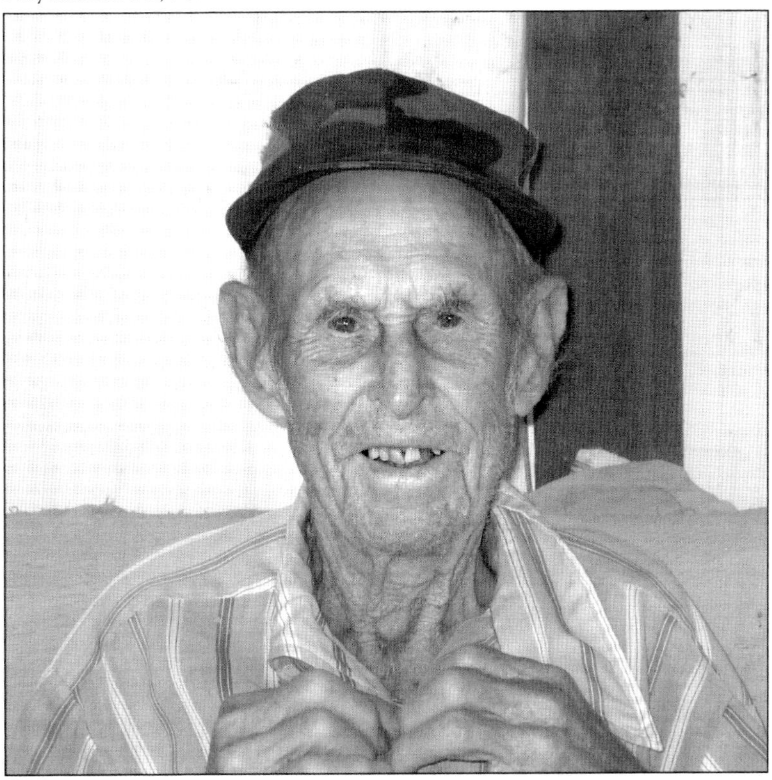

Every year, we lose old-timers who shared their knowledge of the desert. Ed Thedell (pictured) was a veteran from Utah whose experience with the care and tending of vegetables, fruit trees, and cacti made him an invaluable neighbor. His generosity, green onions, and freshly baked bread will always be missed.

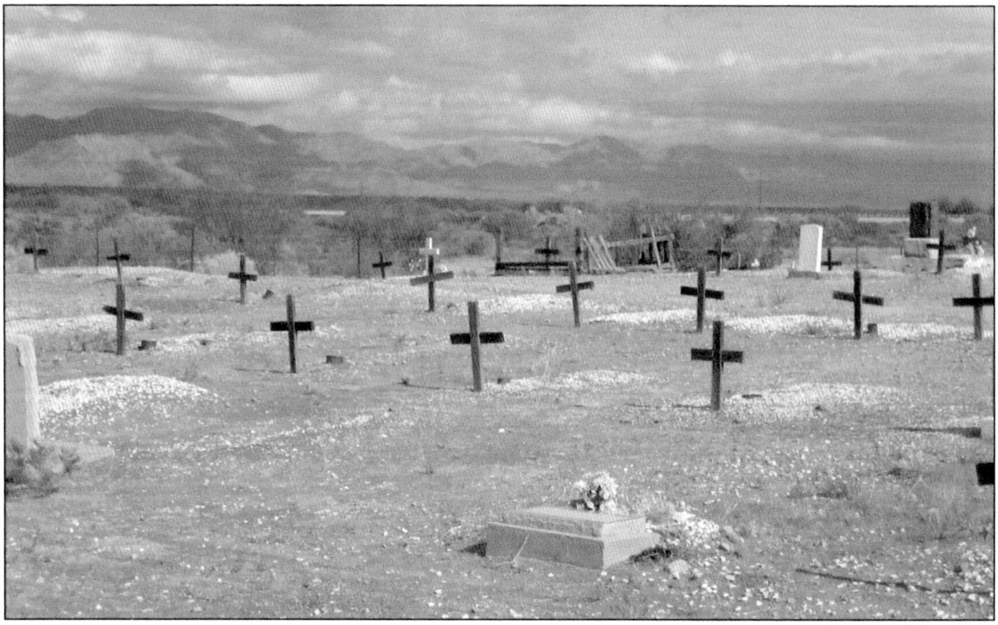

Many members of the pioneer families—miners and settlers whose images appear earlier—are buried in the Wenden Cemetery. In recent years, their final resting place had become forlorn and sadly forgotten. In early 2008, the historical society organized a community cleanup to restore and renovate the cemetery. Nearly all the community service organizations participated and continue to pitch in on this ongoing project.

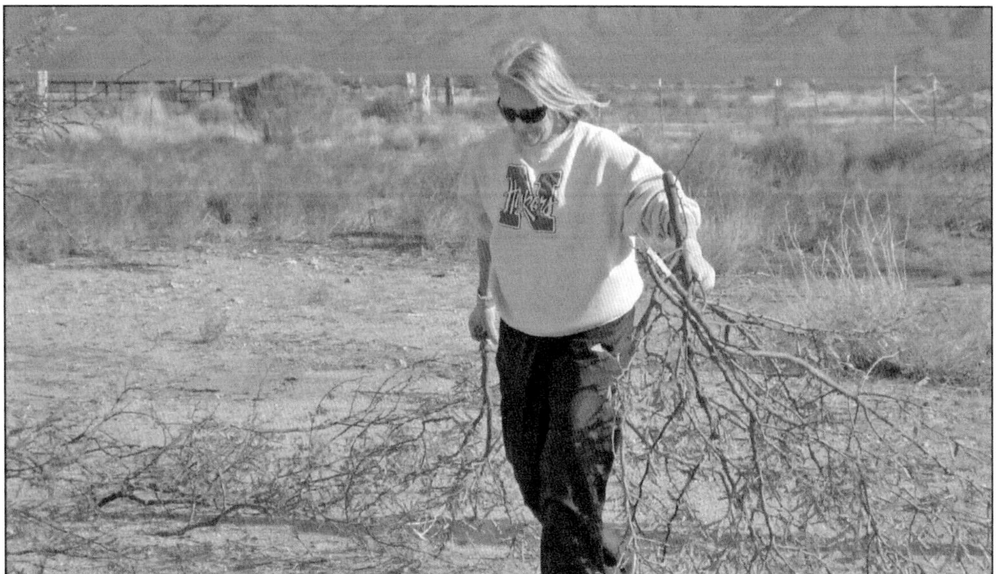

Funding for the Wenden Cemetery project was secured with the help of Supervisor Mary Scott from a 150-year-old historical trust established soon after the formation of the Arizona Territory. The sale of public lands in Wenden created the trust. This creates the possibility that some of those interred directly contributed to the recent restoration project. Pictured during the 2008 cleanup is Louise Wolfe.

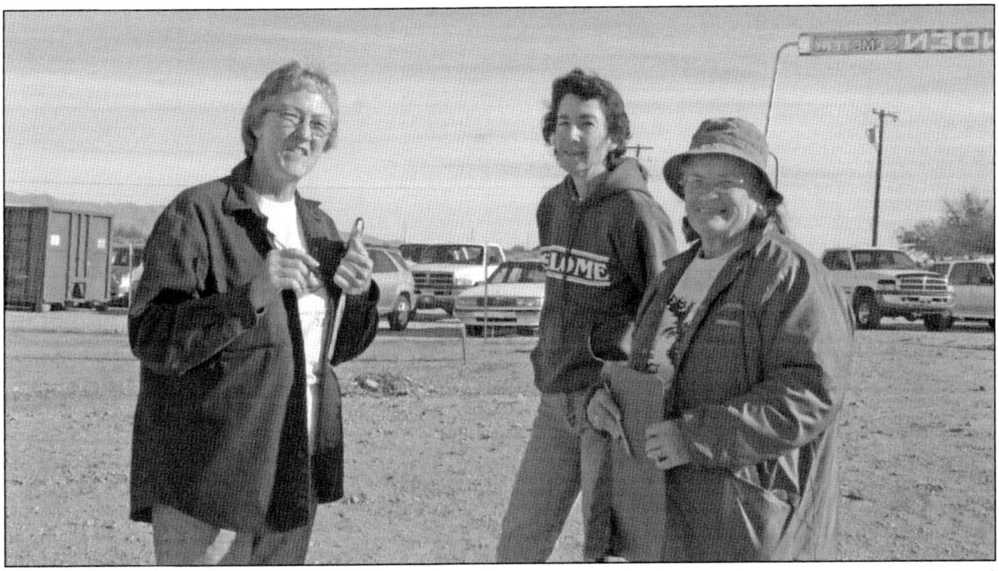

The Master Gardeners organization developed a xeriscape landscape design requiring minimal care and water usage, which should maintain the cemetery's refreshed look for years to come. John Bennett, director of La Paz County Parks Department, served as the consultant. Pictured during an exploratory visit in 2008 are, from left to right, Eileen McFarland, Susan Dewar, and Loreena Cluck.

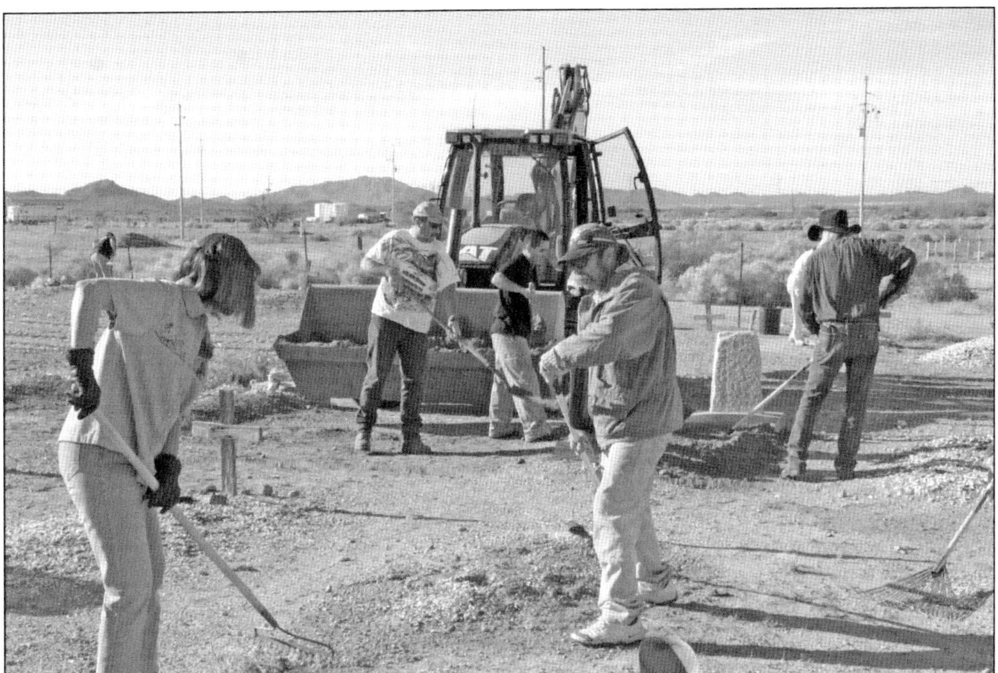

The Wenden Cemetery cleanup in January 2008 proved to be one of the largest volunteer turnouts in years. Residents from all over the McMullen Valley arrived for work with picks, shovels, and rakes. Kelly Stacy came with a front loader, and LKH Farms contributed a truckload of dirt to repair grave sites. Among those pictured are Ilene Wood (left front), Steve Howard (center), and Dennis Patterson (right rear).

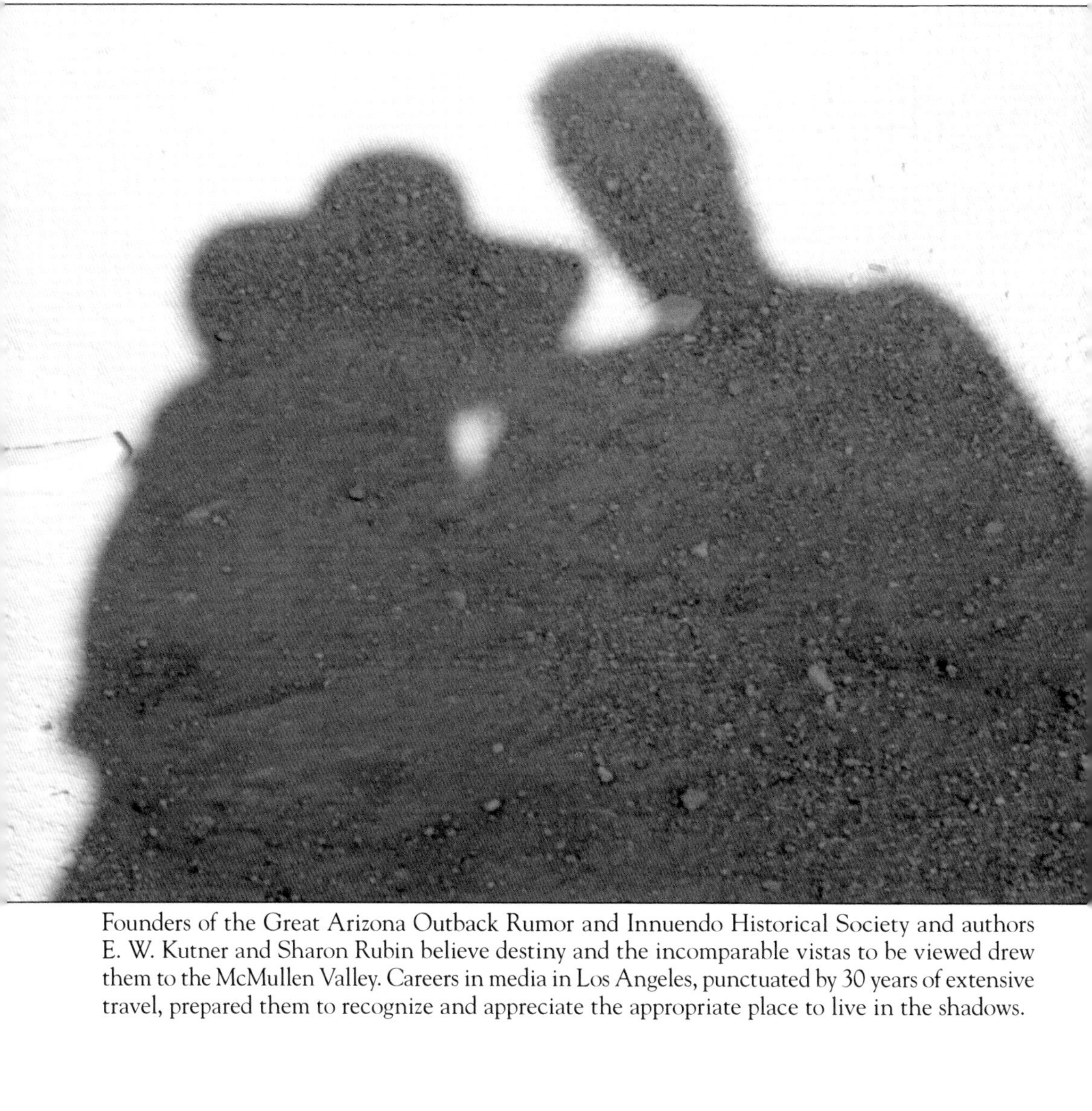

Founders of the Great Arizona Outback Rumor and Innuendo Historical Society and authors E. W. Kutner and Sharon Rubin believe destiny and the incomparable vistas to be viewed drew them to the McMullen Valley. Careers in media in Los Angeles, punctuated by 30 years of extensive travel, prepared them to recognize and appreciate the appropriate place to live in the shadows.

BIBLIOGRAPHY

Bentley, Toni. *Sisters of Salome*. New Haven, CT, and London: Yale University Press, 2002.

Cardwell, Lawrence. "Welcome to Salome—Most Famous Little City in the West." *Arizona Highways Magazine*: April 1949.

Joy, Betty Hammer. *Angela Hutchinson Hammer: Arizona's Pioneer Newspaperwoman*. Tucson: University of Arizona Press, 2005.

Kelli, Cactus. *Pioneer Women, Miners and Thieves: Golden Nuggets of History from the Great Arizona Outback*. Salome, AZ: The Great Arizona Outback Rumor and Innuendo Historical Society, 2007.

Lawton, Mary. *Schumann-Heink: The Last of the Titans*. Whitefish, MT: Kessinger Publishing, 2005.

Maddox, Eddie Jr., and Roger Baty. *Where Heroes Trained*. Tucson: Fenestra Books, 2004.

Myrick, David F. *Santa Fe to Phoenix: Railroads of Arizona*. vol. V. Berkeley, CA: Signature Press, 2001.

Niehaus, Gladys. "Dick Wick Hall Days." *Arizona Highways Magazine*: September 1960.

Nord, Albert. "Old Episcopal Church." *Ribbitt News*: April 2004.

Seabright, J. M. "The Arizona Man Who Made Salome Dance." *Dearborn* [MI] *Independent*: May 19, 1923.

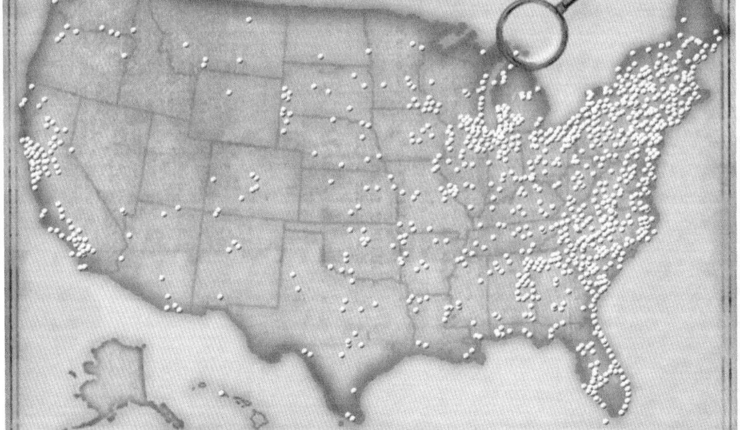
MAP SEARCH